PRAISE FOR MATTHEW P. MAYO'S WORK:

"Mayo is a breezy yarn-spinner, the kind you'd like to sit around a pot-bellied stove with on a cold night."

—Bookgasm.com

". . . I can't recommend it highly enough. The man knows the West and, better still, knows how to tell a story."

—Andrew Vietze, award-winning author of
Becoming Teddy Roosevelt

"An excellent variety of great stories, told in superb narrative style."

—John D. Nesbitt, Spur Award–winning Western
author of Trouble at the Redstone

"Mayo brings the West alive. . . . *Cowboys, Mountain Men & Grizzly Bears* puts the reader right in the middle of the action. Mayo is a writer to keep a lookout for."

—Larry D. Sweazy, Spur Award winner and
author of The Rattlesnake Season

"[Mayo] is a consummate storyteller with a lively, entertaining voice. . . . *Bootleggers, Lobstermen & Lumberjacks* is American history at its most violent and authentic."

—Howard Frank Mosher, award-winning author of A Stranger in the
Kingdom, Where the Rivers Flow North, and Walking to Gatlinburg

"Matthew P. Mayo, a prolific author of Western fiction, pulls out all the stops of his pulp style. . . ."

—The Boston Globe

"Mayo's Grittiest Moments books read like Loren D. Estleman and Jim Thompson got together to rewrite a Stephen Ambrose history book."

—Jeremy L. C. Jones, Booklifenow.com

OTHER BOOKS BY MATTHEW P. MAYO

Cowboys, Mountain Men & Grizzly Bears: Fifty of the Grittiest Moments in the History of the Wild West

Bootleggers, Lobstermen & Lumberjacks: Fifty of the Grittiest Moments in the History of Hardscrabble New England

Haunted Old West: Phantom Cowboys, Spirit-Filled Saloons, Mystical Mine Camps, and Spectral Indians

Maine Icons: Fifty Classic Symbols of the Pine Tree State
(with Jennifer Smith-Mayo)

Vermont Icons: Fifty Classic Symbols of the Green Mountain State
(with Jennifer Smith-Mayo)

New Hampshire Icons: Fifty Classic Symbols of the Granite State
(with Jennifer Smith-Mayo)

SOURDOUGHS, CLAIM JUMPERS & DRY GULCHERS

Fifty of the Grittiest Moments
in the History of Frontier Prospecting

MATTHEW P. MAYO

TWODOT®

GUILFORD, CONNECTICUT
HELENA, MONTANA
AN IMPRINT OF GLOBE PEQUOT PRESS

A · TWODOT® · BOOK

Copyright © 2012 by Matthew P. Mayo

TwoDot is an imprint of Globe Pequot Press and a registered trademark of Morris Book Publishing, LLC.

Project editor: Meredith Dias
Text design: Diana Nuhn
Layout: Joanna Beyer

Mayo, Matthew P.
  Sourdoughs, claim jumpers & dry gulchers : fifty of the grittiest moments in the history of frontier prospecting / Matthew P. Mayo.
     p. cm.
  ISBN 978-0-7627-7064-9
  1. West (U.S.)—History—Anecdotes. 2. Gold mines and mining—West (U.S.)—Anecdotes.
  3. West (U.S.)—Gold discoveries—Anecdotes. 4. Frontier and pioneer life—West (U.S.)—Anecdotes.
  5. West (U.S.)—Biography—Anecdotes. I. Title.
  F591.M393 2012
  978'.02—dc23

                                                                                    2011039924

Printed in the United States of America

10 9 8 7 6 5 4 3 2 1

To my wife, Jennifer—
my bonanza, my lucky strike!

I'm sick to death of your well-groomed gods,
Your make-believe and your show;
I long for a whiff of bacon and beans,
A snug shakedown in the snow;
A trail to break, and a life at stake,
And another bout with the foe.

—Robert Service, from
"The Heart of the Sourdough"

CONTENTS

Acknowledgments xvi

Introduction. xvii

1. Coronado's Hollow Quest 1
   Trusting dubious sources, Spanish conquistador Francisco Vásquez
   de Coronado leads two thousand soldiers and slaves thousands of
   miles northward from Mexico to find the fabled Seven Cities of
   Gold. Nothing works out as he had hoped. (1541)

2. LeBreau's Raw Luck. 7
   In 1790 a three-hundred-man French expedition finds a mother
   lode of gold in New France (now southern Colorado). Intending to
   return, they bury their massive hoard but are soon beset by disease,
   Indian attacks, and cannibalism. (1790)

3. Black Hills Mystery Message 13
   Ezra Kind carves his last words into a stone slab: "... seven of us...
   all ded but me Ezra Kind killed by Ind ... got all of the gold we
   could carry our ponys all got by the Indians I hav lost my gun and
   nothing to eat and indians hunting me...." (1834)

4. Gold Field Paupers 19
   On January 24, 1848, James Marshall finds gold while building
   a sawmill for Captain John Sutter. Within months, gold seekers
   trample their crops and steal their livestock, food, tools, and land.
   Thousands find fortune; Marshall and Sutter die broke. (1848)

5. Desertion! 24
   Armed with a single musket, Army Lieutenant William Tecumseh
   Sherman barges alone into a cabin housing eighteen soldiers who
   deserted their posts for the gold fields. (1848)

6. Barely by Sea 28
    Forty-eight gold-seeking passengers aboard the Dolphin, *a shabby,
    rotting, one-hundred-ton schooner, jump ship in Baja and straggle
    through parched, cactus-riddled land with no water or food, save
    for meat hacked from a dead horse. (1848–49)*

7. The Chilean War 34
    *Dr. Concha and his peones defend their gulch against claim-
    jumping Americans new to the California diggings. A court
    order is ignored, and a bloody battle ensues. (1849)*

8. Death Valley Daze 39
    *A 107-wagon train of emigrants ventures toward the Mojave
    Desert to avoid the Sierra Nevada. Some of the wagons opt for a
    rumored shortcut. Their next four months are hell, and they name
    the place through which they trek . . . Death Valley. (1849)*

9. Bruff's Journey 44
    *Joseph Goldsborough Bruff's thirteen-wagon expedition to
    California's gold fields becomes snowbound in the Sierra Range.
    His gold-crazed men push on ahead, promising to return for
    him. They never do—and winter closes in. (1849–50)*

10. Salting the Claim 49
    *Desperate to off-load their worthless claim, three partners attract
    the Chinese miners from a neighboring claim. The suspicious
    buyers are duped—all it takes is one shotgun, two shells filled
    with gold flake, and a dead rattlesnake. (1850)*

11. Mine Camp Justice 54
    *In the California camp of Indian Bar, the Swede and a friend
    steal gold dust. The friend flees, but the Swede is caught digging
    up his hidden loot. A miners' court finds the big man guilty, and
    a noose is rigged. (1851)*

12. Weaverville Tong War 60
Rival Chinese gold-mining gangs attack each other with medieval weapons in a bloody ten-minute battle. Eight are killed, six injured, and a bystander takes a bullet to the head. (1854)

13. The Ill-Fated Grosh Brothers 66
Ethan Allen Grosh and Hosea Ballou Grosh discover one of the mightiest silver lodes ever, but tragedies dog them. Soon their old friend, Henry Comstock, lays claim to their lode. The rest is history. (1857)

14. Pikes Peak or Bust! 71
Eager to reach the Pikes Peak gold fields, one expedition of '59ers takes the problematic Smoky Hill Trail, renowned for Indian attacks and little food and water. Soon it is known as the "Starvation Trail." (1859)

15. Sinkpit of Degradation 77
Soon after his eureka moment, the founder of the hardest-living mining town in the West freezes to death in a blizzard. Friends bury his remains in the spring and name the diggings after him. (1859)

16. Pardon Me 82
Mine camp badman Sam Brown is accidentally jostled by a stranger in a Virginia City, Nevada, saloon. The stranger apologizes, but Brown cuts out the man's heart with a bowie knife, wraps himself in a blanket, and takes a nap. (1860)

17. Boone Helm, Man-Beast 87
Starving in the winter in the mountains of Oregon, this savage brute shoots a companion and eats one of the man's legs, then hacks off the other and continues his journey, looking for a new mining camp . . . and new opportunities. (1862)

18. Backshooters 94

A prospecting party unearths the richest gold strike in North America. But George Grimes, one of the party's leaders, will never enjoy his fortune. Within days of the discovery, he is shot in the back. (1862)

19. Doomed from the Start 99

The Yellowstone Expedition sets out in search of color along the Yellowstone River drainage. Soon the unrelenting, warring Crow Indians bedevil the men. For most, this search for gold does not end well. (1863)

20. The Lost Adams Diggings 105

Two starving prospectors are found in the desert of east Arizona by a US Army patrol. The men tell of the massacre of their party at the hands of the Apache chief Nana. They also speak of a hidden canyon bursting with gold nuggets as big as bird eggs. (1864)

21. Snowbound and Starving 111

During the brutal "Hungry Winter," Virginia City, Montana Territory, rich in gold but poor in provisions, is socked in under seven feet of snow, and a much-needed wagon train of flour from Salt Lake City is caught in an early blizzard. (1865)

22. Fire in the Hole! 116

As shifts change on the morning of April 7, 1869, the Yellow Jacket Mine catches fire eight hundred feet down. Timbers collapse, and the fire spreads quickly, killing at least forty men. Some bodies are never recovered. (1869)

23. A Living Hell 122

The owners of the Ophir Mine, Comstock District, Nevada, imprison four miners for three days at eleven hundred feet down in a sweltering tunnel—to ensure that word of their latest strike doesn't leak out and harm their investors' share prices. (1872)

24. Black Hills Betrayal 128
Six years after the region is ceded by treaty to the Sioux,
Lieutenant Colonel George Armstrong Custer treks into the
Lakotas' sacred Black Hills region and discovers gold. Treaties
are broken, and Indian wars erupt. (1874)

25. Trespassers Removed! 133
The Gordon Party of prospectors secretly builds a fortified
stockade in the Black Hills. By April the army evicts them,
but thousands of prospectors stream into the Black Hills soon
after. (1875)

26. Snow Angel 139
Businesswoman Nellie Cashman hears of twenty-six miners
stranded in a snowstorm in the nearby Cassiar Mountains. The
Canadian Army refuses to mount an expedition, so she sets off
with six men and pack animals carrying fifteen hundred pounds
of supplies. (1875)

27. Deadwood's Badman 145
With promises of safe, well-paying jobs as stage performers in his
famous Gem Theater, Al Swearengen lures dozens of women to
the mining town of Deadwood, Dakota Territory—and forces
them into lives of slavery as prostitutes. (1877)

28. Heart of a Sourdough 151
Though a millionaire, Tombstone founder Ed Schieffelin is
happiest prospecting. Years later he is found dead in his Oregon
cabin, age forty-nine, flopped over ore samples flecked with gold.
His journal reads: "Struck it rich, again, by God!" (1877)

29. Lost and Found . . . Too Late 157
Prospector Joshua Ward, his wife, and their two little daughters
strike it rich. But no one will know for thirty years, when their
arrow-riddled corpses are found in their hidden cabin—along
with a fortune in gold coins stashed in the fireplace. (1878)

30. Quit While You're Drunk 162
*Crazy Bob Womack digs for twelve years around Cripple Creek.
By 1890 he establishes the El Paso Mine. Though it would earn
three million dollars in the coming years, he sells it while drunk
one night for three hundred dollars. (1878)*

31. Rags to Riches to Rags 167
*Horace Tabor, a Leadville, Colorado, merchant, grubstakes two
prospectors seventeen dollars—and a year later reaps one million
dollars for his share in their diggings. Tabor leaves his devoted
wife for a younger woman. But all too soon, poverty plays them
false. (1878)*

32. Wrong Place, Wrong Time. 172
*Vigilantes mistakenly lynch young James Williams for a horse
theft he didn't commit. When his body is cut down, in his pockets
are found ore samples and a partial map—to a lost Spanish silver
mine. (1882)*

33. Rich and Ungrateful 177
*Noah Kellogg's jackass wanders off one morning, lost in the hills
near Coeur d'Alene, Idaho. The miner follows—and finds the
beast staring at a three-hundred-million-dollar silver lode. But
the beast's braying proves too much, and extreme measures are
taken. (1885)*

34. Beyond Endurance 183
*Tom Williams and an Indian boy named Bob travel for forty-four
days to tell the outside world of a gold strike. Their dogs die, they
wait out a blizzard at Chilkoot Pass, and after five days without
food or fire, they continue. Then the going gets tough. (1886)*

35. Hells Canyon Massacre 189
*In May 1887, dry gulchers shoot and stone to death thirty-four
Chinese prospectors in Oregon's Hells Canyon. The whites who
do it are brought to trial, but none are convicted. (1887)*

36. Don't Mess with a Sourdough 194
*A young Indian kills a much-loved old sourdough for a bit of food
and his meager poke. The prospector's chums find out and hang
the boy, then leave the corpse swinging in the breeze as a message
to other would-be killers and thieves. (1888)*

37. Luck of the Irish 200
*Three Irishmen secure an overlooked claim between two mammoth
mines in gold-rich Cripple Creek. They mine at night under their
cabin and find enough ore to fight twenty-seven lawsuits. But they
get more than they bargain for. (1890)*

38. Curse of the Dutchman's Lost Mine. 205
*For saving the life of an old Mexican, Jacob Waltz is given the
secret to hidden gold deep in the snake-ridden Superstition
Mountains. He mines in secret for years. Since then, hundreds
have died searching for the Dutchman's lost mine. (1891)*

39. Pegleg Annie's Ordeal 210
*Annie Morrow and her friend, Dutch Em, are caught in a late-
season blizzard. Days later a rescue party finds Annie, half-naked
and crawling on her belly through the snow. Her frostbitten feet
must be amputated. (1896)*

40. Up and Down with the Earps. 216
*Wyatt and Josie Earp join the Alaska Gold Rush. Within a
couple of years they open a saloon in Nome, then pan throughout
the Yukon. Later they find copper and gold in the Mojave Desert. Other
Earp brothers aren't so lucky. (1897)*

41. Dead Horse Gulch 222
*During the brutal winter of 1897–98, on the Skagway Trail
across White Pass to Lake Bennett, three thousand ill-used horses,
mules, oxen, and donkeys, dead and dying, are dumped into
corpse-choked ravines. (1897–98)*

42. Avalanche! 228
*Though they had been warned of dicey conditions on the Chilkoot
Trail due to a lengthy blizzard, on April 3, 1898, seventy men are
buried under thirty feet of snow. Few are dug out alive. (1898)*

43. Cheechako Death Trek. 234
*Eighteen New Yorkers set out in April 1898 to gain the Yukon
gold fields by traversing Alaska's largest glacier. By April 1899
accidents, disease, starvation, and stupidity whittle the group to
four. They are found starving, addled, and blind. (1898)*

44. White Horse Rapids 240
*Soon after ice-out, thirty thousand eager Klondikers travel five
hundred miles down inland waterways in seven thousand
homemade boats, shooting through the treacherous waters of the
Yukon's White Horse Rapids. Some make it. (1898)*

45. Do It Fast, Do It Now. 245
*Big Mike Heney and his crew blast through mountains, build
trestles, and lay 110 miles of track to form the White Pass &
Yukon Route railway—all in twenty-six months. And the Yukon
will never be the same. (1898)*

46. The Scourge of Skagway 252
*Infamous con man Jefferson "Soapy" Smith becomes the unofficial
mayor of boomtown Skagway, Alaska. The bunko king and his
gang ruthlessly con miners out of their hard-earned profits.
Eventually, townsfolk tire of his heavy-handed ways. (1898)*

47. Claim Jumper Extraordinaire 259
*In the largest-ever case of claim jumping, Alexander McKenzie
of North Dakota heads a big-money conglomerate that swindles
hundreds of Alaskan miners working backbreaking hours, seven
days a week. The outcome is anything but predictable. (1900)*

48. Klondike Hell Ride 265

Within months of each other, two men attempt the same ludicrous pursuit—and live to tell the tale of how they rode twelve hundred miles, from Dawson to the new Nome diggings, in the middle of an Alaskan winter . . . on bicycles. (1900)

49. Nome's Worst Storm 271

In September 1900 a three-day tempest ravages the overpopulated beach at Nome, ripping away tents, equipment, and supplies. An unknown number of miners are swept out to sea, and four ships are peeled apart in the roiling surf. (1900)

50. Blue Parka Man 278

A man wearing a blue parka and toting a Winchester rifle gets the drop on Fairbanks miners. Though he takes their pokes, this highwayman is regarded by many as a gold rush Robin Hood. (1905)

A Brief Glossary of Prospecting Terms 284

Art and Photo Credits 286

Bibliography 289

Index 295

About the Author 300

ACKNOWLEDGMENTS

My thanks to many, including Sandra Johnston, library assistant, Alaska State Library Historical Collections, Juneau, Alaska; Belfast Public Library, Belfast, Maine; Western Writers of America; Western Fictioneers; my stash of old *Real West* magazines (for pulpy inspiration!); Bozeman Public Library; the National Archives and Records Administration; the Library of Congress; the National Park Service; the Pioneer Museum of Bozeman; the Western History Association; all my writer chums; Cherry Weiner, agent extraordinaire; and Erin Turner, top-shelf editor.

My enduring thanks to Francis John Smith, a lovely man still very much with us; to the Smiths, the Burdicks, and the Royers, family and friends all; to Clan Mayo for unwavering support and enthusiasm; and to Guinness, Nessie, and Guy—steadfast and true.

And last, though always first, my special and deepest thanks to my wife, Jennifer Smith-Mayo, who conducts all the historical image research and procurement for my books (and so much more!), and without whom I would wander with my burro, lost in the mountains, footsore and hungry. . . . Fancy a stack of sourdough flapjacks?

—*M. P. M.*

INTRODUCTION

Not too long ago while roving the West with my wife, I tried my hand at gold panning, albeit in a touristy way. I found there is something singularly thrilling about the prospect of spying sudden "color" in the pan—something akin to the breath-stopping feeling experienced in Vegas when a pull on a one-armed bandit reveals two cherries, then a third blinks into view. Had my presence not been required at a family engagement, the simple dip-and-swirl motion of panning would have kept me busy long after my hands stiffened from the late-summer chill of that Northern Rockies stream. Alas, we had schedules to keep.

Already a fan of literature of the gold rush era, that brief bit of panning further idealized my view of the solitary pursuit of prospecting for gold. As we drove away, I pictured myself in a flop-brim felt hat, rough-cloth trousers, worn leather boots, a pick slung over one shoulder, my other hand tugging a burro's lead rope, the animal carrying everything else I owned in the world. And we would roam the West, always looking for the next big strike. Or little one. Or the merest promise of one. It's a romantic notion, to be sure, and not one that is shared by too many folks of my acquaintance—at least not by my wife—but it's enough to periodically prod me with the question, "What if?" Hmm, what if, indeed. . . .

In the United States, the first substantial discoveries of the yellow metal happened in 1829, in the Georgia Rush, when more than twenty-five thousand people stampeded into the region, overrunning the land claims of the Cherokee Indians. From there, gold seekers found what they sought along the East Coast in Virginia and on into the interior. As Easterners ventured farther inland, and ever westward, more gold was found, along with its attendant boom-and-bust fortunes.

For me, the wonder of the great era of "rushes" (which, for brevity's sake, also includes the numerous nineteenth-century quests for silver, copper, lead, and more) is that the allure *of the promise* of gold prompted so many settled people to uproot themselves and disrupt their families. Though they knew they might never again see their loved ones, they risked it all for the possibility of striking it rich in California's gold fields. Such was the promise sold to them by none other than the president of the United States himself, James K.

Polk, who in 1848 intoned before Congress: "The accounts of the abundance of gold in that territory are of such extraordinary character as would scarcely command belief were they not corroborated by authentic reports of officers in the public service."

And should that stirring statement fail to rouse the spirit of gold lust in the hearts and minds of the public, the *New York Tribune*'s own Horace Greeley chimed in with his declaration of import: "Fortune lies upon the surface of the earth as plentiful as the mud in our streets. We look for an addition within the next four years equal to at least One Thousand Million of Dollars to the gold in circulation." And lo, the California Gold Rush was on, and '49ers—who took their name from the year in which most of them trekked westward—by the thousands journeyed toward the Pacific.

At midcentury, for good or ill, America's infatuation with precious metals entered a new and frenzied age that showed the indomitable spirit of humans, their curiosity, their devil-may-care derring-do, and their foolhardiness. The Argonauts weren't just after monetary wealth—they also sought the promise of greener grass and a life yet unlived. Who among us hasn't dreamed of chucking it all for the unproven-but-exciting? What if, what if . . . ?

For every person who struck a mother lode in some far-flung gulch in California or Montana, there were thousands who frittered away their meager grubstake in a fruitless search for a glimmer of color. If they lacked the special blend of blind optimism, self-reliance, and raw skill needed to tighten their belts and keep on digging, come what may, one hoped they at least had the good sense to recognize failure for what it was and beat a retreat back to wherever they hailed. Sometimes, though, they never had the chance, as getting there for many proved the biggest challenge of all. Just as often, the gold seekers experienced bad weather, bad luck, or bad people—sometimes all three at once. Others, either through circumstance or bullheadedness, kept on searching, kept on digging, kept on prospecting long past when reason dictated they pack up camp and head for home. One might almost think they liked the search more than the discovery.

And that sort of dogged dedication brings us to the sourdoughs, those California and Alaska gold rushers who wore their yeasty bread starters around their necks in little crocks in nippy weather (else it go dormant in the cold). This afforded them plenty of raw leavening material for their tangy "sour dough" breads, biscuits, and flapjacks, which beat the heck out of chawin' unleavened hardtack. But a sourdough was also something more. The name came to define a certain type of seasoned prospector who had gained sage wisdom through living with and learning from the land, the animals, and the native people of a place, such as the Mojave Desert and the Yukon.

And what of claim jumpers? That term defines a breed of usurper who would rather wait for an honest miner to prove up on a claim, then use an excuse—ranging from barely legal means to lead means (often a bullet)—to move in and filch the promising plot. And that went on in spades wherever gold was sniffed.

Dry gulchers are closer to the bottom of the villain pile. They are sleazy beasts who deceive an unwitting claim holder, devalue his property, then pay pennies on the dollar for it. A more menacing and more employed definition is that a dry gulcher is someone who kills from a distance, precisely so he can avoid a fair fight. Sadly, these vermin abounded in the formative years of frontier prospecting.

These are but two examples of the types of folks who made vast amounts of money "mining the miners," as the practice came to be called. Others, perhaps less criminal in intent but no less rapacious in their execution, were merchants, livestock peddlers, freighting and transport companies, soiled doves, flimflam artists, and many more. They plied their trades through cornering markets, price gouging, falsely inflating demand, and generally profiteering—which they defended as merely making a living wage.

Discoveries of precious metals and the equipment and techniques used to free them from the earth, while fascinating, are incidental elements to the primary task of this book, which is to help illustrate the unfortunate, bizarre, and extraordinary events that came about because of man's quest for riches on the frontier. This book is not intended as a comprehensive history of the western precious metal rushes. Rather, it is hoped, through reading the individual episodes, the reader will come away with a deeper understanding of those formative days, their important place in America's history, and their significance to the lives of those who lived during that time, from coast to coast and beyond.

As with previous books in my series, *Cowboys, Mountain Men & Grizzly Bears* and *Bootleggers, Lobstermen & Lumberjacks,* I have used poetic license by adding dialogue and supporting characters where I felt it prudent for the sake of the narrative or where it was necessary to do so, owing to a lack of firsthand accounts. The overall effect is intended to be a collection of exciting, narrative-based retellings (with a dash of pulpiness) of episodes from the history of frontier prospecting in North America, which began in earnest with the discovery of gold at Sutter's Mill—a major spur to the backside of an already cautious-but-creeping westward expansion. It set to glistening the dreams of sudden fortune in the mind's eye of tens of thousands of people for whom a taste is never enough.

Close to two centuries later, that thrill-of-the-hunt urge continues to lure people to prospect throughout North America. Several massive gold deposits, some of the largest found in decades, were recently discovered in Alaska. But their finders are in a pickle: Extricating the gold will harm these remote pristine wilderness areas. Though the earth is a finite resource, we humans have rapacious and infinite appetites, especially for the unknown and the unseen. It is this bittersweet urge to seek, embedded in all of us, that is the flame in the heart of the treasure hunter.

And that brings me back to my own ill-fated gold-seeking endeavors. As mentioned, I have tried my hand at panning for gold, and I am afraid that the pursuit is not something I appear to be any good at. Or, to quote the old, grizzled sourdough: "Where it is, it is. And where it ain't, there I be." Thus far, it appears I have a solid grasp of where it ain't. But then again, I try to keep in mind that it's the people who continue to ask, "What if?" who have all the adventures in life. So, I believe I'll keep asking that very question while I roam the West in my mind—with a pan, a pickax, and a burro who never complains. That's color aplenty for me. See you on the trail. . . .

—*Matthew P. Mayo*
Spring 2011

1

CORONADO'S HOLLOW QUEST
(1541)

Trusting dubious sources, Spanish conquistador Francisco Vásquez de Coronado leads nearly two thousand soldiers and slaves thousands of miles northward from Mexico to find and pillage the fabled Seven Cities of Gold. He gets as far as modern-day Kansas before strangling his native guide in anger and disappointment.

Francisco Vásquez de Coronado refused to believe that the existence of the Seven Cities of Cibola was nothing more than a fanciful dream. It could not be, if only because so many people believed in it, wanted it to exist, needed it to exist. And so, he told himself for the hundredth time that day, it must exist. Were they not Spaniards, after all? That fact alone, it seemed to his young, proud mind, should be enough to fulfill any desire for riches they could conjure.

Coronado closed his eyes a moment and heard the sounds of men shouting, of pigs squealing, of the steady clopping of hooves on packed earth, and farther off, the ring of steel and the shouts of men practicing their swordplay. No, he smiled at himself, *I am nothing more than a man. I cannot conjure and make real the Seven Cities of Cibola any more than I can turn day into night.*

But I do have faith in God, he thought, opening his eyes. *And that alone will go a long way toward seeing us proved right. I have also risked, at great personal expense, my wife's entire fortune, and I have put my neck on the line for my friend, Viceroy Antonio de Mendoza, who believes so strongly in this venture that he has also committed much of his own money. This expedition must succeed.*

With that thought fixed in his mind, Coronado turned toward the stables, where he spied one of the very men he wished to see. "You there, Estevanico! I would like a word with you."

The tall, broadly built man, a Moor called Black Stephen, strode toward him, suspicion narrowing his eyes even as his mouth formed an ill-accustomed smile, revealing stark white teeth. "*Si*, here I am."

"I have decided I would like you to lead the expedition, in a manner of speaking. I will send you out first, as a scout. You know what we are looking for. When you find Cibola, send back a courier bearing a cross—two hands in length if the tales we have heard are only in part true, but a larger cross should be sent if the stories prove modest compared with the wonders you find."

The large black man stared at Coronado a moment, then nodded. "This I can do."

Coronado had just spent one of the worst winters he had ever lived through. It had begun not with the Tiwa, but with the death of Black Stephen, the Moor, who had failed to send back to them any word of riches before he was killed by savages. Coronado still wondered if he should have taken that as a portent of things to come. For then they came up against the dozen pueblos that constituted the village of the Tiwa. He had never met such an unpleasant people, who were not forthcoming with their supposed riches, their food, or assistance in any way. Coronado consoled himself with the fact that surely the Tiwa had known to not expect mercy for such blatant disregard of the Spanish, their superiors. Despite this, his army had been forced to lay low a significant number of the screaming savages. Coronado did not feel easy with the victory. And more to the point, his men were beginning to lose their patience with him, with the quest for riches.

He still recalled the busy days before they had set out from their base in New Spain, where everyone had been making ready for the trek. It was a heady time to be a conquering warrior and a seeker of fortunes. Since then, they had traveled more than one thousand miles over unforgiving terrain—land so wind-stripped that forage was nonexistent for the stock, rock so jagged that a man could scarcely walk across it, let alone hundreds of hoofed beasts. And yet

The Spanish explorer Coronado was convinced of the existence of the fabled Seven Cities of Gold—and trekked thousands of miles into what is now Kansas in pursuit of them. He found no golden riches and eventually, in anger and frustration, had his native guide strangled for misinforming him. *Courtesy Library of Congress*

at other times, it was a sea of rippling grasses as far as they could see. Then had come the war with the Tiwa, native people of this forsaken place.

Too many times he had heard the "Seven Cities of Gold" mentioned, and now, like his men, Coronado was beginning to doubt the existence of such places. And just when their patience had stretched to the snapping point, along came this native with news of Quivira, an eastern kingdom of such wealth that its capture would more than justify the mighty trek eastward it would require to get there.

Coronado regarded the thin Indian whom his men called "the Turk." It was possible that the man was lying, of course. More than probable, actually.

But why would he lie? Should he be found out, the Turk had his life to lose. And yet there was something about the grubby man, an earnestness that intrigued Coronado.

"You are called 'the Turk,' is that correct?"

"*Si*, yes, yes. I . . . I am not lying, sir. You know this to be true?"

"That is what I should be asking you, man."

"I tell you, sir, the people there, they eat out of gold bowls and drink wine from gold cups. They sleep on cloths of spun gold! There is that much, I tell you."

"Turk, how came you to have such knowledge of this place, Quivira?" Coronado was glad he had kept his helmet on when he had come in from patrolling the soldiers. He was sure it gave him a more daunting appearance before this quivering savage. Now, after so much disappointment and very little in the way of gold discoveries, here was this wretched-looking man offering to guide him and his men to one of the cities of gold.

"These Seven Cities of Cibola, that is but a dream," the Turk said, looking down at the tabletop as if deep in thought. "But Quivira," he looked up at Coronado again, heady memory welling tears in his red-rimmed eyes and trembling his lips. "This place exists. And I can take you there. I alone can take you there."

"Bold talk from an Indian, I say." But Coronado's heart pulsed in his throat, and he felt his ears redden under his steel helm. If this man were telling the truth, then all this effort spent seeking the Seven Cities will have been for naught. And yet it would not matter, for he will have been proved right. "Where is this place?" Coronado's voice sounded stretched and hoarse.

"It is a long time from here, toward that way." The man pointed eastward.

Coronado recalled all this as he sat on his horse, staring down at the collected thatched structures in which dwelled the Quivira. Yes, they were a tall, rugged-seeming people, mostly naked, but they appeared to be in good health. And little wonder, he thought, in begrudging admiration. For the landscape was by far the most promising and bountiful he had seen since beginning this expedition two years before. Not only did these people indulge in rich meats from the endless supply of those wild-roaming, humpbacked cattle, but their land was thick and black and fertile.

They seemed to grow crops with ease. And his men had reported that the plums were the equal or better of any they had seen in Spain. But he and his men had ridden back and forth, surveying the entirety of the kingdom of Quivira and its neighboring regions. And in all that surveying, they had found no gold, save for one little bit that on inspection seemed to have come to a native from one of his own men.

They would leave this place soon, and they would leave it empty-handed. Having spent months riding another thousand miles from the Tiwa village to Quivira, he would return to New Spain and have to tell his superiors that it had all been for naught. As the anger welled in him, filling his throat and blurring his vision, he thought once more of the Turk. The man to whom he had acted as a friend and a confidant for the entire trip, the man he had trusted above all others—this man had lied to him.

As if bidden, one of his officers rode up. "Sir, it's the Turk." The youth was nearly out of breath.

"What has he done now?"

"We have found out that he has secretly told the Quivira and their allies to rise up against us, sir. To kill us!"

Coronado felt anger, to be sure, instant and hot and flashing, like a strike of lightning. But he also felt a powerful weariness. Would this madness never end?

"Soldier, I want him tied and secured in a tent tonight, under guard. We will not allow this to continue." He narrowed his eyes and looked beyond the young soldier. "We will end this foolishness once and for all. Tonight, strangle that damnable rat of a man."

When the soldier left, a slow smile spread across Coronado's face, the first in a long, long time. And it would be the last one he would experience for some time to come. For it was to be a long trek back home, southwestward, to New Spain. Perhaps, he thought, we will find gold on the journey. . . .

Though his was by no means the first or last Spanish quest for gold in the New World, Coronado's quest for the Seven Cities of Gold is most memorable for a variety of reasons, not the least of which is that it portends so much of what happened to numerous subsequent expeditions for gold. That

the very reasons for such massive undertakings were so often based on little more than hearsay passed from one slave to another is incredible. But the tellers, who had little to lose, relayed information that they knew the listeners, their captors, wanted to hear. That information, in turn, made the slaves important in the eyes of people whose decisions held sway over their lives. Couple that with the Spaniards' hunger for the glory of instant fortune, not to mention instant elevation in the eyes of God, and you have a recipe for a greed-fueled expedition of historic proportions.

Following Coronado's failed quest, there were at least six further documented Spanish expeditions that searched for a fabled golden city. All of them ended with the seekers returning home, humbled and empty-handed—or worse, as they frequently perished in the field, their armor-clad remains discovered hundreds of years later by Indians and lone prospectors.

While the famed Seven Cities of Gold have never been found, it is now widely believed, due to the presence of Indian and Spanish artifacts dating from Coronado's time, that Quivira did indeed exist and was located in what is now central Kansas, along the banks of the Arkansas River.

2

LEBREAU'S RAW LUCK
(1790)

In 1790 a French expedition of three hundred miners, geologists, soldiers, and laborers finds a mother lode of gold in New France (now southern Colorado). They mine for months, then bury their massive hoard. Before they can leave the mountains, they are beset by disease, Indian attacks, dwindling supplies, and cannibalism.

◆

LeBreau lay still, listening for any sound to indicate that the Indians would soon renew their attack. He hadn't so much as twitched a muscle in hours. He knew others were alive, but they too must have had sense enough to keep still. The battle had been a vicious bloodbath.

The savage Indians had kept them pinned, would not let them leave the mountain for weeks leading up to the battle. Their food stores had dwindled, and a handful of rampant diseases had done even more to lay low many of their men. All about him, LeBreau had seen officers ordering about their lessers, putting great effort into moving the gold ore they had spent so long in unearthing.

He had been told that the gold would be buried in three locations. The officers, of whom LeBreau was one, had each been required to make a copy of the detailed map on a piece of silk. Should the worst happen, it would still be possible that the gold would one day make its way to France.

Already their original number of three hundred men from the year before had dwindled to less than one-third of that. And by the time they had finally decided to bury the gold and leave the mountains, their food stores had thinned to several bug-infested sacks of flour and a few barrels of salted meat, though no one knew what animal it might once have been. Wild game was not as plentiful as it had been. LeBreau assumed it was because his people had been up there for so long, pounding away with their rifles.

At first the Indians had been friendly, but LeBreau reasoned that since the French expedition had killed or driven away anything remotely edible and then attempted to make off with the gold, the savages had grown angry.

"Rightfully so," mumbled LeBreau.

"Shush, you!" whispered a voice from a few feet away, cracked and straining to be heard. "Do you want to rouse those savages again?"

"Well, we can't sit here forever. Do you know how many of us are left?"

A dragging, rustling sound drew closer. Neither man spoke. LeBreau squinted into the slowly graying morning, but it was still too early to see who—or what—made the sound.

Then a third voice said, "There are less than twenty of us, as near as I can tell."

"That can't be! But we were three hundred. . . ."

"It's true, I swear it. I have been risking my neck to find survivors. I found less than twenty, counting you two men. Do you know of others?"

"No," said LeBreau. "At least I do not."

"As soon as daylight comes," said the mysterious voice, "we have to get down, out of these mountains, and get to the river. Once we're on it, we can travel it to safety and leave this wretched place behind. I for one will never leave France again."

LeBreau knew then who his companion in the dark had been all night—it was Perton, the fat complainer. During the battle, while LeBreau and a handful of others had been busily reburying the gold and correcting their original maps with the new details so that they might again find the hoard, he had seen Perton doing his best to avoid contact with anyone—French or Indian. The man was a weasel.

Hours later the third man's figures were proved correct: There were but seventeen of them left. Seventeen of three hundred. The Indians had taken most everything of worth, including all their food, the stored, dried meats. The men did find one partial sack of flour that had been ripped apart and ground into the dirt by hundreds of frantic feet. That was all. And the men were hungry. They dared not make a fire to warm themselves or cook on, but one man contented himself with squatting near the spilled, begrimed mess, licking his bloody, grungy fingers and dipping them into the flour. Other men saw this and joined him.

The seventeen tired, wounded men straggled down the mountainside, doing their best to avoid clearings, should the Indians decide to return. It had occurred to them all that perhaps the Indians had never left. Some men wept at the thought of being weak, nearly unarmed, and of such low numbers that should the savages return, slaughter was assured.

They did not have long to wait. LeBreau watched as one man, trembling from fatigue, hunger, and lack of sleep, tried again and again to retie the knot on his arm sling. LeBreau rose from the riverbank log, intending to help him. He heard a rustling behind the frail man, then something poked through the man's shirt as if he had another hand hidden away. At the same time, a great clot of blood burst from the little man's mouth, his eyes seemed to push out of his skull, and he pitched forward, and LeBreau saw arrows protruding from his head and back.

"Run! Run! The Indians are back—" but his shouts were a waste of breath, for already they were overrun. The air filled with screams and the hoarse cries of Indians wielding clubs and bows and wide-bladed knives already slick with the red-black life-juice of his comrades.

LeBreau's guts hurt, a sharp pain pulsed and flowered in his side as he staggered and stumbled through the scant riverside flora, trying to move fast but knowing that if he were wounded it might not matter. He chanced a peek down at his side and noted no blood. Sweat stung his eyes and rolled down his nose into his beard. Of course, he thought. I only have a stitch in my side, no wound . . . yet. He chanced a look backward and saw two forms gaining on him, both of them, he hoped, were Frenchmen.

LeBreau continued moving, keeping the Arkansas River in close sight, and heading downstream with it. Screams of the savages and the savaged haunted his trail like hounds on a scent. Soon, much to his relief, even those sounds receded. By nightfall he allowed himself to stop, though in truth his mind had done so hours before and his body had screamed for relief for far longer than that.

The next day LeBreau was awakened by something moving slowly through gravel and dried sticks. It stopped and started several times, all the while coming close enough that he finally opened his eyes but did not move. It was one of his fellows. But the man had not yet seen him.

"Hey!" whispered LeBreau.

The man whimpered and bolted, though barely moving faster than if he had been shuffling along.

"Hey," hissed LeBreau louder than before.

The man stopped and looked at LeBreau. "You . . . you're not an Indian."

"No, no. How many of us made it?"

The man shrugged, shook his head.

LeBreau sighed and looked upstream. The other man came along and sat down beside him.

Hours later LeBreau watched as three more of their party straggled up to them. The last one said that he was sure no others were left alive. At this news, LeBreau, without much thought, felt inside his shirt with his cracked, bloodied fingers for the folded cloth map he kept hidden there. It was still with him.

For days after the attack, the five men argued quietly, then finally all agreed on skipping the larger group's initial plan on returning to the city from which they began the expedition, New Orleans. Now but five, they had no food, no hope, no gold; they guessed they still had Indians dogging their feeble moves, and even their modified plans of heading to the French post at Fort Leavenworth seemed unattainable. Berries and tree bark and mosses were not sufficient to keep their bodies functioning. Soon they were too weak to continue, and they sat in a daze, leaning against trees, staring at their mud-covered hands and legs.

"We must have meat, men, or we will none of us last another day." LeBreau looked at the haggard group, and no one seemed to disagree. "We'll draw straws."

"What for?"

"To see who will forfeit their life for the sake of the others."

Again, LeBreau expected someone to protest, but no one said much. In due time he grunted into a standing position and hunted up a handful of suitable sticks. He arranged them in his hand, concealing the ends.

"Now, whoever draws the shortest straw knows that he must make the greatest sacrifice anyone could ever make in life—that of helping one's fellow man."

All too soon the straws had been handed out, and a tall, thin man sat back against a rock and sobbed. He had been one of the men who had refused to go on. And now he was to be eaten by his fellows.

After the first time, LeBreau was surprised at how unfeeling he could be toward slicing meat off a man, someone he had known for quite some time. But now that the third had been chosen, he felt only gratitude that he had not been one of the short straw men. His last traveling companion, however, left much to be desired.

The man was obviously not right in the head. He raved and tried to sing as they traveled onward, forcing LeBreau to resort to violent means to keep him quiet. This only served to shock the fool, who would then crumple to the trail and cry. Soon enough, even the lighthearted fool could not go on and he sank to the earth for the last time, refusing to budge.

Shortly thereafter, and months after they fled from the Indians, LeBreau staggered farther along the Arkansas River and finally reached a trading post. While recuperating there, the nearly dead LeBreau learned from a search party of the death of his crazed companion. The news saddened him, and with it came the realization that he was the sole survivor of the three-hundred-man expedition, and of the secret of the bloody hoards of gold. In all that time, he kept his map folded and hidden away.

After a lengthy recuperation, and with much relief, LeBreau eventually made his way back to New Orleans. On his return to France, he presented the map to the French government, where it was promptly put in storage and not considered again for forty years.

LeBreau's Lost Mine at Treasure Mountain, near what is now the Summitville ghost town, is regarded as Colorado's most famous—and most elusive—lost hoard. The members of the expedition marked trees and built elaborate cairns to help them decipher their intricate maps that they were confident would later lead them back to their multiple tons of buried, gold-rich ore. It has been surmised that rockslides over the long years have covered the original hiding pits. At that time, depending on the version of the story, the hoard was valued at somewhere between five million and thirty-three million dollars. It was documented well enough that the French regarded it as a potential source of revenue when they ran into financial difficulties in the 1830s.

Several well-provisioned expeditions were sent to hunt for it over the years by the French government and privately by LeBreau's family as well (it seems that he made a copy of the map for himself), though none ever managed to turn up the hidden stash. If they had, it may well have precipitated a gold rush to the Rockies decades earlier than the California rush.

BLACK HILLS MYSTERY MESSAGE
(1834)

As his last act, prospector Ezra Kind carves into a sandstone slab his grue-some tale: ". . . seven of us all ded but me Ezra Kind killed by Ind beyond the high hill got our gold guns 1834 . . . got all of the gold we could carry our ponys all got by the Indians I hav lost my gun and nothing to eat and indians hunting me . . ."

◆

The little train of seven men leading their laden ponies picked its way across tumbledown slopes in the Black Hills on sacred ground belonging to the Lakota Sioux. They knew it for what it represented to them—land rich in gold ore. They had been making good time, but the late summer light proved deceptive. Much like the tremendous boon of gold they had found, the hours of daylight in June seemed to unspool before them as if they would never end. Then all too soon darkness found them. They had been intent on making it to the river in hopes that by walking downstream, the water would hide their trail.

For weeks over their campfire, they had discussed the possibility of Indian attack, as well as the fact that the Indians didn't seem bothered by having them around but that their removal of gold might not be welcome.

"Could be they're figuring that if we make it out with our gold, we'll tell the world and pretty soon they'll lose their land to whites." Ezra Kind's statement hung like thick smoke over the campfire. It made certain sense, and yet it wasn't anything the men wanted to hear.

"Aw, we'll make it out of here. I can feel it in my bones."

"Only thing my bones is telling me is that they're tired and they make popping sounds when I wake up in the morning."

The men laughed as they turned in for the night. The next day would be another long one, bringing them one day closer to the waiting arms of their families.

Late the next afternoon, their first notion of danger came too late to be of use as a warning. Wood's strangled cry ended in a rough bubbling sound. He'd been at the rear of the straggling train, and all six of his friends looked back in the day's waning light to see his pony thrash its head, the reins whipping free, and Wood nowhere in sight.

Before they could yell to him, raw shouts unlike anything they had ever heard descended on them from all sides, and to a man they knew this was the Indian attack they had dreaded since coming into the Black Hills to prospect a year before.

The six men scattered, bolting for nearby boulders, bushes—anything of size that might yield protection from their attackers. Ezra tried to keep his pony between himself and what looked like a swarm of Indians from the far bank of the river. He scrabbled for his long rifle, but his pony, Pretty Boy, danced and thrashed. One whip of its head pulled the reins from Kind's calloused hand. He shouted, "No, dang you horse!" and lunged for the bolting beast.

He fell to his knees in the cold, flowing steam and realized that, for the time being at least, the savages had ignored him. He cut his eyes back upstream in time to see Robert Kent and Tom Brown, close friends, both succumb to at least six Indians at once, so numerous did the savages seem. The two men hadn't a chance, and even though he was in the same grave danger, Kind watched in bowel-loosening horror as an Indian hatchet cleaved the skull of Brown. Another Indian knocked off Kent's felt topper and grabbed a handful of the young man's hair. He jerked Kent's head backward and dragged a dark blade across the man's throat.

All grew silent and still to Kind, crouched in the stream, several feet from the bank, river water dripping from his beard, his hand on the hilt of his knife, still sheathed at his waist. Then the world pounded back at him with its full ferocity. He was aware of a lull in the attack as the Indians busied themselves with the bodies of his friends. He felt sure he saw them all die.

Maybe he could wait there in the water until they left. He glanced behind himself, and his heart crawled back up his throat—the riverbank at this spot was barren of undergrowth, no overhanging knot of roots and no boulders. He sidestepped, hugging the bank, when he saw a movement diagonally across from him—it was Pretty Boy, on the far bank, cropping grass and looking for all the world as if nothing had happened, save for the sagging load on his back that had shifted and slumped to one side.

He knew then that he had a chance of escape, if he could get to the pony. He still had his knife, so he could cut free the load of gold and supplies, keep his gun, then ride hell-for-leather on out of there, praying that no arrows found their mark in him or the horse.

Kind decided he could not wait for full dark. He crouched low until his belly and his chin hair again soaked in the water. Uneven, random shouts pierced the coming dark, and he realized that at least one of the voices was not an Indian but a white man, speaking English and sounding like pain was steady and agonizing. Then that too subsided, marked with an Indian cheer, as if in triumph.

He was but a few feet from the still-grazing horse when he heard another shout, this time much closer. In the near dark he glimpsed a form rushing at him, shouting in that strange tongue, and Pretty Boy bolted from the ruckus. Other Indian voices, raised in a fevered pitch equal parts anger and excitement, and all bloodlust, filled the night sky like a song from hell.

Ezra Kind rose from out of his crawl and ran downstream, dodging branches and boulders and keeping the river close at hand. He spied an outcrop to his right and waited until he passed it, then bolted quickly behind it and away from the river. Sweat stung his eyes and his sides ached, and still he kept running, staying low and praying that the Indians didn't see his dash away from the water.

For two days Ezra Kind hid himself in whatever crevice he might tuck himself into, sleeping as he could, haunted by sounds, by the slight rustling of a bird, hopping on its thin legs from rock to rock, pecking at bugs. It was unaware that a man, starving and near-hysterical, wanted nothing more than to snatch it and

In this 1889 image from Rockerville, Dakota Territory, three sourdoughs pose while panning for their fortunes. Note the sluice through which gravel is washed and separated. *Courtesy Library of Congress*

devour it whole, uncooked, beak, feathers, claws, and all. But Kind held still, fearful that the Sioux ringed his hiding spot.

By the third night he managed to overcome his fear enough that when the moon, damnably bright and silver the past couple of nights, disappeared behind a roiling mass of black clouds that had been building all day, he made his way down to a flat. He felt softer earth under his feet, dropped to it, and snatched young green grasses by the handful, so ravenous was he. The taste, while far from a haunch of deer, was at least more substantial than the pebbles he had been sucking on in an effort to slake his thirst.

The moon had begun to peek out from behind the clouds, and for once he welcomed its light. He had been sitting in the staggered little tumbledown of rocks for half an hour when he thought once again of something that had troubled him his entire life—of dying alone, lost and forgotten. His worst and longest-lived fear realized. And then, as suddenly as that most depressing of thoughts enclosed him in a blanket of grief, another idea occurred to him. He would make his own tombstone so that he might be remembered. A fine stone, to be sure. And he would tell what happened to the rest of his group as well. But how to do it? And with what?

It took but a few minutes to find a suitable flat rock, somewhat square, and with a surface smooth enough that he might be able to gouge into it on both sides. He arranged it on his outstretched legs, grasped his thick-bladed hunting knife as if he were going to dig a furrow with it, and set to work:

came to these hills in 1833 seven of us. DeLacompt, Ezra Kind, GW Wood, T Brown, R Kent, Wm King Indian Crow. all ded but me Ezra Kind killed by Ind beyond the high hill got our gold June 1834

He flopped the stone over, repositioned it on his lap, and recommenced his carving for posterity:

got all of the gold we could carry our ponys all got by the Indians I hav lost my gun and nothing to eat and indians hunting me

Ezra Kind looked at the second side of the stone, then with a last effort, slid it upright between two other rocks into a crevice that seemed made for the task. He slipped his knife back in its sheath and leaned back against the rocks, oddly more at peace than he'd felt for days, feeling now that he didn't much care what happened to himself.

No indication has ever been found that Ezra Kind made it out of the Black Hills alive. But he left behind the first written record of whites inhabiting and mining the Black Hills, an intriguing slab of history for future generations to ponder. The Thoen Stone, named after the men who found it, has

instigated much intriguing speculation. On March 14, 1887, Louis Thoen and his brother were removing stones from a local quarry when they found the carved tablet. Though the stone's authenticity had been questioned from the start, it is now widely accepted as a genuine record. This is especially so since a series of genealogical inquiries regarding the names listed on the stone have turned up specific connections to men who ventured west and were never again heard from. The original Thoen Stone can be seen at the Adams Museum in Deadwood, South Dakota.

It is fruitless, though tempting, to consider that had Ezra Kind and his six fellow miners made it to civilization with their rich ore, it may well have triggered the West's first gold rush, which in turn could have prevented Custer's unfortunate 1874 Black Hills foray (predated by Kind's by some forty years) into sacred Sioux lands, thus altering the course of events that precipitated the Battle of the Little Bighorn and the death of Custer and his men.

4

GOLD FIELD PAUPERS
(1848)

On January 24, 1848, James Marshall finds a nugget of gold in the American River while building a sawmill for Captain John Sutter. Though both men are large landowners, within six months frenzied gold seekers trample their crops and steal their livestock, food, tools—and their land. While thousands find fortune at their expense, Marshall and Sutter die bitter and broke.

◆

You there, what are you doing?"

The two men looked up from skinning the first of two cows laid on the ground. Nearby, the half-stripped remnants of a small hay barn echoed with the prying efforts of three grubby men slowly disassembling the rest of it.

Captain John Sutter sat on the seat of his wagon and looked all around himself in amazement. Where once stood handsome plank fencing and ship-shape barns, lush grasses of field and pasture with horses, cattle, and sheep grazing contentedly, now there were tents and ragged lines with stained clothing wagging in a slight breeze of the early spring afternoon. He saw no animals, save for the two dead cows before him, and the last of the barn that was fast becoming a lumber pile again.

He looked again at the butchering duo. "I said, what are you doing? Those cattle don't belong to you!"

The two men looked at each other, then stood, their hands on their waists, their skinning knives dripping blood on their clothes. "What's it to you, mister?"

Sutter ground his teeth and jumped down from the wagon. He strode toward them and heard the creaking, hammering, and slamming of the dismantling crew cease. All eyes were on him. Good, maybe he could stop some of this blatant thievery. He didn't slow his pace until he stood toe to toe with one of the men. "I'll tell you what it is to me. These are my beef cows that you are butchering and that is my barn and this is my land . . . and you will be arrested for these offenses." His face grew red and hot, but it felt good to confront these thieves, to catch them in the act for once.

One of the men laughed at him and elbowed the man next to him. "You must be Sutter, right? I heard about you."

"Now see here—" Sutter leaned in and wagged a fat finger in the man's face.

Quick as an eyeblink, the man raised the bloodied knife up under Sutter's jowly chin. "You know, back in Georgia where I come from, a man don't jam a finger in another man's face what he knows he might just lose it—or a whole lot more."

Despite the knife point pricking his jaw, Sutter said, "You dare threaten me on my land? You . . . you . . . thieves!"

He fully expected to be stabbed. But instead the men laughed and bent to their tasks.

Sutter stood there helpless, watching them. Other men who had hoped to see some grand spectacle turned away, shaking their heads and laughing.

At that moment, considering everything that had happened to him since the damnable gold had been discovered on his land by Marshall, Sutter thought that maybe death wouldn't be the worst thing.

John Sutter's foulest dreams were coming true. Months before, when he rode north to see the gold for himself at his sawmill being built by James Marshall, he had been warned by the Indians about the evil the yellow stuff brought out in men.

At first everything about the precious metal, despite the warnings from the Indians, was a secret thrill to Sutter. He could scarcely believe that gold was found on his land. He thought perhaps that he would use it to help him advance his own agricultural and merchant endeavors. But now he knew that would never happen. Instead of lucky, he felt cursed.

Sutter trudged back to his wagon. This beautiful river-bottom land, in a matter of months, had become a place he no longer recognized. Everywhere he looked, trees, shrubs, grasses had all been uprooted, turned over, burned in place. And there were men all over, and great mounds of gravel, and tents and wagons, and piles of tins and bottles and other trash. And everywhere were men, laughing and shouting and taking, taking, taking. . . .

As he rolled away from the butchering thieves, a last stab of anger pierced him and Sutter reined up. "I'll be back! I'll bring the law!"

"What law would that be?" The other butcher spoke, an Irishman, silent until then. And they both laughed again.

As he rode back to his home, his home for who knew how long, he thought, "What law, indeed?" Then all he wanted was to be drunk on his homemade *aguardiente*. Something he would not be able to distill for much longer if the thieves kept uprooting his crops.

"I tell you now, once again, and for the last time, that I don't have magical powers! Now leave me be!" James Marshall had had enough of these men, for weeks now, following him from spot to spot. He'd barely get to sink his pick and they would swarm all about him, more often than not pushing him out of the way.

"Look here, Marshall, you are the man who found gold at Sutter's, am I correct?" The big man who asked the question stood a head taller and a good deal wider than Marshall. He folded his arms and stood waiting like an angry giant, waiting for the smaller man to refute the facts.

Marshall closed his eyes and ran a calloused hand through his beard. "I am that man, to be sure. And so help me, God, I wished I'd never found that cursed nugget."

Another man, tending toward fat and with coarse red hair poking out from under a hat that had the looks of once having been a brown derby, said, "Now that there's sacrilegious. You keep on talking like that mister, instead of leading us to a proper gold spot, and we'll string you up."

By then a half-dozen men had gathered, and they glowered at Marshall, mumbling about the unfairness of it all, how some men have the gift and don't even share it with those who have none.

"Look, you all," said Marshall, his clenched fists shaking with a rage uncommon to someone whose demeanor was most often accepting and conciliatory. "I will not be threatened, you hear me?"

One of the men, wearing a much-used coil of rope as a bandolier, shucked it over his head and sneered black stumpy teeth at Marshall. "You gonna tell us where there's gold at or what?"

Marshall swallowed and stepped backward, his hands held in front of him as if to push them back—all the way to the Pacific, he thought. If I could only do that. "If I had the ability to find gold by magical powers, do you think I'd be out here doing my own rough work?" He glanced from face to face and could tell that at least he had cracked open the door. "And dressed like this?" He gestured at his ragged clothes, the rucksack on the ground that held his scant possessions, the oft-repaired handles of his pick and shovel.

Finally, the big man spoke, "What you're saying may be truthful. So we won't hang you—least not right now. But by gum, we'll be keeping an eye on you just the same."

Marshall was about to say, "Why don't you leave me alone," but he thought better of it. As he bent to retrieve his pick from the ground, with the cluster of men behind him, watching his every move, he wondered how his promising life could have taken such a drastic drop. He doubted he could fall any further.

◆

James Marshall couldn't have been more wrong. He continued to prospect for years, without success, and eventually settled in Kelsey as the town black-smith. About the same time, his drinking habit increased. He took his story on the road and offered lectures as the man who first discovered Califor-nia's gold. For the next few decades, he continued to lose ground, literally, as his holdings were nibbled away by well-moneyed mining consortiums that consumed claims large and small in the region of the initial discovery. In 1872 Marshall petitioned for and was awarded a two-hundred-dollar-per-month pension for his "service to the state." That was soon reduced to one hundred dollars, then was cut out completely within six years due to Mar-shall's drunkenness at the state chambers in Sacramento. He died seven years later in extreme poverty. Within months, a ten-foot statue of young Marshall holding a gold nugget and pointing toward the place of his life-changing dis-covery was erected on his grave. A private group paid twenty-five thousand dollars for the monument.

In June 1841, one year after he arrived in California, John Augustus Sutter gained a Mexican land grant that included nearly forty-nine thou-sand acres then still owned by the Mexican government. It offered tremen-dous agricultural promise and large sections of the region's primary rivers, including the Sacramento, Feather, and American. Sutter imported and bred vast numbers of stock, including cattle, pigs, and horses. And he kept acres of gardens and grew wheat for flour. He also operated a sawmill, stables, gristmills, and more. His was a mighty and growing presence in the region.

Though he was capable of grand and generous acts of assistance and charity—he provided much help for the rescue of the Donner Party—John A. Sutter was also, sadly, a firm believer that the local Indians were inferior to white Europeans. He kept Indians enslaved, sometimes in pens, and used them as laborers to build a rambling, enclosed compound he named Fort Sutter. He surrounded it with ten acres of nut and fruit trees and two acres of roses, and his living quarters were housed within the fort itself.

In the winter and spring of 1848, Sutter's holdings were at their peak. Then, within months of the discovery of gold on his property, most of his workers deserted him for the gold fields. As more people flooded the region from all over the world, they grew desperately hungry and began stealing Sutter's unguarded livestock. Soon entire herds were driven off his land. In one instance, two men sold off a herd of Sutter's beeves for sixty thousand dollars, then left the region, having made their pile.

Instead of becoming one of the world's wealthiest men, as he well could have been, Sutter watched as his empire was whittled away to nothing by thieving strangers. He finally headed east, to Washington, D.C., to appeal to Congress for $125,000, a sum he felt was owed him. Congress dithered. In 1880 Sutter died a broken man in his Washington hotel room, awaiting an answer that never came.

5
DESERTION!
(1848)

Armed with a single musket, Army Lieutenant William Tecumseh Sherman barges alone into a cabin housing eighteen soldiers who deserted their posts for the gold fields.

◆

Twenty-eight in one night! Army Lieutenant William Tecumseh Sherman fumed as he mounted up and led the party of eight officers a-horseback into the cool early-morning California air. He was pleased to be the one in the lead, not only because among the officers he was the most experienced with the region aside from Dr. Murray, but also because it rankled him that these men should swear an oath and then chuck it all with no more thought than one might give to flinging a hat across the room after a hard day's work.

Ah, but he knew his devotion to the cause was not necessarily matched by those men who were not officers, had not chosen the army as a way of life. And who could have predicted that within such a short span of time, their very neighbors, strangers to the Monterey region themselves, would appear one day and dig for gold the next, more often than not churning up seventy-five or one hundred dollars in a single day.

And these poor soldiers—poor was the word—he had to stifle a smile, earned six dollars a month. He sympathized, though he was loath to tell them that. He too felt the sting. Lowly army wages weren't the least of it. But because the diggings had inflated the economy, the men could in no way afford anything the army did not provide them. Their wages wouldn't buy a pound of coffee or a sack of flour, let alone luxury items such as tobacco or ale. No, for that reason, he understood why the men did what they did.

There was, of course, no way the army could compete with the promise the gold diggings offered, but neither should it tolerate such blatant disregard. These men not only deserted, but they stole as well, for all of them took packs of gear and supplies and some of them took their saddled mounts and weapons. And that was unacceptable.

The army was sacred to Sherman and much more than a duty to be cast aside on a whim. Even if that whim was something as tantalizing as wealth beyond one's broadest imaginings. But that, he knew well, was something that would elude every single one of the damnable traitorous deserters. And he would see to it that they returned in shame and disgrace to serve out their time in the US Army.

Sherman figured they had traveled six miles when up ahead in the road, and owing to partial moonlight, he spied several blue jackets. He halted and looked behind him, counting only three other officers. The other four would have taken a different route, that side road, possibly.

"Men," whispered Sherman. "I believe there are six of them, all afoot. Let us proceed." As the senior officer, Sherman didn't wait for any commiseration. They walked the horses, the thick, sandy road surface muffling the beasts' footfalls nicely. When they were within shouting range, they bolted straight at the straggling soldiers. It was all over within minutes. The six men, Germans, were dog tired from walking and so presented no trouble.

"Lieutenant Hamilton, you will march these men straight back to Monterey. Hill and Davis, you come with me. We'll route these devils yet. They'll have headed for the Sauna Plain, beyond the river. It's a wide, flat expanse, and it's doubtful they'll have crossed it yet."

As he expected, Sherman saw the deserters' trail clearly, made even easier after another six miles by the full morning light breaking over the plain. In his mounting excitement at gaining on his quarry, Sherman soon outdistanced his two fellow officers, though due to the flat nature of the terrain, they were still in sight. He spied the old adobe ranch house he'd seen on his numerous waterfowl hunting trips taken out this way in the past, as the cabin sat near a pond. He reined up and patted the horse's lightly sweated neck. "Good lad. Now, what have we here?"

Before him he saw two soldiers retrieving water from the pond and several more loitering at the cabin's front. Sherman gritted his teeth. He hated like the devil to lose this prime chance—there could well be many more men inside that cabin, and that's just where he wanted them: trapped like fish in a barrel, no escape, tired, and with few weapons. The moment was ideal. Except for one thing: Including his fast-approaching companions, Hill and Davis, there were only three of them and potentially twenty-two men in and around that cabin.

He couldn't chance waiting for the other officers to meet up with them. He was sure they had good reason for branching off, no doubt pursuing some of the deserters. But judging by the number of tracks he saw plain as the new day at his feet, Sherman felt confident that he had the lion's share of them right here before him, wrapped up in that cabin. All the scene lacked was a silk bow atop the roof.

Sherman touched heel to his claim mount and proceeded forward, not waiting for his companions. They would be there soon enough. He raised his musket. By the time he gained shouting range of the adobe, the men fetching the water had closed in on the cabin, too.

"You men there," he said, riding up bold and as close as he dared. "Get in the house and don't try anything that you will regret."

The few men, shocked at this sudden appearance of an officer they seemed not to know, exchanged confused glances but didn't do much more than shuffle their feet and stare at him. He could tell by their shifting glances and raised eyebrows that they had caught sight of Hill and Davis, whose mounts' hoofbeats he now heard.

Sherman dismounted in one quick jump and brought his musket to bear on the confused assemblage. He cocked the gun. "Do what I say men ... now!"

Without further urging, the men pushed their way in, and Sherman followed them, so close that he could have driven a fist into the last man's back.

Inside, the space was close, dark, and filled with men. Confused shouts gave way to groans as those who had been sleeping awoke and caught sight of an armed officer blocking the door. Their grand quest, it seemed, was over before it began.

Without hesitation, Sherman backed out of the doorway, shouting, "Fall in. Fall in now!" The captured men assumed that a large contingent of desertion-hunting officers awaited them outside, and they began pushing their way out the door into the morning.

"Two ranks now," shouted Sherman.

Within a half-minute, Hill and Davis rode up in time to help Sherman finish disarming the yawning, defeated rabble.

"Eighteen plus six equals a good night's work, I'd say, gentlemen. Let's hope the others found the remaining four." Lieutenant William Tecumseh Sherman couldn't help smiling.

Hill and Davis nodded, smiling in agreement as the last of the deserters slung their knapsacks and prepared to march back to Monterey.

In the end, twenty-seven of the twenty-eight deserters were captured. This is but one episode in what was, for a time, a daily occurrence, indicative of a major problem for the US Army and US Navy. Both branches of service experienced drastic numbers of desertions during the gold rush. And for good reason—although that may well depend on which side of the badge one stood.

Charged with protecting the civilian populace at the Monterey and San Francisco garrisons, the soldiers became increasingly annoyed by the fact that while they were earning six dollars per month, the very people they were supposed to protect were earning seventy-five dollars and more at the gold diggings. Many soldiers who lost their battle with their conscience and deserted public service often took with them their army-issue gear, weapons, and horses.

Of 1,290 soldiers in northern California in July 1848, 716 of them abandoned their posts in the following year and a half. And the US Navy fared little better, as jumping ship abounded. Even when soldiers were sent to retrieve the deserters, it was not uncommon for none to return, all having fallen under the bewitching spell of California's booming gold rush.

Officers were thought more trustworthy and reliable and so were frequently called upon to pursue and bring back deserters. "None remain behind but we poor devils of officers who are restrained by honor." This sentiment, expressed by Lieutenant William Tecumseh Sherman, was felt by most officers at the time. Though he would go on to become a highly regarded commanding general of the United States Army, in an effort to make enough money to survive during the gold rush, Sherman began a business as a surveyor in his spare time.

6

BARELY BY SEA
(1848–49)

Forty-eight gold-seeking passengers aboard the Dolphin, *a shabby, rotting, one-hundred-ton schooner, jump ship in Baja and straggle through parched, cactus-riddled land with no water or food, save for meat hacked from a dead horse.*

◆

The final straw came when John W. Griffith leaned over the gunwale and saw five sprung boards jutting away from the curved hull of the listless old schooner. "Should have known better," he said to himself, surprised that he could still be surprised. He didn't realize that Dibney was within earshot. Dibney leaned over the side and, not surprised, nodded his head. "What we gonna do about it?"

Griffith tuned around to face the deck, a mass of tangled ropes and debris. Carpenter's tools lay strewn about, and punky spots in the decking were crudely marked with burlap sacking. There were many sacks. "Shouldn't have even gotten on this boat in Mazatlán."

"But you did, Griffith. Now, I didn't ask you what you wished you had done different; I asked, what you gonna do about it now?"

The first man turned to his companion. "You talk as a man who might just have something up his sleeve? Out with it, then. I'm all ears. Nothing else to do, drifting as we are in the rotting ghost of what used to be a schooner."

"That's what I like about you, Griffith, you're always yammerin' on with them fancy words and such. My only thought is that we should get off this thing. We're hugging the coast pretty tight anyway. Why not do it from shore? It's nothing but a straight walk up the Baja coast to San Diego anyway, right?"

"I admire your spunk, Mr. Dibney, but there's one thing you've neglected— we're on board a ship."

"Ha! This ain't no ship; this is a tragedy waiting to happen. I say we make the captain let us off. We'll take our shares of food and water and make our way up the coast."

"That's foolhardy, and you know it."

"I know nothing of the sort. Truth is," the man crowded close and spoke in a low voice, "foolhardy is staying on this thing. Why look up there," he gestured above them to a mainsail ragged about the edges and rent with flapping holes. "And look at that rigging. Why it's a miracle we ain't dead already."

So far, Griffith had managed to keep himself relatively healthy—a short bout of dysentery and some initial seasickness but nothing like what he'd heard had been happening on other boats. With startling speed, cholera and scurvy outbreaks were laying low hale, stout people. He'd been stranded in Mazatlán just long enough that he'd grown worried about ever reaching the gold fields. He had no way of getting up the coast when he heard that the one-hundred-ton schooner *Dolphin* had nearly been abandoned, and had been forced to refit, since her passengers from Panama had jumped ship. There was rumor that for $150, a man might find a spot aboard. She was due to sail soon, all the way to San Diego.

He should have followed his instincts about her, but he hadn't, and now here he was, on shore somewhere along the coast of Mexico, staring at a paltry pile of provisions at his feet, having left the sinking disaster that was the *Dolphin*. He had no doubt that this would prove safer than drowning, but as he looked at the parched inland landscape, he wondered just how much safer it might be.

The sound of voices shouting pulled him from his reverie, and he saw that the lifeboat had once again swamped in the surf, still a dozen yards from shore. The men in the boat spluttered and thrashed shoreward. It was like that with each subsequent load from the anchored *Dolphin*. Even from shore, she looked like a spent beast. But come what may, thought Griffith, at least we have a chance on shore. At least we'll find water.

As if privy to his thoughts, a small man, bald and shaped like a pear, standing next to him but looking inland, said, "We'll be hard-pressed to find water here."

"Hard-pressed, but I'll wager there's a better chance of finding it here than on board that rotting scow."

That had been four days before, when each of the forty-eight men who came ashore still had a half-bottle of water, bitter and undrinkable though it was, a handful of rice, and two unappetizing hunks of hardtack. So that's what we get for paying our fare, Griffith had thought bitterly as he'd looked at the meager provisions.

They found nothing on shore but rock, jagged black rock that gave the landscape a sort of hell-on-earth look. The rocks seemed scorched, and the earth offered no vegetation save for the occasional cactus, hard, spiny little growths that seemed to serve no purpose other than to annoy them. For days the ex-sailors had wandered, their legs weak from months of little activity aboard ship.

On the fourth day, two brothers and a lawyer vowed they could not go on and dropped where they stood. The rest staggered forward, promising to bring them back some form of sustenance, the hope in finding such a boon their only guiding light.

Griffith thought of the personal property he had carelessly dropped along the trail as they trudged up the rocky hell of a coastline. There were things he had packed so carefully, things he had looked at 1,001 times on the journey, the guidebook to the diggings, the maps, the Bible his wife had given him, along with a daguerreotype of her and a journal in which he had vowed to keep a record of his days as an Argonaut.

After another day of trudging onward, he laid aside the journal and the Bible and took a long time doing so. But another of their party, Crane, picked up the Bible and carried it for a couple of days. When Crane also grew too weary to lug it, Griffith took it back from him and so kept his wife's gift after all.

This last item he was thankful that he retained. Other items—the expensive clothing and tools they had saved for and selected with care back in Philadelphia—were all gone now. And he realized with each dragging step that he couldn't care less. He had been tempted more than once to toss away his very boots, so heavy did they seem in this sweltering sun, and yet he knew that to do so would invite sure death, at least sooner than he was sure to meet it. How far could a man get on shredded, bloody feet?

THE WAY THEY GO TO CALIFORNIA.

Once gold was discovered in California in 1848, it was a matter of weeks before people from back east scrambled westward any way they could. Ships and wagons were the most common modes of transport, though fanciful thinking was entertained: One man proposed a steam-powered balloon, the "Avitor." Alas, his idea never got off the ground. Despite that, more than twenty-five thousand people emigrated to California's gold rush country in 1849 alone, and that figure doubled the next year. *Courtesy Library of Congress*

After a week, Houghton's dog, a little bull terrier, whined and moaned so that the men thought he might be on the verge of giving up, too. But when they looked for him and found him on the far side of a small tangle of rocks, the little mite was digging at a patch of earth. "He smells water," his owner said. "Mark my words, so he does." Houghton was relieved, as there had been grumbling among the men about eating the dog. But he had proven his worth by finding the life-giving liquid.

The men helped the dog at first, then pushed the panting lad out of the way and carried on themselves, with their hands and tin cups. And at four feet down, a trickle, then a steady steam of potable water began to fill their ragged hole. Each man cried out of sheer happiness. Houghton let his dog drink from his cup and hugged the little savior until the dog grew tired of the unwanted attention and resumed slaking his thirst.

"Now that we are renewed and fortified," said Griffith, "I propose that at least two of us go back for the three who gave up."

None there could argue, as the thought had been foremost on their minds since they left the haggard trio.

Griffith had become somewhat of a leader of the group, and now he spoke: "We'll make camp here and wait while you, Crane, and perhaps you other two men go back to retrieve them."

Within two days, they returned with the thankful rescued men. Then, as a group, they moved onward. Days passed, and it was only the lack of water that drove them. They happened upon an old nag, more bone and bug-infested hide than horse. Still, it was meat of a sort, and that represented an extension, if not a promise, on the life they were living. The desperate men killed it and cooked it. This would prove to be a turning point for them, as it gave them sustenance to keep trudging forward. It proved to be a turning point of another sort for a man named Melville, who soon became ill from eating the foul meat.

Within days, farther up the coast, the party met again with the remaining crew and passengers of the *Dolphin*, listing at anchor a short distance from shore and looking much worse for the wear. The captain and a skeleton crew were determined to sail her to San Diego, despite her obvious sinking condition.

Though food was scarce and water scarcer still, Griffith's party opted to continue on foot, after turning over the ill Melville, who was made comfortable onboard the *Dolphin*. They later found out that he expired the day before the *Dolphin* limped into port at San Diego. He was buried there, and the ship was condemned and sold for scrap.

The trekking party eventually made it through the mountains to the Mexican village of El Rosario, where they bargained for corn and other supplies. They rested there and were able to continue their journey. After three and a half weeks of dallying with death on a daily basis, the haggard party made its way to San Diego harbor. On telling their tale to others, they found little sympathy, as most West Coast arrivals, no matter the route taken, had experienced a grueling trip.

California-bound ships that made the journey around Cape Horn were often pummeled by vicious winds topping one hundred miles per hour. Some were driven off course, often ending up in Africa. One shipping company, the Vanderbilt Line, lost four of its six ships in 1852 and 1853. Ships weren't only transporting hopeful Argonauts; they were also filled with much-needed supplies. So wealthy were the diggings in those early, heady days of California's gold rush that eggs shipped from the East sold for a dollar each in San Francisco. One ship carrying a load of flour sold its valuable cargo for forty-four dollars per barrel and ended up with a tidy profit of eighty thousand dollars on its return trip.

In an effort to avoid the six- to nine-month journey around Cape Horn, many bound for the gold fields decided on the sixty-mile Isthmus of Panama route. This overland journey was often the worst part of the trip, as travelers had to trek through jungles infested with thieves and disease. Malaria was particularly worrisome, as was dysentery, yellow fever, and cholera. Once the gold seekers made it to the other side of the isthmus, they often had to wait for months for passage on a suspect ship to make the final thirty-five-hundred-mile trip up the coast to San Francisco.

Not all such journeys ended poorly, however. One fellow, Henry Mayo Newhall, left his wife in Massachusetts in 1850 to seek their fortune. He became quite successful in the auction business and wrote to his wife that he was headed back to retrieve her. At the same time, she had written to tell him that she was on her way to meet him in San Francisco. Unaware of the other's plans, they proceeded on their respective journeys, he sailing down the Pacific Coast to Panama, she down the Atlantic Coast to the same locale. And in Panama City, they literally bumped into each other.

7

THE CHILEAN WAR
(1849)

Dr. Concha and his peones are told by Americans new to the California diggings to vacate their Calaveras River claims. The Chileans secure a court order, but a bloody battle ensues. Before it is through, greed and racism win out over fair play, and men pay with their lives.

Dr. Concha paused in digging. He spent a full minute laving his face with clear water from above his rocker. He didn't see the gringo right away. Though it was only a few days after Christmas, the first Christmas he had ever spent away from his family back in Chile, the day had been a particularly bright one, if not hot, and he had been working hard. Sweat stippled his forehead, the same with all the men, his peones, fellow native Chileans who'd come to the diggings as everyone did, with an eye toward gold and the rich lives it might bring them.

Even behind his cool kerchief, Concha couldn't help but smile. If all it took to make a modest fortune at his gold claim here on the Calaveras River was a little sweat, maybe some aches and pains at night, then he could live with that. He thought of his wife back home in Chile, how she would rub the stiffness from his shoulders. Enough of that thinking, he told himself. You are here to work, work hard, and make this gulch pay. And besides, he thought as he looked around at the men all sweating and laboring the same as him, these men are counting on you, Concha. Don't let them down.

"Hey you, Mexican!"

Concha and most of his men swung their gazes toward the top of the gulch. There stood a line of white men, perhaps a dozen and a half, among them maybe six who held long guns, a mix of rifles and shotguns. A couple of others plainly wore sidearms. The speaker cradled a rifle, Concha could see that now, the sunlight glinting off brass.

Concha grunted, exchanged a sidelong glance with a friend, and then pasted on a smile. "Hello, señor. Welcome to our camp. I should correct you, we are not Mexicans but Chileans. There is a—"

"Same damn thing . . . Mexican. Now you listen up—we ain't hard men, and we are fair, so me and the gents here," he waved the tip of his rifle in a broad gesture. "We figure you're on our land. See, we claim this here gulch for our own. And according to camp rules, you got yourselves settled in where you ain't wanted nor allowed. Sort of like fleas on a dog." The speaker looked to his fellows, who laughed and jostled as if they were schoolboys.

Concha felt his grip on his shovel handle tighten. Calm and reasoned, he thought. You can make this all work out. This is surely a misunderstanding, nothing more. His men had all stopped working now and began to walk slowly toward him, carrying their picks and shovels. A fight would do no one any good. Most of them could not speak English but relied on him to convey such talk to them.

But the dark scowls on their faces told him they knew what the white man was on about. He must make sure this ends without violence. So far in the camp they had been treated, if not equably, then at least with indifference, and as a foreigner, Concha knew this was preferable to hostility.

He cleared his throat. "You are new here. We have been here for some time. This gulch is ours, legally. Claims have been filed—"

Again, the white man interrupted him. "We are American and you ain't. Case closed. Now everybody knows that no foreigners are allowed to work a claim here. California is under American control and will soon be a state. And you and your kind are not wanted."

Dr. Concha watched the man's face redden as he spoke. This low brute actually believed the rhetoric he fouled the air with.

"You got fifteen days to clear out. Plenty of time, in my estimation. In the meantime, we'll be right here. Making sure you do as you are told."

"But you are on our land, sir." Concha spoke in a measured, tight tone, but it took every ounce of his willpower not to dash up the slope and pummel this fool with his fists. But he knew he would be shot before he took five steps. And then where would his men be? No, no, there has to be a better way. The law, of course. They claimed this land legally, and it will be defended legally.

Several days later, Concha rode back to the claim. He had slipped away from their camp under cover of darkness on the fastest of their three horses, and his men had done their best to cover his absence, lest the whites grow suspicious. Now he was back among them, smiling and holding a stamped, thrice-folded paper tight to his chest. The men laid down their tools and gathered around him. "I have the writ here from the judge in Stockton. It states that we are the lawful owners of this claim and that as such, we have the power to evict interlopers."

His smile slipped from his face, and he looked at them all. "I have thought long and hard about this, and I believe that violence is normally the worst solution. But in order to avoid it, sometimes men must act swiftly to take the upper hand." His men stared at him, concern and confusion knitting their brows. He looked from man to man before he continued, brandishing the paper before him. "This writ gives us permission to arrest these men. But I feel we must take them by surprise and drive them from our claims."

His men looked at one another, then back to him, and nodded their assent.

They rushed the Americans at dusk, when the whites' hoots and drunken howls were at a peak, just before they knew the fools would go to sleep. And despite Concha's urgings to avoid bloodshed at all costs, two Americans were killed in the melee. As his men secured the other sixteen, he consoled himself by saying that they were in the right and that they had not been the ones to instigate this fight.

They loaded the Americans into a wagon, and though nearly all were in some state of drunkenness, the Chileans took extra precautions to keep them secured and under heavy guard. Every creak of the wheels tensed them, and the night passed slowly. They avoided routes that would bring them close to other whites. They had a two-day trip before them and by the time the first night arrived, they had made less progress than Concha had expected. But there was nothing to do about it. They had to bed down so they might be fresh and put in a full day tomorrow.

During the night, Concha awakened to shouts. For a brief moment he had no idea where he was, so soundly had he slept by the campfire. It had been a long few days, and he was more tired than he expected he would be. But the shouts, muffled thumps, and angry growls of men snapped him awake fully.

And for a brief moment he wished he was still asleep, that the tumult and mayhem about him were all just a bad, bad dream.

The Americans were loose! Somehow they had escaped, and from what Concha could see, they were overpowering his men. Already they were outnumbered, and the Americans began to beat them savagely. He had not yet been seen, for the fire had burned down considerably. He crouched low and backed away from the fire. Weighing his odds of survival against the help he might be able to rouse from the law in Stockton, Concha swallowed hard, hating what he was doing but knowing it might well be their only chance at survival. He backed farther into the scrubby growth, then turned and ran low and fast for the tethered horses. And then he rode for help.

◆

"Ahem, hem, hem. . . ." The squat man in the midst of the crowd stood up from behind the judge's makeshift bench and rapped his knuckles on the boards. No one listened. He shouted, "Shut your mouths, all of you!" That did it.

"That's better," he continued. "Now, after spending most of an hour of good, honest digging time listening to both sides on this skirmish, and having thought about it good, long, and hard for nearly another ten minutes, it is the finding of this miners' court that these here foreigners," he waved a hand at the bound and bruised Chileans who had been forced to stand, "are to all be punished." The Chileans' wrists were bound behind their backs, their eyes, cheeks, and lips puffed with plum-colored bruises and crusted with blood.

The gathered miners hooted and hoorah-ed until the judge shouted them down again. "These two here," the judge pointed to the two Chileans closest to him, "they're to be hung for killing the two Americans when they kidnapped 'em and tried to haul 'em off to Stockton—as if that old judge knows what in hell he's up to."

One Chilean tried to rush the judge's table, but a miner dashed forward, punched him square between the shoulder blades, and sent him sprawling to the dirt.

The judge shook his head. "Them others are to receive the lash, by God. Teach them to monkey with Americans!"

The cheers continued as the Chileans feebly fought their bonds and tried to plead their case. Though they had explained to the best of their ability that the claims were lawfully theirs and that they had a writ to prove it, it did no good. The whites were too stirred up.

Two of their number were lynched, and the others who had been captured were whipped until their backs were flayed open, leaving runnels of blood and raw flesh.

Even that wasn't enough. Two of the flogged men were pointed out by the half-drunken Americans who had been kidnapped and humiliated by the Chileans as being particularly unforgiving adversaries. For this, they were held down, their backs raw and bleeding, and their ears were sliced off.

<hr />

Dr. Concha fled from the fight that night on the trail. Days later he was dry-gulched outside a dance hall in San Francisco and died of a gunshot wound. Despite their perceived superiority over the Chileans, the newly arrived Americans had no legal right to assume the Chileans' claims, as evidenced by the fact that Dr. Concha was able to secure a writ from a judge in nearby Stockton, enabling him to evict the interloping Americans. Unfortunately, such blatant acts of racism were supported by local and regional laws that prohibited anyone not of "American" descent from owning land. Whites as the conquering newcomers also treated Mexicans as second-class citizens, much as they did with blacks, Indians, Chinese, and anyone else who didn't look or sound as though he or she was from Western Europe.

Outrageous acts perpetrated against the Latino population gave rise to outlaws such as Joaquin Murietta, who, along with his gang, routinely attacked, robbed, and killed Anglo miners in the heart of California's gold country in revenge for the alleged theft of his claim, the rape and murder of his wife, and the lynching of his half-brother. The legend has far outgrown the source materials to the point where reports and sources conflict. Regardless of these fuzzy facts, the saga of Joaquin Murietta is the basis for the world-famous legend of Zorro.

8

DEATH VALLEY DAZE
(1849)

In October 1849 a 107-wagon train of emigrants ventures south toward the Mojave Desert to avoid the Sierra Nevada. In November twenty-seven wagons opt for a rumored shortcut. The next four months bring unequaled hardships for the party, and they name the place through which they trek . . . Death Valley.

◈

Try as he might, Manly could not recall the names of the children in the Arcane and Bennett families. He and Rogers had traveled with them now for months, stuck with them even as the group fractured into smaller groups, as with the Jayhawkers' departure some weeks before. That group of young men felt hampered by the slower-moving members of the Arcane and Bennett parties, but Manly and Rogers knew that those families would need their help in this increasingly hellish place. They had all wished the Jayhawkers luck, and each group vowed to return for the other should they find help first. But for now, it was all Manly could do to put one foot in front of the other. He was sure he knew the children all by name. As he walked slowly, just a few yards behind Rogers, he shook his head. Of all the things that his mind should fix on, this was the silliest. Must be the lack of water making his brain act like cotton batting.

He thought about asking Rogers what their names were, but he dared not speak, for the heat was so intense that to open his lips would risk evaporating what little moisture was there. He had rolled a bullet around in his mouth for most of the morning, then had traded it for a pebble some time ago.

What hell on earth is this? he thought, looking down at the irregular patchwork of cracked earth at his feet. Wished we had never struck out on our own, away from the initial wagon train. And then each faction of our group fractured further and attempted to make its own way. It looked as if all would be lost. Manly could still hear Rogers's voice echoing in his head from their

Death Valley earned its ominous name in 1849 because it offered such brutal terrain for the Arcane and Bennett Party to cross in winter. Temperatures there in the summer have reached 134 degrees Fahrenheit. Despite its harsh and demanding climate, gold and silver were mined there in the 1850s and borax in the 1880s. *US Geological Survey*

last break, less than an hour before. He had said that it would take a knapsack full of miracles to make it out of this place alive. And Manly feared his friend might be proved right.

As he trudged on, Manly thought back on the last month. He had scouted ahead of the party, climbing peaks and using his telescope in an attempt to find an acceptable route. But all he saw, peak after peak, was more of the same flat expanse between mountains, with no evidence of water or forage for the beasts. He did his best to maintain a hopeful demeanor around his fellow emigrants, but when he'd found himself alone, Manly wept.

Back at the camp, they had begun killing the oxen, as they were of little use now that the wagons could hardly be pulled. Even if the terrain would permit it, the beasts were in such poor condition that they could scarcely keep themselves mobile. They had found no fat on the oxen once dressed out. The animals that had been spared, at least for the time being, were still charged with dragging the few remaining wagons. They were so footsore that the emigrants had had to fashion moccasins for their hooves out of the hides of the dead oxen. It seemed not to help the beasts all that much.

Five days after their water ran out, the Jayhawkers still had not reached the Amargosa River. They dropped from exhaustion where they stood and called it camp, not knowing if any of them might have the ability to rise again the next morning once they felt rested.

As they sank to the cracked, hard earth, one man looked at the bedraggled band of young men, his companions. He wondered how many of them regretted leaving the main party for this more treacherous route. He suspected most of them did. Who could have foreseen that Mother Nature would dish up such hard resistance? In truth, he thought as he looked at the panting, slack forms of his friends, he held out little hope that they would have any reason to rise ever again, so parched and drawn and gaunt did they all feel.

In the morning, with their slumber having somewhat restored their strength, the men stood with their hands outstretched toward their meager fire, daring to hope that the day might bring them some form of good fortune. They were quiet for some minutes, when they began to look at each other, startled and confused. What was happening? They looked up. The sky had clouded imperceptibly while they sat or stood, dejected and not wanting to continue onward. In a short while, snowflakes dropped down on them, lightly at first, then in more profusion. They grabbed at the falling flakes with their puckered, parched mouths and swollen tongues.

"The blankets, shirts, anything, spread them out!" shouted a burly fellow. The order proved a good one, as it soon resulted in catching enough snow to ease—at least for a few minutes—the stinging pangs of thirst that had tortured them for long days.

Manly trudged on and, staggering, again lapsed into a daze of recent memory. He recalled that Indians had killed three oxen in a raid that they should have expected. The travelers were to blame, and they knew it. Days before the attack, someone in his party had stolen melons from an Indian's patch. They should have known better.

The attack was but one more setback on their treacherous trail. And though they felt sure they were closer than ever to the settlement over the mountains, the route to get there had proved nearly impossible. They had nearly lost a wagon at the steep cliff marking the head of a canyon. That unfortunate situation forced them to send two scouts ahead—Manly and Rogers—to trek out on foot over the mountains to find food and bring back help. Manly recalled how startled they had been when the meat of the ox sacrificed for their trip nearly all fit into their two knapsacks. Based on such grim realities, the two men figured they had ten days to return, or face a ghastly welcome.

Little did they know, it would be weeks before they might return.

Since then, he and Rogers had crossed mountains and down valleys, then climbed mountains again—only to stare at a vista stippled with endless peaks. There seemed to be more mountains than ever. Here and there they found signs of their friends, the Jayhawkers, who had passed that way before them. And they came upon the dead body of Mr. Fish, one of that strong trending group.

The single body of water they found was a sizable lake, but it proved undrinkable. It had been foul, alkaline, and off color. And shortly they found that their thirst had increased to such an extent that they were simply not able to chew or swallow their ox meat—they had no saliva with which to moisten it.

Sleep eluded the men, eating food was no longer a possibility, and so they continued their ragged pace, knowing that if they did not persist, the one hundred or so men, women, and children left behind would perish in that living hell, awaiting their return. Ahead they found ragged remnants of the Jayhawkers party and gave them hunks of their ox meat in hopes that it might sustain them long enough for help to return. Manly recalled that as he and Rogers prepared to leave the meager camp the following morning, several Jayhawkers, with eyes that could no longer force tears, pressed scraps of paper into their hands. The notes bore the names and addresses of relations. Nothing was said as the men tearfully took their leave, stuffing the papers into their pockets as they walked away.

Though they did not realize it, the two haggard men, Manly and Rogers, had crossed the Mojave Desert, and as they emerged from it, they found a pass through the San Gabriel Mountains. There they were able to shoot several birds. Farther on, they emerged overlooking a verdant valley a thousand acres in size, dotted with grazing cattle. Soon they found themselves guests at the table at a Spanish ranch, where they were fed a hearty meal, their

desperate hunger overriding the guilt they felt at indulging in a repast they wished they could share with their friends back in the vicious desert.

They spent the night and in the morning bought two horses, dried meats, flour, beans, and wheat from the rancher. They retraced their steps and headed back toward Death Valley. Before heading back into the mountains, they bought another mare and a one-eyed mule. It was determined that the horses were too weak for doing much more than carrying the men, so the mule carried the bulk of the provisions.

Their eventual arrival back at the Arcane and Bennett camp, where they had left their friends, at first offered naught but fear and foreboding. As they approached, they came upon the body of one man, a Captain Culverwell. But as they trudged onward and finally reached the camp, they were greeted by men, women, and children, gaunt and tired, but still alive. And soon the haggard band made its trek out to safety. Manly and Rogers traveled more than five hundred miles to save the members of the Arcane and Bennett Party, with much of that time spent crossing the Mojave Desert. In the months to come, Manly would rescue several more groups of wayward emigrants from Death Valley. Today, three landmarks there bear his name: Manly Peak, Manly Beacon, and Lake Manly.

The Jayhawkers, meanwhile, had continued on their ragged, every-man-for-himself journeys but soon found that some level of mutual aid was more beneficial to all. One of them, though, did wander away from the rest, convinced he could find water in unseen puddles. He never returned to camp. So hungry were they that nothing was left of an ox they had slaughtered, save for one charred horn, on which a man gnawed. Eventually they too reached a peak in the San Gabriel Mountains, the final impediment to their trek. And they grazed on the perpetual snows there as if they were cattle on grass. They eventually made their way over the mountains to safety, though the footprints they left in the snow bore bloodstains.

9

BRUFF'S JOURNEY
(1849–50)

Joseph Goldsborough Bruff's thirteen-wagon cross-country expedition to California's gold fields becomes snowbound in the Sierra Range. His gold-crazed men push on ahead, promising to return. They never do. Starving in the spring, Bruff staggers west.

They'll be back, you just wait and see. Wait and see." Joseph Goldsborough Bruff grinned at the ribby, little dog, though he knew it wouldn't make one whit of difference to the animal. Or to himself, for that matter. Truth was, he knew no one was coming back for him. Had known it for a month. What makes a man maintain a clawhold on hope such as this? he thought. He eyed the little dog with a greed he despised in himself. Ever practical, Bruff knew that should he resort to eating his dear little dog, the poor beast wouldn't make but a single meal, so small and wasted was he. Bruff was beyond allowing the guilt over such thoughts to hamper him.

"What a way to welcome in the new year, eh dog?" Bruff dragged at the slushed snow in front of his tent with a broken shovel, his bony hands trembling on the handle. He stopped frequently to blow on his throbbing fingers and hug them to his chest. Nothing could help make the task easier, he knew. Under better circumstances, the boy he was burying, a four-year-old, might have been a little red-faced corker, running through a happy house, upsetting his older sisters with his hijinks. But this lad's lot had been anything but happy.

As he dug the little grave, Bruff reflected on how he came to be here, on what he might have done differently. His thoughts returned to the men of the company, the Washington City and California Mining Association, that he had organized. Sixty-three men in thirteen wagons, and they had made it all the way across the country, alive and intact, when so many others had failed, fallen out over squabbling and laziness.

The group had remained intact as a company because of him, and he didn't mind telling them that. On the journey he brooked no complaining nor put up with sloth, not if they were to all make it to the gold fields. By gum, he'd vowed, they were going to make it there as a company. And they had. Nearly so, anyway, until snow hammered them to a halt in the Sierra Range. And it was there, with provisions running dangerously low, that they finally had to make a painful decision: Someone had to stay with the wagons loaded with valuable gear and, most importantly to Bruff, his own journals, notebooks, and gathered natural samples. The party simply could not go on as it had been, with the heavy wagons making such slow progress. It was decided that the men would pack light and move on, though they assured Bruff they would send someone back for him.

At the last minute, one man, his friend Poyle, agreed to stay with him. That had heartened Bruff, most definitely. But neither man guessed they would be forced to live this way for long. Soon more fall snowstorms drove at them from the angry heavens above. Bruff's rheumatism bent him forward as if he were constantly looking to pick up something off the muddy earth of the tent floor.

After a few weeks, a man appeared one day while Poyle was off on a hunting trip. The stranger bore with him a thin, pasty four-year-old boy, asking if he would take care of the boy until he could return. Bruff recalled taking the measure of the man, looking him up and down and deciding that the rascal had nothing but deceit writ large on his pocked face. He sent the man on his way, knowing that the boy would fare no worse with him than he would with the man.

That had been weeks before, and now Bruff resumed the slow task of digging the boy's grave. The snow had been the easiest part to get through, but the earth was not as iron-hard as he had expected. Still, it was hard enough. It took him most of the morning to hollow out a hole in the cold, hard earth deep enough and long enough to accommodate the thin boy. The night before, he had washed the lad's frail body with handfuls of snow, then wrapped him in the cleanest cloth he could find, a section of white bedding. The entire time, his tears had flowed freely and it surprised him, for he had never been a man given to showing his emotions. He suspected his weakened state was responsible, and he no longer cared.

Soon he had the wee body laid in the grave and filled it in, saying over it what words he found suitable. He topped the grave with stones piled high, and on a plank he carved, "William, Infant son of Lambkin—an Unnatural Father, Died Jan. 1, 1850." Bruff slept the rest of the day, too tired to try to find food, too achy from the crippling rheumatism made worse by the cold and wet weather.

It was the barking of his bull terrier that brought J. Goldsborough Bruff awake. He lay still for a long moment, too startled to quiet the dog. Then he heard it—the chuffing of a grizzly bear, just outside the tent. He dared not utter a sound—the beasts were unpredictable enough without goading them into a frenzy. He edged forward, taking care not to breathe, and reached for his rifle with his right arm.

He checked it and, quiet as he dared, with the bear chuffing intermittently and the dog's barking tightened into a throat-filled growl, as if the little animal had been eating gravel, Bruff peered through the opening between the tent flaps and wished he hadn't. There, in the bright of the moon reflecting off the banked and heaped snow, he saw a large bruin, not ten feet away. It stopped its rough noises and stared at him, pinning him to the spot as one might a moth to a board.

For the longest five minutes of his life, Bruff and the bear stared at each other, unmoving. Finally, when Bruff felt he could no longer stand the beast's piercing gaze, the light reflecting off its dark, liquid eyes, the bear swung away and walked out of sight. After some minutes, Bruff shushed the dog and brought the tired creature inside the tent. Finally, toward daylight, Bruff and the dog slept.

It had been more than a month since Poyle had been in camp, and the only thing left of the last doe he shot was the memory of it. It is April 1, Bruff told himself, shaking his head slowly as if to rouse himself from the hunger-induced stupor he found himself in more and more frequently. Surely someone would come. And yet, did he need that person and his charity? Had he not lived through a winter in the mountains?

"I must walk out of here, though I am bent and weak; I must make the attempt." Even as he spoke these words, he knew he did not have the strength to do so. Thirty-two miles was but a couple of days of solid effort for a healthy man. He tried to raise a smile. He had always been a hale fellow eager to try his hand at new and interesting challenges in life, but this time, he was nothing more than a man made old far beyond his years, bent by rheumatism.

"April fourth, little friend," he told the dog. The dog sensed change and pushed his way out the tent flap. With much difficulty, Bruff shouldered the sack containing his too-heavy notebooks, and with his rifle, he looked at the grimy camp for what he prayed was the last time. He glanced once more at his precious specimen collections. "I will make it back for them," he told himself. "I must. The world must know what stuff we are made of."

Then he turned and, step by pained step, he walked his way out of the camp. Thirty-two miles lay before him. He shook his head as he paused, not ten feet from the tent, already exhausted.

Days passed as he stumbled along the trail, so weak he could scarcely stay upright. As he tried to cross a chilling freshet, he staggered, then fell into the water. He crawled up the riverbank and somehow kept moving forward. Toward afternoon, he collapsed against a dead oak tree and knew that he had reached the very end of his hope, his endurance, his life.

Some time later the dog's hoarse barks roused him from his stupor. He saw something moving toward him. Oh God, he thought. Please don't let it be a bear. I would rather die alone here of starvation than succumb to a bear mauling.

The bear spoke, and he realized it was a man. He squinted his eyes and concentrated harder. It looked like his friend, Poyle. Could it be? Yes, yes, he saw that it was. Good old Poyle. Bruff knew that someone would come back, someone would return for him. He tried to rise, but could not do it. But he did manage to clasp his friend's hand in his, and smile.

It had been just over ten months since the Washington City and California Mining Association expedition, organized and planned to a T by Joseph Goldsborough Bruff, had made its Missouri River crossing, each of the

sixty-three men filled with a bravado and confidence that had flagged little until they reached the Sierra too late in the season. They should have waited out the winter, as did so many other travelers, before attempting to cross the mighty range at the onset of the unpredictable winter months. But their optimism and inflated opinion of their abilities deceived them. Some of the members of Bruff's party who went on ahead made a halfhearted effort to return for him. But inclement weather, the allure of gold, and Bruff's prickly disposition all conspired to keep them away, most only too glad to be out from under his thumb.

For two years following his brutal winter, Bruff roved with his note-books in tow, from camp to camp, detailing the exploits of mine-camp life. He desired to publish the ultimate, authoritative, and genuine guide for gold seekers, though he himself found no gold. Eventually he booked passage aboard a ship and sailed back to the East, by way of Panama. When he finally made it to New York City, he was robbed. The thieves stole everything from him but his precious journals. Despite his story, he found that no pub-lisher wished to take a chance on releasing the journals.

Bruff spent his later years as the supervising architect for the US Depart-ment of the Treasury in Washington, D.C. During his lifetime, Bruff could find no ready market for his copious, heavily illustrated journals. They were eventually published posthumously, under the title Gold Rush: The Journals, Drawings, and Other Papers of J. Goldsborough Bruff. Today historians consider them some of the most useful firsthand accounts of the California Gold Rush.

10

SALTING THE CLAIM
(1850)

Desperate to off-load their useless claim in Tuolumne County, California, three mining partners attract the interest of Chinese miners from a neighboring claim. The suspicious would-be buyers, savvy to claim salting, are still duped—all it takes is one shotgun, two shells filled with gold flake, and one dead rattlesnake.

◈

Clarence tossed his pick and sat down hard on the river-worn log beside one of his other partners, Rufus. "I have had about enough of wading in gumbo. This has to be the lousiest claim anyone in the history of gold panners has ever claimed."

Rufus didn't respond, just kept working the rocker. Their other partner, Burton, came wading up, his leather boots slick with water. "What is he on about now, Rufus?"

The two men exchanged a glance, but Clarence caught them.

"You know as well as I do that there ain't nothing of value on this here claim of ours." Clarence pointed a calloused finger at the hard earth between his feet.

"I'm inclined to agree with him, at least this one time," said Rufus, winking at Clarence. "And truth be told, I'm not so sure I can take another winter here."

"Keep yammering on about it, fellas, and we'll have even less than nothing when we play this thing out."

"Played out? Why, this thing already—"

Burton advanced on the younger man and poked him in the chest hard enough to sprawl him backward off the log. Clarence jumped to his feet in a shot and squared off, ready to hammer the older, wiser partner into a sobbing mess.

"You better pack a lunch, kid," said Rufus, laughing. "Cause this could take you all day."

"Not even," said Burton, lowering his voice and keeping one eye on the riled youth. "Now calm yourself, Clarence, and look here—I have an idea how we can off-load this useless claim and take our profits and try our luck elsewhere."

"Profits?" said Rufus. "You got to be kidding. The only ones making any of those are them Chinese over on the next claim," he jerked his head to his left, toward the arm of gravel bank separating their claim from the smaller but more profitable adjoining claim. "They been doing all right."

"Yeah, and wouldn't it be just fine if we could sell 'em this one." Burton eyed his partners and smiled.

"How—" Clarence looked about ready to start a new fight, so Rufus cut him off.

"You got a plan, Burton?"

The big man nodded, still smiling. "I been thinking on it. Ain't much else to do out there, moving dirt from one place to another all day."

"They know we ain't doing as well as them, though."

"Yeah, but they don't know how bad it's been. And they won't, as long as you keep from bellyaching every time you're tired, Clarence."

The younger partner looked at his feet, shifted a smooth black rock from one boot to another, but said nothing.

"You talking about salting, ain't you?" said Rufus, his eyes narrowing.

Burton leaned closer and waited for both men to lean in toward him. "Hell, yes, boys. Hell yes."

"I don't know, Burton." Rufus stood up, doffed his flop-brim felt hat, and scratched his nearly bald head. "Them Chinese is savvy. They'll know we salted if we tell 'em where to dip their sample pans. Trick is to get it where they're going to be, and unless you're a mind reader, and one who can read a Chinaman's mind at that, then I don't see how—"

But Burton kept on smiling, standing there with his arms folded across his chest and nodding his head as if he had all the answers. "I thought of a way."

"Only way I can figure is to salt the entire claim," said Clarence, as if Rufus hadn't spoken. He looked at both men as if he had just decided the matter.

"How you going to do that, dummy?" Rufus shook his head. "We ain't dug enough gold out of here in a year to salt a weasel's backside, let alone toss it all over this claim. In case you forgot, this claim is one of the larger ones around these parts."

Clarence resumed toeing the rock at his feet, his face burning a deep scarlet.

"Now, Rufe, the boy's on the right trail but the wrong game is all." The big man patted Clarence on the shoulder. "I got a way to salt it . . . right in front of them!"

"You never . . ." said Rufus, but he was smiling.

A few days later, Burton turned to Rufus. "All right, now? You got it? They'll be here any minute. I need you back behind that shoulder of gravel. I'll do my best to make it work out right."

"Still don't see why I don't get to do it and not Rufus." Clarence looked down at his boots.

"Dammit, Clarence. I been over this with you a hunnert times or more. I'll need you here, in case any of them Chinese need us to fetch something. Just keep your mouth shut and let me and Rufus do what we need to. Got me?" Burton looked at the boy until Clarence returned the look and nodded.

"Good. Now get set, 'cause here they come." Burton checked his double-barrel shotgun and snapped it shut. Under his breath, he said, "We get one shot at this."

The four Chinese miners from the neighboring claim walked to the edge of the claim silently, lined up side by side, and eyed Burton and his shotgun. They all held pans, two of them smiled, the other two offered slight bows. One of them smoked a short pipe, blue smoke drifting upward into the clear fall air.

"Come on in, boys. Here's the claim, in all its glory. We're sellin' up, all tuckered out. Got families to see, places to be, as the man in the newspaper says."

The four men took tentative steps onto the claim.

"See you got your pans, good, good. Tuck in, anywheres you like," said Burton, nodding at the stream before them.

"Yeah, we ain't salted nothin'," said Clarence.

The man with the pipe stopped short, narrowed his eyes at the two men.

"Boy speaks the truth, neighbor," said Burton. When the man turned back to the stream, Burton jammed the butt of the shotgun into Clarence's side.

"Ow, hey!"

"You shut your mouth, boy. You hear? Any talking and I'm the one to do it." Burton turned back toward the prospective buyers, his smile back on his face as if it had been there forever.

After a quarter hour, the four men had tried their hand at sampling various spots but failed to find a speck of color. They turned to Burton and Clarence, two of them shaking their heads.

"Why don't you fellas try one more spot before you call it a day, huh? Try over there, maybe." Burton gestured with the shotgun toward a far corner of the claim.

A smile crossed the pipe-smoker's face.

That one can sniff a salted spot, thought Burton. Or at least he likes to think so.

"No, no, no. That corner no good. We try there." The man with the pipe pointed back behind Burton and Clarence.

Before Burton could offer a weak argument, a long, fat rattlesnake, one of the largest any of them had seen, flopped down the embankment right about where the Chinese miners were headed to give the claim one last shot.

"Holy mother of God!" shouted Burton, pushing the visitors aside. "Get back, fellas, get back!" He positioned himself in front of them, though still a good distance from the snake, and let loose with both barrels—BOOM! KABOOM! The snake, dead a full day by then, offered little fight. "Clarence, get that thing out of here—these men aim to dig here and we can't have them messing with that nasty thing."

The boy slipped in and dragged off the three blasted parts of snake, tossing them over the bank as the four visitors smiled and nodded and bowed to Burton, thanking him for shooting the wretched snake.

They set to work sampling the general location where the snake had been and turned up a touch of color in one panful after another. It wasn't much, but it was enough, they determined, to make an offer on the claim.

◆

"Less than I would have liked," said Clarence, as he stuffed his spare socks into his rucksack.

"I swear boy, you'd gripe if they strung you up with a new rope." Rufus smiled and shook his head. "If you really don't like the deal we come to, why, you're welcome to spend another winter here."

Rufus winked at Burton, who said, "Wouldn't catch me here any longer than I need to be." He slung his own sack onto his back and turned to face his partners. "Especially not with all them snakes around these parts."

Their laughter could be heard up and down the river valley.

◈

Claim salting, or the planting of rich ore samples in an unproductive mine for the express purpose of attracting unwary buyers, is an ancient practice. One of the first recorded instances of a claim being salted out West was, oddly enough, also the location of the first discovery of gold that touched off the firestorm that became the California Gold Rush.

On the morning that John Sutter arrived at the famous mill he hired James Marshall to build for him, Marshall had the mill hands scatter various bits of gold in the millrace so that Sutter might "discover" some of the ore for himself. That one of the children of the crew's cook, Mrs. Jenny Wimmer, happened upon the gold before Sutter did is of little consequence, for Sutter already had high hopes of exploiting the unexpected potential windfall.

As mining became more widespread, so too did claim tampering. Numerous cases of out-and-out fraud dot the pages of gold rush history. Use of a shotgun was a preferred method, as shells could be packed with gold dust and then blasted far enough into the raw earth of the claim that was up for sale. Before greenhorns became savvy to the ways of salting, a few well-directed blasts from a shotgun usually were sufficient to sell a potential buyer on the golden possibilities of an otherwise useless claim.

In one notorious instance, the owners of the worthless North Ophir Mine on the Comstock cut silver dollars in half, then pounded them into unrecognizable shapes, and distributed them in a shaft. Shortly thereafter, stock of the mine rose and rose—until one sucker scrutinized one of his silver lumps and realized it bore the words, "ted States of."

11

MINE CAMP JUSTICE
(1851)

In the northern California mining camp of Indian Bar, on the Feather River,
Swede and a friend steal hard-earned gold dust from their two partners. The
friend flees, but Swede is caught digging up his hidden loot. A miners' court
finds the big man guilty, and a noose is rigged.

Word circled the mining camp of Indian Bar as a buzzard will a gut
pile. Within an hour the assemblage of miners, ranging in age from
boys too young to sprout decent lip hair to men too old and bent from years
of hard labor in the diggings, gathered around the trembling, seated William
Brown, also known as Swede. Their glowers forced his eyes groundward and
set his teeth to grind. A drop of sweat clung to his long nose tip.

The judge, old man Mikelson, stood before the assemblage, nodded at the
men of the jury and at the man charged with acting as the defendant's lawyer,
and thumbed the lapels of his black, boiled-wool frock coat. He only wore it
on special occasions; otherwise it was kept tightly rolled in a snatch of canvas
tarpaulin. The murmuring men quieted, and he nodded.

"Now men, you all must know why we are gathered here. Seems a couple
of months back, William Brown and another no-account pilfered eighteen
hundred dollars worth of hard-earned gold dust from their former partners,
Riley and Horace here." Mikelson inclined his head toward the two wronged
men and half smiled.

"Now see here, you can't go talking like that, why you're—"

"Talking like what, McDonough?" Mikelson stretched to his full height.
"Just because you were told to be his lawyer don't mean you don't know as well
as me that this here Swede stole the money with his partner. Why, he admitted
it to Horace and Riley already. Didn't you, Billy Boy?"

Someone had handed Swede a full bottle of whiskey at the beginning of the proceedings, and he had been availing himself of it with increasing frequency. Consequently, his head had begun to bob and wobble, and every few minutes a pinched sob arose from his trembling mouth.

It was possible, some of the men thought as they studied him, that he had just nodded his head. They looked to one another for confirmation, passing their own bottles of liquid lightning back and forth among them.

"Now," resumed Mikelson, working his lapels harder than ever. "Men of the jury. Seems to me you have but one decision you can come to, and that is not only guilt, but I'd guess death, too."

At the harsh word, a wave of surprised murmurs rippled through the first few rows of the crowd. The hundreds of men in the rows beyond had become rowdy. It seemed their bottles were emptying.

Brown suddenly looked up and seemed to focus his eyes. "What? What is this?"

"Get off with you now, you dozen jury men. And don't keep us waiting all day, neither." Mikelson regarded his pocket watch. "It is one o'clock. This is a working camp, after all. Lots of men have folks depending on them to earn a day's wage—honestly." This last comment he directed at the defendant, whose mouth worked the air like that of a banked fish.

For long minutes the entire crowd waited, Brown in the center. Finally, the jurors returned. Mikelson snatched the paper from the foreman and unfolded it. He nodded, then cleared his throat. "By the power vested in me by my fellow miners on this here day in December of 1851 at Indian Bar, I declare that the Swede known to all of us as William Brown is guilty of theft of personal property in the form of gold dust amounting to about eighteen hundred dollars."

"I didn't take it all," said Brown, weaving in his seat.

"Hell, we all know that, Billy, but you're the only one fool enough to come back and dig up the rest you hid. That rascal partner of yours got away and you didn't. Them's the breaks."

Swede shook his head as if to dispel a fly but kept his mouth closed.

"Now, where was I? Oh yes, so, the jury of your peers, these here twelve men," the judge gestured with a gnarled hand toward the grim-faced dozen,

Freshly minted prospectors, eager for a chance to strike it rich, pause briefly for a photograph in their journey to the newest mine camps and gold fields. *Courtesy Library of Congress*

who to a man stood looking at their boots, hats in hand, "have determined that in one hour's time, you are to be hung from your neck until you are dead."

"What? What is this? But I only took a little gold dust. . . ." Brown spun around in a circle. The bottle, nearly emptied, slipped from his grasp and clunked to the ground. "I never killed a man in all my born days, jah. It's the truth." He spied Horace and Riley and lurched toward them. "Horace, Riley, my old partners, tell them that I never kill no one. Right?"

But other men forced him back toward the judge. Someone shouted, "Aw, hell, give him three hours, at least. Man's got a right to make his arrangements, ain't he?"

This comment met with murmurs, then shouts of assent that reached such a climax that the judge could only nod in agreement.

"Three hours then. We'll be back here at—" he pulled out his pocket watch and regarded it a moment. "At a quarter past the hour of four o'clock."

As the crowd dispersed, Swede spoke to his captors. "I would like . . . more whiskey, please. And paper and pen. I wish to write letters to my good friends and family back home, in Stockholm."

Little Dicky Filkins, much moved by the proceedings, as evidenced by the quivering of his lower lip and the welling of tears in his eyes, nodded and rushed off to retrieve the ink and paper. Swede's whiskey request was fulfilled by a nearly full bottle that Horace thrust at him.

"What you doing that for?" said Riley, his eyes wide.

"Old times' sake. Don't worry, it'll come out of my share."

"You bet it will," said Riley, shaking his head and walking away.

When they rigged the noose around his neck, William Brown made as if to lift his hands, but they were bound behind his waist by a kerchief wrapped tight about the wrists. A tall, somber man whose jaw muscle worked like a second heartbeat whipped the coil of rope upward over the stoutest limb of the gnarled tree that had served such a purpose twice before. Fittingly, it grew just outside the entrance to the camp's cemetery.

"Shouldn't have let him get so drunk," said Horace, just loud enough for Riley to hear.

"Man's own business how much he drinks," said his partner, not taking his eyes from the swaying Swede.

"Yeah, but a man ought not go to his maker all liquored up."

"I guess that's how a fair number of men meet the Lord, wouldn't you say?"

Horace nodded, not taking his eyes from the condemned man, their one-time partner. He had to admit, though, Riley had a point. He also allowed how it was good to have their money back.

Just then, William Brown jerked upright and stood taller than he had been. He shook his head, his eyes focused on the judge. "I would like to pray."

"I expect you would. Well, no time like the present." He nodded and said in a quieter voice, "Best get on with it, Billy."

Brown lowered his head, closed his eyes, and began whispering to himself. The only sounds the gathered miners heard from him were the soft whisper of words only he could hear. Fifteen feet behind him, eight men had assembled, grasping hold of the slack rope.

Soon, Brown's lips stopped moving.

The judge nodded once toward the eight men. The small amount of slack in the rope tightened, and they stormed backward at a brisk pace. William Brown rose up into the air. The creaking of rope and limb were drowned out by a ragged chorus of whoops and cheers from the mostly drunken assemblage. It had been a long afternoon of waiting.

Swede spun and kicked; strangled coughs and spittle flew from his pink, distended tongue. His body swung in a wide arc, his legs spasmed and the toes of his worn boots tapped at the air as if he were engaged in a new, energetic dance step.

After nearly a minute of this, with little change, the judge shouted over the cheers to the minders of the rope, "Work him, by God! Work him up and down, that's the only way!"

The eight hoisters gritted their teeth, and their cheeks filled and emptied with the effort of dragging William Brown up and down, over and over again. The drunken revelers cheered with each successive raising as the Swede's frantic efforts at survival grew less energetic. The more sober of the gathered spectators watched as the doomed man's throat finally collapsed from the rope's crushing grip.

After ten minutes of sustained effort, it was apparent to all that William "Swede" Brown was no longer among the living. His tall form hung limp, his big boots pointed inward, toes touching. His face had purpled long minutes before, and his head seemed to have swelled to twice its natural size, made even more unbelievable by the impossible narrowness of his crushed neck.

His eyes, white orbs, shot through with veins of red, stared downward, perched as they were above a snot-caked ginger-color mustache. But the worst sight of all was the man's purple-black tongue, filling his mouth as if he were choking on a beef tongue. The sight repulsed many onlookers, particularly the women, who walked away, shaking their heads.

"Well, that's that." Riley turned toward Horace, his eyebrows arched high.

Horace continued to stare at the slowly swinging body as a tall, somber man lashed the rope tight around the trunk of the tree. "Damn shame, is all," said Horace as he walked away, his hands in his trouser pockets. His fingertips touched the buckskin pouch holding his share of the recovered six hundred dollars in dust. His fingers closed tight around it, and he gritted his teeth, fighting down the urge to rip it from his pocket and fling the sack far from him.

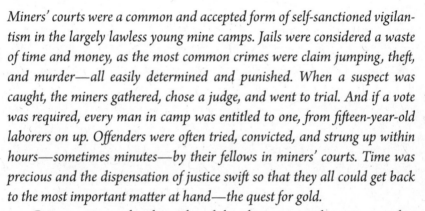

Miners' courts were a common and accepted form of self-sanctioned vigilantism in the largely lawless young mine camps. Jails were considered a waste of time and money, as the most common crimes were claim jumping, theft, and murder—all easily determined and punished. When a suspect was caught, the miners gathered, chose a judge, and went to trial. And if a vote was required, every man in camp was entitled to one, from fifteen-year-old laborers on up. Offenders were often tried, convicted, and strung up within hours—sometimes minutes—by their fellows in miners' courts. Time was precious and the dispensation of justice swift so that they all could get back to the most important matter at hand—the quest for gold.

Crimes not considered worthy of the ultimate punishment were often settled by flogging, mutilation (ears were frequently cut off), and banishment from camp. If a banished man returned, he could expect further punishment, or he might just be hung. In the Klondike food was so precious that stealing from a man's larder was a hanging offense.

The concept of preventive hangings was also popular. One Colorado miner, when inebriated, would fire his pistols at passersby. His skittish campmates grew weary of this drunken practice, and it was determined that it would be better for everyone involved if he were hung in order to avoid potential fatalities. So they strung him up.

12

WEAVERVILLE
TONG WAR
(1854)

Rival Chinese gold-mining gangs stun locals by attacking each other with medieval weaponry in a bloody ten-minute battle. Eight are killed, six injured, and a bystander takes a bullet to the head.

◆

Ihave no idea what in the world is going on with all these folks today, but I tell you what, I'm gettin' gone while I can." Old Ned Theakston tugged his hat brim down, and with a quick nod to the man beside him, he slipped through the growing crowd and headed toward any place that might serve up a drink or three. Hardworking man takes the first day off he's had in weeks, thought Ned as he walked away from the increasing noise with long steps. You think his fellow miners would cut him a wider swath. . . .

"It's on! It's on today!" A boy, not yet of age to shave, by Ned's reckoning, shouted as he ran barefoot down the dusty summer street of Weaverville, California.

"Hold on, boy, hold on." Ned grabbed hold of the boy by the shoulders. "Now what's all this? You're runnin' down here like your hair's afire."

The kid smiled, eyes wide, as he squirmed in Ned's grasp. "You ain't heard? Why, it's them Tongs—the Chinese. They been ordering all manner of crazy weapons for weeks now."

Ned let go of the boy, who seemed to be enjoying his role as informer to an old man who hadn't yet heard the biggest news to hit Weaverville since Orton's strike some months before.

"Go on, boy. I can't read minds."

"My pappy's a blacksmith."

"Mine was a peach grower, 'til he died. You don't hear me crowing about it all over the streets of Weaverville."

The kid looked at Ned for a moment, then said, "Mister, you been in the diggin's too long. I got to go." The boy resumed his frantic run down the street, shouting, "It's on! Them Tongs'll be at it any time now!"

Ned continued toward the Jackdaw Saloon. "I'll take a beer for now," said Ned, leaning against the bar and scanning the room. When the barkeep set down the glass, he said, "Hurry it up, mister. I got to lock up."

"A saloon that locks up in the middle of the day? Now I have seen it all," said Ned as he quaffed his beer, in no rush to head back out into the July heat. He reflected on the frantic boy's news. Of course he had heard of the unrest of the two Tong groups.

As if reading his thoughts, the barkeep, a jowly fellow with a starched collar and black arm garters, came around to the front of the plank bar. "Finish 'er off, old-timer."

"What's the hurry?" But Ned knew he'd get the bum's rush if he didn't comply.

The fat man sighed. "Hurry is that I aim to get a good spot to see the Tongs duke it out."

"That again," said Ned.

"You don't wanna see it, fine. But I aim to."

Ned set down his empty glass. "Reckon I'll tag along."

As they headed toward the sheep pasture just behind Weaverville's main street, Ned asked the man just what this hubbub was all about.

"You mean to tell me you don't know?"

"Nope. Got enough on my mind with trying to find gold and all."

"Then you ain't been in town in a spell."

"That's a fact." Ned smiled at the statement. It was a source of pride to him that he could go long stretches at his diggings without seeing his fellow man. "What's it all about, then?"

"No one knows. Only thing they say is that the Cantons and the Hong Kongs are fit to bust over something, so they're going to have at each other," the chubby man smiled at Ned, and continued, "using all manner of weapons like you'd find in China."

"Like what?" Now Ned was intrigued. He'd been an apprentice to a gunsmith decades before, but that had lasted about as long as anything else in his life—do a little of this, a little of that, call it good, and move on. Could have been worse, he thought. Could have been Chinese. Them fellas were always getting the short end of the stick, getting treated as if they were less than dirt. He'd never been able to understand a lick of what they said, but he figured they felt the same about him.

All the while they talked, with Ned easily keeping up with the hustling fat barkeep, people from town streamed past them. Soon, though, they arrived at the edge of the field, and the bartender pointed a chubby finger toward one end. "See there," he read aloud the banner, "Canton City Company."

It stretched across the front of a group of what looked to Ned like hundreds of Chinese. Many of them had nearly shaved heads, save for their long pigtails. Some of them wore odd-looking hats like a miner's pan, but they all seemed to have a weapon of some sort. They were too far from him to get a good look, though.

They were spread out, in what looked to him like a pretty solid formation along one end of the field. Seemed to Ned like these boys knew a thing or two about fighting.

"And lookee that!" the bartender shouted, pointing toward the other end of the grassy sward.

Ned saw a smaller group, less than half, if he had to guess, of Chinese. Most of them wore bright red hats. Like the superior number at the far end of the field, this group was dressed in the loose-fitting garments the Chinese favored, but they all held various weapons, the likes of which Ned had never laid eyes on. Some of them looked like spears with long wooden handles ending in hooks and odd-shaped pitchforks. Some of the men held shields made of straw, woven tight and shaped into a circle big around as a proper campfire. In their other hands they held steel swords and shook them menacingly.

All of a sudden, the sound of many drums and gongs rose up from each end of the field, followed by the shouts of enraged men. The crowd of onlookers, what seemed to Ned was about the entire town of Weaverville, gave up an even louder wave of noise. The bartender leaned close to him and shouted, "Hold onto your hat, old-timer!"

Then both sides rushed at each other, the two unevenly matched masses of men looked to Ned as if they would explode when they hit, so hard did they run

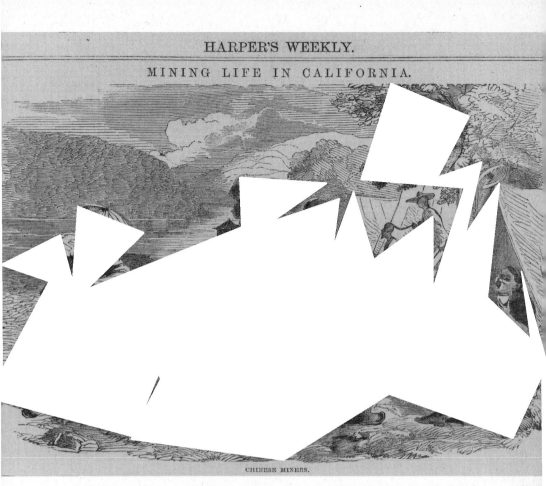

MINING LIFE IN CALIFORNIA.

CHINESE MINERS.

In the nineteenth century, the Chinese, more so than many other nationalities, supplied much-needed labor in America's burgeoning mining industry. Despite their substantial contributions in civilizing the West, the Chinese experienced brutal racial oppression. *Courtesy Library of Congress*

and so fierce and determined did they look. Then they stopped and stared at each other for a few moments. Even the crowd was silent. But only for a moment. Then came jeers and howls and a whole lot of bad words that made him embarrassed to see women and children in the crowd. He pinched his own mouth closed, lest any should see him and think he was responsible for even one of those foul words. Chinese or no, a man doesn't deserve such name-calling, he thought.

The sides had retreated. They went through the drums and gongs and howling and then again came the hard running at each other. And again they stopped short of colliding. What are they on about? thought Ned. That's odd behavior. But then again, he thought, I'm no Chinaman, so what do I know?

One voice from the crowd broke out above the rest. "This time, make it count!" Ned looked up at the nearby man. It was that tall Swedish fellow. Then the loudmouth shot off his pistol—straight into the crowd of Chinese.

It was as if someone lit a fuse. The Chinese groups tore at each other like wildcats, slamming and screaming and thudding into one another. It was a violent, harsh clash of men, and no one in the crowd of non-Chinese watchers was prepared to see such a vicious display. It only occurred to many as they stood there that none of them knew what the fight was about.

The battle raged up and down the field, spilling into the rows of gathered spectators, who joined in here and there. Ned had no intention of getting injured or worse for someone else's fight. He saw at least two dozen Chinese men sprawled on the grass, some of them moving, their arms reaching toward the blue sky and shaking. Others whipped their heads back and forth; some of them were as still as stone, crumpled where they fell. All of the fallen bore the red-black staining of blood on their clothes.

As he struggled to free himself from the crowd, Ned felt the tension-thickened air about them loosen somehow. Everyone seemed to calm down, the shouting and screams diminished, and pretty soon all they heard were the moans of the wounded.

"Well now, old-timer," said the bartender, his big, jowly face leering close by Ned's. "That was a bit of excitement, eh? And I don't think it lasted more than ten minutes."

Ned was about to tell the fool a thing or two when someone nearby shouted, "Someone shot the Swedish fella!"

People pressed in close around the tall man stretched out at their feet. Looked to Ned as if he'd been shot in the head, his chest not rising or falling. Dead, thought Ned. And he doubted it could have been a Chinaman who did it—they all were using their oldtime weapons. But might be that the Swede's shot had killed one of the Chinese. So someone in the crowd must have done him in.

Ned looked around and saw quite a few Chinese faces, as they made up quite a big part of the camp's population. If I were you, he thought to himself, I'd get out of here. Then he took his own advice and walked back to his claim.

So much for a day off, he thought. *Next time I decide to give myself one, I'll work through it.*

◆

Though Weaverville, California, was established in 1850 by white miners, within a few years, more than two thousand Chinese called it home, many of them finding modest success working claims that other miners had given up on.

Due to an accusation of cheating by one group, or Tong, in Weaverville's Chinese-only gambling establishment, on July 15, 1854, two Tong gangs from Weaverville's burgeoning Chinatown attacked each other with medieval weaponry. It was a short but bloody battle that left eight dead, six injured, and a bystanding Swede, who'd earlier been calling for Chinese blood, dead with a bullet through his head.

Though the Tong factions got along well after the battle, the non-Chinese members of the community retaliated, afraid that the Chinese were getting too powerful. Part of the town's Chinese quarter was razed, resulting in an exodus from Weaverville of a number of Chinese miners.

Today Weaverville is home to the Temple of the Forest Beneath the Clouds, the oldest continuously used Chinese temple in California. The impressive temple, museum, and grounds are maintained as a state historic park and are open to the public.

13

THE ILL-FATED GROSH BROTHERS
(1857)

Ethan Allen Grosh and Hosea Ballou Grosh, discoverers of one of the mightiest silver lodes ever found, are dogged by tragedy and don't get the chance to whoop it up. Their old friend, Henry Comstock, lays claim to the Grosh Brothers' lode. The rest is history. But Comstock gets his. . . .

We are sitting on a monster ledge, Hosea, do you hear me?" The two brothers were not prone to histrionics, but nonetheless, they trembled with the excitement of possibility. After eight years of labor and scattershot successes at various mines, it looked as though their ship had come in. "It's mid-August now," said Ethan Allen Grosh to his brother. "As we agreed, we'll leave within the week and head to Philadelphia to find investors, and for proper assaying."

"What about Henry?"

"Comstock? Our blustering friend and frequent visitor? Why, we can hardly prevent him from continuing his regular visits—we just won't be here. It's a wonder he gets anything done, what with all the chatting he gets up to. Which leads me to another point, Hosea."

Ethan Allen Grosh lowered his voice and leaned closer to his brother, though they were both alone in their cabin for the present. "It goes without saying that we shall need to keep this quiet, at all costs. As we always have."

"But this time," said Hosea, smiling, "we have more reason than ever."

The two quiet brothers smiled, shaking their heads in disbelief. After all their work, it was coming true, they could just feel it.

Ethan heard his brother scream and, dropping his own tools, he scrambled up the ragged gravel path. He found Hosea trembling, his face sapped of color, and his forehead beaded with a sickly sweat. Then he looked down to where Hosea was staring, and his entire body went cold. This, he thought, is not good. Not good at all.

His brother had driven his own pick into his boot and deep into his foot. Already, he could see the blood, thick, red-black, and mixed with the dirt crusting Hosea's boot. If ever there was a wound ripe for infection, it was this. As he watched, Hosea wobbled, then slumped backward and sat on a low rock.

"It's just a foot wound," said Hosea, as he tried to smile. "I've had worse and you know it." But Ethan was unconvinced. This was a brutal mess and would considerably alter their plans to leave in a few days. He secretly wondered if they might ever be able to leave.

As if in reply to his worried thoughts, Hosea said, "I'll heal up, don't you worry. Nothing like this can stop a Grosh, and especially not when it's taken us eight years to get to this point. No, sir. We're going all the way together. All the way."

"Then you best get rid of that hole in your foot, brother." Ethan forced a smile.

<hr />

Ethan leaned in close to his brother's ear. Hosea's rasping, halting breaths worried him with their irregularity. He pushed the sweat-matted hair from Hosea's forehead and said in a whisper, "I can do no more for you, dear brother. It is up to God now. You will soon be with our dear mother. God rest you both."

He fancied he felt the slightest of squeezes from Hosea's hand in his. And as he watched his brother's face, he knew he was past pain now, as the dreaded infection had taken over his body in the two weeks since his accident. He recounted their last conversation of two days before. They were in agreement—he would have to get the ore samples properly assayed. Ethan would do this for his brother's sake, to prove that their years in the West had not been in vain.

He laid his head on the blanket at his brother's side, still holding his hand. When he awoke a few hours later, Hosea's body was cold.

"Late November is not the best time to set out on such a journey, Ethan."

Grosh looked at his younger traveling companion, Robert Bucke. The man hadn't said it, but it felt as though he had heard the very words with his own ears. It was his guilty conscience, he knew, for the words sounded just like his brother's voice, perhaps their father's.

I know that, thought Ethan, but there is little to be done about it. I need to get to California and prove up on this ore, or I might lose the place come spring. I haven't a penny to my name and had to work the placers from Hosea's death on September 2 until now just to get enough to outfit this trip. But Ethan said nothing, hoping that his brother's spirit would help guide them on an expeditious and safe trip across the Sierra Nevada—even so late in the year.

His companion continued cinching their provisions to the back of the mule and kept his peace, trying not to think of the snow that had begun to fall before daybreak.

Nearly a month to the day after they had set out, the mule began to sway and fight to stay standing. Were it not for the depth of the snow at times, holding the beast upright, it would surely have toppled to the ground miles before. It seemed to Ethan that the animal must have pneumonia. He wanted to care more than he did, but he himself felt so very cold, he could do little more than stare at the swaying, raspy-breathed mule.

Grosh looked over at Bucke. The young man looked nearly as bad as the mule. "We'll camp here. Rest the mule," said Grosh.

"Ethan, that mule is not going to make it. It's already dead." Bucke regarded Grosh and shook his head. "It just doesn't know it yet."

"What do you propose we do, then?" Grosh might feel horrible and cold and despondent, but he'd be cursed if he was going to let this junior trail partner talk him down like that.

"We have to kill the mule, Ethan. Our provisions are so low that we'll not last much longer ourselves, and that mule is starved. It's been subsisting on what twigs and bark scraps we've been able to scrounge up for it. That's no way to treat the poor beast."

Grosh, still flaming inside, stared at the young Canadian for a long minute. Then his anger flickered out, and he closed his eyes. "You're right, of course, Robert. Would you . . . ?"

The younger man nodded, and Grosh turned away, hugging himself and marveling at what was turning out to be a season of utter folly.

A week later found them trudging through snow deeper than any they had seen. And as they reached Lake Tahoe, they were socked in at their paltry campsite by a blizzard so violent that, after the squalls eased some days later, no sign of the trail could be seen. Most of their provisions were long gone, and they were unable to carry much of the stringy meat of the slaughtered mule. Soon, they grew so weak that they each had to dispense with everything they carried but their blankets. For Grosh, this meant his property maps and sack containing the ore samples. He tied them up tight in a section of canvas and stuffed them into a hollow pine, stoppering the hole with a stone. He carved a mark in the tree and then trudged on.

Eventually, even their blankets became sodden and useless, and they let them drop. They had no way to make fires, and for four days they wandered, unable to find a trail, huddling in freezing temperatures. At night they heard wolves close by, howling and snuffling, and saw sign of one bear. They soon could go no farther, and in a jumble of rocks, without speaking of it, they each came to the conclusion that their end had been reached.

As if in response to their unspoken agreement, they heard shots fired close by. With a bit of struggle, Bucke was able to stand. The two men stared at each other for a moment, then Bucke nodded and hobbled off in the direction of the shots.

Robert Bucke returned after half an hour with a party of miners who had been out hunting. The group carried the two men to Last Chance, their rustic mine camp. A doctor of dubious skills determined that the frostbite on their feet was untreatable, then performed amputations. Grosh lost both legs, and Bucke, one foot and part of the other. Ethan Allen Grosh never regained consciousness and died some days later, on December 19, 1857, just a few months after his brother, Hosea. Bucke was more fortunate and spent the winter at Last Chance. In the spring the miners pooled enough money to send Bucke back to his hometown of London, Ontario. He eventually became a medical doctor.

Unlike so many of their fellow '49ers, the Grosh brothers were well educated and had much experience in assaying, geology, and mineralogy. They worked diligently, and in the course of eight years, from 1849 to 1857, they wrote more than eighty letters from mining camps back home to their father in Pennsylvania, unwittingly providing rich documentation of the rough-and-tumble lives miners led.

When he learned of the demise of Ethan Grosh, the brothers' erstwhile friend, Henry Comstock, claimed their cabin and land for himself, though he didn't think much of the paperwork and ore samples he found in a locked trunk in the cabin. As more miners moved into the area, Comstock paid them all visits. When Peter O'Riley and Patrick McLaughlin made a rich strike on property that Comstock had previously claimed "grazing rights" on, he threatened them until they cut him and his partner, Immanuel "Manny" Penrod, into shares of the claim.

Since the richest diggings lay far underground, each sold their claims to larger, well-funded consortiums for fractions of what they would one day be worth. Patrick McLaughlin received thirty-five hundred dollars. He squandered it and ended his days toiling at a variety of menial jobs. "Manny" Penrod sold his shares for eighty-five hundred dollars. Peter O'Riley retained his interests and collected dividends totaling forty thousand dollars. He eventually went broke and died in a California insane asylum. Henry Comstock sold all his shares for eleven thousand dollars. He opened and lost several businesses and resumed prospecting before shooting himself near Bozeman, Montana, in September 1870.

To date, the Comstock Lode, though it really was the Grosh brothers' discovery, has offered up nine million ounces of gold and 220 million ounces of silver, making it one of the world's largest silver strikes. Combined, the Comstock's gold and silver have a total value, at today's prices, of approximately twelve billion dollars.

14

PIKES PEAK OR BUST!
(1859)

Eager to reach the Pikes Peak gold fields, one expedition of '59ers, which includes the three Blue brothers of Illinois, takes the problematic Smoky Hill Trail, renowned for Indian attacks and little food and water. All too soon, it will become known as the "Starvation Trail."

On that sunny February day in 1859, standing beside his two brothers, Alexander and Charlie, Daniel Blue felt as though nothing in his life could possibly ever go wrong again. He was young and healthy, and he was headed off to the gold fields of Colorado. He and his brothers were convinced by accounts that popped up on a daily basis, even here at their home in Illinois, of rich gold strikes where a man could dig for a few days and claim his life's fortune. Daniel could scarcely wait to leave. Their plan was to buy a pack pony, load it with provisions bought with their pooled savings, then walk to the diggings.

They'd each read the available guide books and felt they had learned everything they might possibly need to know to make a go of it. It being February, they figured on arriving at the diggings in time to get to serious work come the spring melt.

"With any luck, little brother," Alexander had said, cuffing Daniel on the back of the head, "we'll make our fortunes and be home again by fall. Just in time to hire *other* folks to help with the harvest."

Daniel secretly liked that idea just fine, but he didn't want to tell either of them, or their two companions who were to accompany them, that it was the journey getting there that he was most looking forward to. For he knew, despite the pie-in-the-sky accounts, that once they arrived at Pikes Peak, life would be a series of days filled with hard work that began before daylight and ended after sundown. Much like life on the farm. So, for the time being, walking for a couple of months with his brothers, hunting and foraging along the way, why that sounded just about right to Daniel.

At Manhattan, Kansas, the three brothers and their two friends joined with another team of nine members, all sharing the notion that banding together could only help since they were heading into Indian country. Daniel and his brothers liked the idea, though only for the practical aspects. He felt guilty thinking so, but Daniel couldn't quite shake the notion that he would have preferred to spend the time with the smaller group. Now the party was so large that any comment made was either ignored or passed around for far too long, chewed on and spit out like tough jerky.

Within days, Daniel was pleased to see that he would get his wish, for at the jumping-off place for the Smoky Hill Trail, one of the newer men of their group mentioned that he had already traveled that route. His claim was met with skepticism by some of the men, but he finally won some of them over by telling them that it had proved the shorter route to the gold fields.

And so, in the face of indecision, the party agreed to split. Daniel and his brothers soon found themselves part of a whittled-down, seven-man party. They continued ahead, and the others stayed behind near Fort Riley to hunt buffalo before moving on.

Within days, the first of their travails began.

"Charlie, where's the pony?"

"What?"

"Charlie . . . the pony," said Alexander, looking up from the campfire. "Where's the pony?"

"I thought you were going to take care of it. I did yesterday, and the day before."

Alexander growled through his gritted teeth at his younger brother. "That's because it's your job. Has been for oh, how long now? Since we bought him?" He looked back at his brother, as did the other men, with not a sympathetic eye in the bunch.

A Pikes Peak prospector shows off his cozy homestead in the middle of his claim. Shortly after gold and silver were discovered there in 1858, prospectors and speculators snapped up promising claims long before hordes of gold seekers from the East arrived. *Courtesy Library of Congress*

"This is just great," continued Alexander. "Not only did we lose our way off the trail two days ago, but the pony's gone and it has most of our provisions still packed on it—because you didn't even see fit to unpack it."

Another member of the group said, "Doesn't that tell you something, Alexander?"

"What?"

"Ponies that just walked all day long and are still loaded with provisions don't usually wander too far. If we don't find it soon, it's a safe bet the Indians stole it."

The very idea smacked them each with its awfulness. Not a day had passed on the Smoky Hill Trail when they hadn't seen some sign of Indians, though much of the sign seemed old to their untrained eyes. They each wondered what more could go wrong.

◆

According to Daniel's pocket journal, the day was March 18, and the blizzard had hit the day before. He'd never felt so cold, and they had to stop frequently to huddle for warmth, despite the urgings of Alexander, who said they were only fifty-five or so miles from Denver.

The little lost band of gold seekers had no way of knowing it, but they were still 170 miles from Denver. The one thing they did know was that their provisions were nearly gone. The next morning, with the snow falling and the wind whistling at them from seemingly every direction, three of their party of seven bade the three Blue brothers and a man named Soley good luck and struck off on their own, in hopes of saving themselves. As they slowly walked off into the snow, they promised to send help for them should they find any. The unspoken truth was that the men were too afraid they might soon run out of strength to do much of anything, let alone range a long distance. But they all gathered their stamina tight about them as though it were a tangible thing, and together the remaining four men moved forward as their flagging strength allowed.

For days the four survived solely on roots, grass clumps, and snow. Soon Alexander and Soley were too weak to continue. Carrying them or dragging them behind in a litter was out of the question, as the other two Blue brothers were near exhaustion themselves.

"I am going to say something that you won't much like, but it needs to be said." Alexander licked his lips and shielded his eyes from the bright sun bouncing off the snowpack before them. "If one of us dies soon, the others must use that man as nourishment. So that they might stand a chance of being rescued."

For a long time no one in the small band said a thing. Through silence, they reached mutual consent. They did not have to wait long to test their resolve. In the night, Soley died. Despite their pledge, the three Blue brothers, so weak from hunger and exhaustion, lay in their simple dugout camp, refusing to commit to the necessary and grisly task. Eventually, after three days, they did.

Alexander Blue died next. And his two brothers, with great reluctance, cut him up and ate him. This they did in grave silence, staring at the taunting vision of Pikes Peak in the far distance.

Despite the nourishment, they were still too weak to move onward. Their only hope was that some other travelers might find them. But they also knew they were lost, and any trace of them was unlikely to be discovered.

It was some time in early May, he was later told, that Daniel Blue, the sole survivor of their small party, was found, near death, by Arapaho Indians, who brought him to an express company's office. From there, he was taken to Denver, where he arrived on May 11. There his story was met with downcast eyes and hands over mouths. "There but for the grace of God go I," muttered more than one chilled miner. Daniel found out that only five of the larger initial party had reached the diggings, and ten men remained unaccounted for and were presumed dead.

The Pikes Peak Rush in Colorado and the Virginia City Rush in Nevada took place in 1859, a decade after the California Rush. The participants, called the '59ers, swarmed into the Pikes Peak region of western Kansas Territory and southwestern Nebraska Territory.

In 1858 and 1859, 150,000 people, ill-prepared and desperate for gold, trekked west to Colorado any way they could—some on horseback, some pulled by dogs, some pushing wheelbarrows, most on foot. One-third that number turned around before they reached the Rockies, and twenty-five thousand more headed back once they realized the work required of them in the gold fields was much more than they were led to believe by huckster newspapermen and guidebook authors who had never traveled the routes they purported were safe and expeditious. The people who chucked in the towel and returned east, called "go backs," didn't go home empty-handed—they brought back young blue spruce trees, the descendants of which can be seen far from their indigenous Rockies, thriving all over the East.

The tragedy of the Blue brothers' expedition was one of the worst in a long series of preventable events that occurred on the Smoky Hill Trail, the central route to the Pikes Peak region. The route was promoted in guidebooks to be shorter, more expeditious, and more plentiful with wood, game, and water than others. In truth, it was none of these.

The way was so poorly marked that numerous gold seekers became lost and were never heard from again. There were reports that the remains of at least one hundred men could be seen along the trail and that Plains Indians wiped out entire parties. One hundred men from the Smoky Hill route, lost and starving, descended on a trading post at Cottonwood Crossing, accosted the owner, then stole one hundred sacks of meal, flour, and other provisions. Newly fortified, they proceeded to the emerging gold fields.

15

SINKPIT OF DEGRADATION
(1859)

Often referred to as the hardest-working, hardest-living mining town in the West, Bodie is born with the discovery of a modest bonanza in gold by a man who, soon after his eureka moment, promptly dies in a blizzard in November 1859.

◆

"Open up! Open the camp!" W. S. Bodey rapped on the log door of the dugout with a rag-wrapped fist. "Let a man in!"

Soon the door swung inward, and "Black" Taylor, the half-Cherokee, peered at the snow-covered specter before him. "Bodey?"

"Who in hell do you think I am? Queen of England?" the little man shook himself as a dog might, then shuffled into the warm cabin. As he huddled shivering over the tin stove, his teeth chattered and his clothes and beard dripped and steamed on the glowing heat source.

"Where you been?"

Bodey glanced at his diggings partner, then looked back to the stove, muttering to himself. Finally he said, "You recall something about me fetching supplies? By God, but you are short-minded."

"Okay, okay. But I was worried, you know. Where are the supplies, anyway?"

"Well, Taylor, that's mighty big of you. What say we have some coffee and when the storm lulls, we can go back for 'em."

"Okay, but coffee will have to wait, then."

"Why's that?"

"We don't have any until we get the supplies back here."

"Okay, okay. I'm going to get some shut-eye, but wake me when the storm lulls."

Taylor watched Bodey stretch out on his bunk, then he plunked down on his own bunk and promptly fell asleep.

Several hours later, Bodey awoke first, and hearing no blowing wind, he called to Taylor. "Get up, you varmint. Let's go get our grub."

Taylor roused himself and yawned. "You got the strength to get there and back?"

Bodey pushed himself up off the cot. "I guess to hell I do. By God, I'll take a round or two out of you, you say that again."

Taylor smiled. "Thought that would wake you. Come on. Sounds like the storm's over."

He swung open the door and after a minute of steady digging, managed to punch a hole through the drifted plug of snow that had piled up before the door. Once outside, both men strapped on their snowshoes and Bodey motioned over his shoulder for Taylor to follow him.

Within minutes of leaving the dugout, Taylor felt the sting of wind-whipped snow crystals and realized the storm had indeed merely lulled. And now it looked to be gathering itself for another charge. "Bodey! Let's go back! We'll come out later!"

"You kidding me?" Bodey shouted over his shoulder. "We wait, we'll never find it in all this snow. Or critters will beat us to it." Bodey trudged onward.

Taylor sighed and followed as the storm increased in intensity.

"We been at it for two days, Taylor." Bodey nearly whispered the words. He seemed to his companion half the robust man he had been, his wiry strength now replaced with a frail, shivering old man. "Face it, we're good and lost. So turned around. . . . Can't find hide nor hair that I recognize. Our dugout's got to be close at hand, but . . ." Bodey let his hand drop to his lap. He sat shaking his head, his eyes watering and his face a swollen black mask of frostbite and defeat.

Taylor bent low and with a grunt heaved the man over his shoulder. "We'll get there, Bodey. I'll get you home. . . ."

Taylor had to stop frequently, and soon he had to stop altogether. By then, Bodey had become insensible and stayed wherever Taylor propped him, staring straight ahead and shaking his head, his swollen, cracked lips moving as if he were thinking of saying something. But no words came from him.

"I have to leave you here, Bodey. This is a good little thicket. I'll lean you against this tree, but stay here." Taylor looked Bodey in the face, squinted, and tried to get the man to pay attention to him. It didn't work. He spoke anyway. "You got to stay here, Bodey. I'll be back for you." He pulled Bodey's coat collar high up around his face, folded his arms before him. "Stay warm and stay put."

Taylor leaned back on his heels, exhaustion pulling at his shoulders, telling him to lay down, just for a few minutes, and rest. Then he would be better able to find their dugout. "No, no, no," he said, gritting his teeth. Taylor stood and with one last look back at Bodey, set off in a direction he thought correct, though he didn't know why he felt that way.

Hours later, Taylor recognized a thatch of trees and hurried forward. Only it wasn't the cabin. Before him in the snow, at the base of a tree, lay Bodey, sleeping where he'd left him. Bodey's eyes were closed, and his mouth had a bit of a smile to it. Otherwise, he looked as he had when Taylor left him hours before.

Taylor bent down, touched his friend on the face, and realized Bodey was dead, stiff and frozen.

He sat staring at his partner for a few minutes, then stood, promising himself one more chance to live. While I still have strength, such as it is, he thought, I have to try. Bodey would want me to. For the second time that day, Taylor staggered away from his friend, knowing that a dead man might be the last person he would ever see. As he ventured forth through the snow once again, he muttered, "I'll be back, Bodey. I'll bury you right. Promise. . . ."

Tremors and an aching tiredness overcame him. Fighting it was the most difficult thing he had ever done. He staggered for what seemed like hours, with darkness creeping in once more. He faced a third night lost in freezing temperatures.

As sudden as a slap to the face, Taylor recognized the lay of the sloping land before him, though it was covered with stiffened peaks of drifted snow. He knew that he was less than a half mile from the cabin. He fell forward and tried to rise, but could not, no matter how hard he tried. His legs would no longer hold him upright. He began crawling through the snow, praying that he didn't veer off course as the dark descended and the snow began again.

Twelve hours later, he found himself at the cabin.

Black Taylor made good on his promise, and the following spring, 1860, he scoured the area until he found W. S. Bodey's body. He buried him where he lay, not far from the spot where Bodey and several other men found gold the previous fall. As with Bodey, Black Taylor was not to enjoy any prosperity from the gold discovered there. He was killed in 1862 by Indians near the town of Benton.

The spelling of W. S. Bodey's surname has appeared in several variations over the years. Early residents of the town named after him felt that a less literal spelling might be more suitable. Thus, the name "Bodie" came into being. The town of Bodie inspired a number of emotions over the years. One particular quotation seems most apt, attributed to a little girl who penned it in her journal on the eve of her family's move to the famous mine camp: "Goodbye, God. We are going to Bodie."

Bodie, considered one of the wildest mine camps in the West, thrived for several years, and then, when little gold could be found, the population dwindled and Bodie was on the verge of becoming a ghost town. But in 1875 the Bunker Hill Mine collapsed in on itself, revealing fresh gold ore. Miners rushed to the town, and by 1877 one mine owned by the Standard Company dug up three-quarters of a million dollars in gold and silver. By the next year, twenty-two mines were using steam-powered equipment in their operations. By 1880 the population had swelled to eight thousand, then ten thousand a few years later. At the height of its five-year boom, from 1877 to 1881, whiskey was freighted in on wagons one hundred barrels at a time.

Bodie eventually slipped into a slow decline that lasted well into the twentieth century. Today the town is owned and operated by the State of California, as it has been since 1962, and is in an official state of "arrested decay." On visits, one can peek in windows and see homes and businesses as they were when the last residents left more than fifty years ago. Nothing in the town, which now has no living residents, may be disturbed or removed.

Bodie is also famously considered one of the most haunted spots in all the West. It is said that anything removed from the town, no matter how small, causes grief and misfortune to the person who took it. So much so that throughout the year, park officials receive packages from guilty parties containing stolen items and notes asking for forgiveness from both the park and the ghosts who are said to haunt the town. They claim to have experienced terrible luck since they pinched their Bodie keepsakes.

Two decades after the first discovery of gold was made there, the bones of the man for whom the town was named, W. S. Bodey (some reports have his given name as Waterman, Wakeman, or William), were paraded down Main Street and then reburied in the fancy new town cemetery. The new grave was never marked, however, and the exact location of Bodey's body is a mystery.

PARDON ME . . .
(1860)

Mining camp baddie Sam Brown is accidentally jostled by a stranger in a Virginia City, Nevada, saloon. The stranger apologizes, but Brown cuts out the man's heart with a bowie knife, wraps himself in a blanket, and takes a nap.

◆

McKenzie eyed the mug of beer and knew he would never make his fortune mining in the Comstock as long as he spent most of his time and all of his money in the saloon. But it was so much cooler inside on such a scorching August day in Nevada. And he had to say that of all the places he'd had beer on a hot day, this Virginia City saloon—he'd forgotten just which it was—seemed to be the best of the lot. The barkeep set the mug down on the bar top in front of him and didn't bother to tell McKenzie the cost. He'd bought several already and had no plans on this being the last. He slid his two bits on the counter and caught the bartender's eyes as he glanced to McKenzie's right.

But the miner didn't care to see what attracted the man's attention. He was too busy raising the mug of copper-colored liquid to his mouth as he turned from the bar to resume his seat by the back wall. It was a fine spot from which to take in what little activity could be found on the street.

But McKenzie turned to the right, the wrong way. His elbow and arms drove into a man standing beside him, sloshing half his beer on the stranger's back. "Ho there, ho there, your fault or mine," said McKenzie, not quite glancing up as he stepped backward to avoid the sloshing beer. He looked up and immediately wished he hadn't.

McKenzie knew he wasn't the tallest, broadest man you were apt to find in the place. In fact, if you were to press him, he'd admit to being on the small side. But as he looked up at the man he'd bumped into, he knew he'd found the biggest man in the bar. And what's more, he knew who the man was.

If it was possible for the watery beer to lose its dubious inebriative effects in an instant, that's what happened to McKenzie. The several previous beers seemed to evaporate from him as he stared up at the wide, reddening face of Sam Brown.

"I—" was all that McKenzie would utter.

Brown's massive left arm lashed out and curled around the smaller man's neck. Quick as a finger snap, he dragged McKenzie toward him, lifting the now flailing man off the floor so that their faces were nearly of the same height. McKenzie felt something pop in the back of his neck. His nose and lips were now mashed into the big killer's bushy, ratty ginger-colored beard, the hairs of which poked into his mouth, up his nose. Even in his thrashing, distressed state, McKenzie gagged at the stink of the man's breath; the rank odor of rancid food warring with the fumes of whiskey clouded him.

He saw the brown and black stains on the killer's teeth, and as his eyes searched higher on Brown's face, they locked with the man's own eyes. And what he saw there stunned him for the brief moment before he felt the "Pop!" of the bowie knife as it poked through the skin of his chest. A wash of heat like a jump in a hot spring boiled up in him, from his boots to his nose. He tried to speak, tried to scream, but his mouth had filled with something thick and warm.

The big man gripped his neck in his hand and pulled him backward a few inches. Brown grunted, and through the man's copious whiskers, McKenzie saw the big man smile, those rotting teeth revealed in full as his mouth broke into a broad grin.

The bartender had run back down the bar and left through the back room's alley door. The three other patrons were too stunned and scared to do much of anything but keep their seats and stare as Sam Brown gutted the little Irishman. As far as they could tell, McKenzie hadn't done much more than bump into the big man. If ever there was an accident. . . . Then, as they watched, it got worse. Brown clamped his hand tight around McKenzie's neck, pulled him backward, and spun the big bladed knife around in a circle inside the man, carving a hollow where McKenzie's heart pounded its last beats but seconds before.

Kellman didn't dare breathe, let alone move, as he watched McKenzie's body slip from Brown's grasp and clump to the floor. The sound of the man's head smacking the boards, a dull clunk the same as a rock makes as it smacks another just below the surface of a stream, was a sound he suspected would stay with him his entire life. Brown took no notice of his surroundings as he looked down at his steaming, dripping knife, not a speck of metal of which could be seen through the thick blood stringing from it and pooling on the floor and the man's boot tips.

He dragged the knife across his pant leg, both sides of the blade smearing against the already grimy fabric of his pants, and with a practiced hand, he jammed the blade back into its sheath, on the right hip, opposite his revolver. Kellman continued to watch as the big, wide-shouldered killer stepped over the dead man's tangled legs and trudged to the billiards table as if he had just returned from a long day in the mines and was eager for nothing so much as a quick snort and a soft bed.

Since no one had yet uncovered the green baize surface of the pool table that day, Brown snatched up the old blanket covering it and sloppily shrouded himself in it. Then with a long sigh, he flopped backward on the table. Kellman stared at the man a few moments more, disbelief warring with reason in his mind. Surely none of this had just happened. This sort of thing just couldn't happen in a modern mining camp. And yet . . . his eyes traveled back to where poor McKenzie lay, blood pooling about him—more blood than Kellman thought could possibly come out of a man, should he become unstoppered like that.

A snore from Sam Brown brought Kellman back to his senses. He heard a growing murmuring just outside the half-opened door. People were coming close—what if they awoke Brown and he saw Kellman sitting there, having seen the entire thing? What if the people outside somehow thought he had done it? He'd not been in town all that long and had no real means of support. Fact is, he thought, he was just out here looking for grist for his mill, as it were, for a chance to soak up the real and heady nature of a mine camp. He hoped to break into journalism and thought that perhaps time spent here might give him a bit of color to write about—and then it occurred to him. This was exactly what he needed.

But the killer snored again, and Kellman knew that if he didn't get out of there, he might not get to make a career out of anything. He glanced at the front door, then at the back door just behind the bar, and seeing he was equidistant from each, he froze one second more. A renewed round of murmuring voices drawing closer, followed with a burst of snoring from Brown, found Kellman bolting for the back door. The entire trip across the room, he expected to feel a blade or a bullet pierce the vulnerable span between his shoulder blades.

It wasn't until he was three buildings down and had ducked into an alley that he bent forward, hands on his knees, and emptied his gut into the gravel of the Virginia City alleyway. Already his mind worked on a lead sentence. . . .

◆

Sam Brown was, in many ways, the stereotypical bad man of the Old West. When he walked down the boardwalk in Virginia City, men, women, and children hastened to clear themselves out of his path. And for good reason— he was a known murderer whose inner fire drove him to kill repeatedly. Mine camps were ideal places for men of his ilk, undesirables keen on a free lunch. Virginia City was but one of many such mine camps and towns where Brown played his one-sided game. Having served time in San Quentin for multiple murders, after his release in 1859, Brown wandered the California gold fields, causing havoc and distress wherever he went, before venturing to the Comstock Lode and Virginia City, Nevada. At the time, Mark Twain, writing for the city's paper, the Territorial Enterprise, *referred to Brown as the worst killer in Virginia City.*

In May 1860 Brown joined a posse called the Carson City Rangers, riding under Major William Ormsby, a group set on tracking and punishing a band of Paiutes for crimes against whites. Sadly, the Rangers were all but eliminated in an ambush. Brown, thrown from his own mount in the melee, leaped atop a mule whose wounded owner was attempting to ride to safety. Brown pushed the bleeding man to the ground, sunk spur, and rode off. He never picked fights with anyone who was armed or who showed any sort of backbone. Instead he chose to dry-gulch his victims and knife or shoot them when they least expected it, most often in the back.

But what goes around, comes around, and for Brown that happened on the night of his thirtieth birthday. Primed with booze and a solid meal, he told a friend that he wanted to kill a man before the night was through.

Brown chose a well-respected Dutch emigrant named Henry Van Sickle. Unfortunately for Brown, the Dutchman had no intention of dying at the hands of a cowardly killer. After receiving return fire from Van Sickle, Brown hopped on his horse and fled, with the irate Van Sickle in hot pursuit. The Dutchman eventually caught up with the thug and let loose with both barrels of his shotgun, removing the top third of Sam Brown's head. Now that's a birthday present.

17

BOONE HELM, MAN-BEAST
(1862)

Near the gold-mining burg of Antler Creek, Cariboo, British Columbia, this savage brute murders three miners for their gold. Later, caught in the winter in the mountains of Oregon, Helm shoots a companion and eats one of the man's legs, then hacks off the other and continues his journey, looking for a new mining camp . . . and new opportunities.

◆

A tall man with a head like a rough-cut stump, his matted hair crowning a dense brow ridge that topped two staring eyes, stepped onto the trail twenty paces from the three miners leading a mule and two horses, each animal laden with full panniers.

"Ho there!" The big brute raised a thick paw in greeting, but there was no smile on his face. Cradled in the crook of his arm lay a double-barrel shotgun. He squared off in front of them and hoisted the shotgun, ramming the butt against his gut. In his other mitt, he gripped a revolver.

At the same instant, another man stepped onto the path from the low side of the road. He held a drawn pistol, cocked it, and shouted, "Throw up your hands!"

The three miners exchanged glances with the two strangers, then with each other. They clawed for their six-shooters as they scurried to get behind their pack animals. The second dry gulcher opened fire. The three miners fired over the backs of their pack animals, the sharp crack of pistol shots whizzing and creasing the still afternoon air. Within seconds, the three pack animals, despite their heavy loads, spun and danced in all directions at once, kicking and braying and neighing and lunging. Their antics exposed the three miners and distracted them from their attackers, who advanced and continued firing.

In short order, two miners went down, their torsos perforated and their blood leaching into the dust of the trail. The third had spun and bolted up the trail, firing back at them as he ran. He hadn't gone twenty feet when the bigger of the two attackers dropped him with a single shotgun blast. The miner's feet drummed the dry earth for a moment, then stilled.

"Get them three beasts rounded up—they're hauling about thirty-two thousand dollars in ore. I heard one of these fools telling another last night."

"So, that's where you got to."

"Yep, now do as I say. I'll tend to these fools. Two of 'em are still twitching, so I reckon I'll finish 'em off."

"You gonna go through their pockets afore I get back?"

"Just do as I tell you, or you'll get the same as them." He waved his revolver toward the three prone men in the road.

The smaller man holstered his pistol and straggled after the three pack animals. They hadn't gone far, burdened as they were with ore.

"And be quick about it. We got to bury that ore for now, then get out of here."

"Okay, Boone."

Soon, the small man heard three shots.

◆

The six men toting the stretchers bearing the three dead men came to a stop in front of a tent saloon in the little town of Quesnel Forks. A crowd gathered and stared at the stiffened, stunned-looking victims.

One fat old man shuffled close. "I recognize them boys. Just here yesterday with their ore all loaded."

He eyed the sheriff, who said, "No sign of their gold, nor much in the way of valuables in their pockets, though their guns were still with them. They made a good show of it, too. All the chambers were emptied."

"Boone Helm, I'll swear it was him," said the old man. Most of the gathered people nodded, so he continued. "And someone said another fellow's traveling with him, dry-gulching folks all over the hills." The old man dragged a ratty coat cuff across his mouth, smearing chew juice into his already stiffened gray-yellow beard. He looked past the low buildings toward the hills beyond, as if the bandits would be visible.

"Well, who is Boone Helm?" a thin woman asked, without looking up from examining the dead men.

"Why, my God, woman, where you been?" The old man tucked his thumbs in his coat's breast pockets and puffed up. "He's a known killer from south of here, a gambler. Last heard tell he'd escaped from the San Francisco Vigilance Committee by the skin of his teeth."

The woman finally looked up at the sheriff. "This true?"

"Yep, and now if you'll all excuse me, I have to round up men interested in pursuing the killers, though I expect they'll have headed for the border by now."

"Any pay in it?" said the old man.

"Yes, Billy, I expect we'll be able to raise some sort of compensation." The sheriff walked away, then turned back. "For able-bodied men, that is." He shouldered his rifle and headed for the saloon.

Elijah Burton was in a bad way, that much he knew. His eyes felt as if someone had stuck them with hundreds of sewing pins. He staggered forward, then dropped to his knees and scooped up snow, smearing it on his face in a vain attempt to quell the hellfire that burned there. "Boone!" he listened for a moment. "Boone Helm, have you gone off and left me?"

"Shut your yelling mouth, Burton. I've done nothing of the sort. I ain't like you."

"What's that supposed to mean, Helm? I am in agony here, gone blind, likely from lack of food."

"It's snowblindness, you fool. And you know what I meant. We up and left them other three 'cause they were too weak to keep up with us."

"We left them alive and able to see, Helm. There's a difference."

"Big difference? Tell them that. Own up to what you've done, Burton. You're no better than the rest of us. Come along like you're the boss of the outfit."

"I am, I am the boss of the outfit. I hired you all to make this expedition over the mountains—"

"I am my own king, and don't you forget it, Burton. You are less than dirt. We both of us took the provisions from them. And now we're in the same boat as them when we left them with no food."

Teamsters with loaded ore wagons took great risks to transport the valuable rock to banks in towns and cities. Often one or more men would "ride shotgun" to fend off attacks from dry gulchers, such as notorious badman Boone Helm, looking to make an easy payday. *Courtesy Library of Congress*

"But they . . . they could see, could build a fire. . . ."

"Yes, I expect they did just that as soon as we left them behind. I expect that once their fire got to a great height, they roasted a pig or a beef on it, don't you?"

Burton crouched in the snow, trembling, his clothes sodden and begrimed. He began crying, his raw, red eyes swollen and leaking. He clawed at the ground for snow and smeared the muddied mess into his eyes.

"You ain't gone blind from lack of food, Burton. It's snowblindness is all."

Burton paused, then reached out with his filthy hands like claws held before him. He walked forward on his knees toward Helm's voice. "Boone, Boone, lead me along the trail. We're nearly there, I know it." Lead me out of here. I'm sure I'll recover in a day or so. Boone? Where are you? Boone?"

The click of the hammer on Boone's rifle was the last thing Burton heard, other than Helm's laughter blurring with his own screams as he shouted, "No!"

Two men leaned against the backside of a boulder in a vain effort to keep out of the sun. The silence suited the bigger man just fine. When sober, as he was now, he was known for his long, moody quiet spells.

Finally, though, the smaller of the two cleared his throat. "Is it really true, what they say, I mean, about you?" The small man looked at his companion slowly, fearfully, as if he were afraid he had asked something that would cost him dearly. He'd never worked with Helm before, but he'd heard the stories.

Instead of slipping into the rage the younger man had expected, Boone Helm cracked a wide smile. "I guess everything that's been said of me is seeded in truth, if you snaked it back far enough. Though I'd wager you are talking of making a meal of a man, eh?"

The smaller man lost even his squint and stared at Helm, wanting for all the world to have never asked what he did. Curiosity, his mother used to tell him, would get him killed one day. He guessed this might well be that day. Finally, though, he nodded, not able to contain his inquisitive nature.

Helm continued. "What would you have done? He was dead and I wasn't. It was colder than a gravedigger's ass, and I was wearing rotting moccasins that was more hole than shoe. I'd wager that if you were in my spot, you'd a taken your knife to your dead pal's leg, too."

The other man swallowed, then in a quiet voice, said, "So, you ate of him, then?"

"Hell yes, I ate Burton's sorry hide. Much as I could. I wasn't about to die, not when I had a way of preventing it right there before me."

"How far were you from a town?"

"Oh, less than a hunnert miles, for sure."

"So . . . what did you do for food . . . after that? Did you hunt?"

Helm forgot he was hiding in wait for the pay wagon and let out a quick burst of laughter. "I didn't need to, you foolish pup! I hacked off his other leg with my bowie here." He pushed back his coat hem and rested a hand on the hilt. "Rolled her up in Burton's old red shirt, then I took to the trail. I had enough left over to feed a stray dog in the street. I guess some of them folks must have been right about me, 'cause that dog and me, we had that much in common. We both didn't turn up our noses at a free meal."

Boone Helm's smile faded from his face with all the speed of a sunset, and he leaned down toward the smaller man. "You 'bout finished with your questions? 'Cause I'm hungry."

No color was left on the young man's face. His eyes hung wide and unblinking. He nodded quickly and wanted to step backward but couldn't seem to recall how to make his feet do his bidding.

Helm's smile spread across his face again. He shook his head, choking back a laugh as he pulled a wrinkled flour sack from his coat pocket. He pulled out two biscuits and offered one to his companion.

The little man stared at it, then up at Helm, who said, "Go on, take it. I thought it would be obvious to you I don't like to dine alone."

He dropped the biscuit into the little man's shaking hand and stifled a laugh with a mouthful of biscuit.

Boone Helm would finally meet his much-deserved end stretching hemp in 1864 in front of a crowd of six thousand in the town of Virginia City, Montana, as part of Sheriff Henry Plummer's Gang of Innocents. His last words are reported to be: "Let 'er rip!"

But long before that day came, Helm, victim by victim, built the reputation for which he will long be remembered as a vicious, lowlife thug of the frontier, a man whose total murder count is unknown, though more than one dozen murders are attributed to him.

Alferd Packer was another badman of the West who also indulged in murder and cannibalism. In the winter of 1874, when crossing the Rockies with a group of gold seekers, the members of his party became snowbound and fell to fighting among themselves with pistols and hatchets. Months later, Packer, as the expedition's sole survivor, emerged from the mountains, well fed and in possession of a significant wad of cash and other valuables. Packer was found guilty of murder and cannibalism and sentenced to forty years in prison, though to his death he maintained his innocence. In his later years he was also reportedly a vegetarian.

18

BACKSHOOTERS
(1862)

In August, in what became known as the Boise Basin, a prospecting party triggers the richest gold rush in North America—bigger than the California and Klondike rushes together. But George Grimes, one of the party's leaders, will never enjoy his impending fortune. Within days of the discovery, he is shot in the back.

◆

George Grimes walked on, his pack feeling heavier with every step. But the countryside was beautiful and rugged, and he was enjoying himself, breathing in the crisp mountain air.

He smiled and thought back on all the time he spent prospecting. If he ever struck it rich, he'd probably miss moments like this. But the odds of striking pay dirt were slim, so there was little worry of missing out on a walk in the woods. Though if there was something to the tales he'd heard, this trip could be the one. He'd met Moses Splawn, the old Indian fighter, and after hearing his stories about the gold in this place, he'd decided to form the party, grubstake it, and hire Splawn on as their guide, naturally.

They'd seen Shoshone Indians and had taken care not to run afoul of them. They'd continued on their way, but he knew the Indians probably ran off and alarmed others. Would it come to a fight in the woods? In territory so foreign to them that they might well lose their lives? Who would ever know? How many of their relations would mount an expedition to find them?

They could well die here in the treed slopes, and none would be the wiser. The Indians would get what they want, which was to be left alone. And he'd be dead. Was it worth it? He tried to push the thought out of his mind, for it reminded him of his dear Marietta, and she always brought up that question. She loved him, she said, not money or the things it might buy. But she wasn't the one who had grown up with less than nothing. Not the one who had grubbed for food.

So, if Moses Splawn is right, he thought, then we might be able to call this trip our last. For the region, so says Splawn, holds much promise. Time will tell, thought Grimes. But first things first: I need to get to work and dig a few test sites to see whether the Indian tales of gold that Moses told us are true.

"And I am telling you that it was an Indian attack."

Moses Splawn stared at the young man struggling to gain control of his breath and tell his story all at once. "It'll never come out right if'n you don't get on the good side of your breathing, Wilson."

The man nodded, swallowed, and dragged a hand down his face.

"Now suppose you tell me again what happened."

The young man nodded. "Me and Grimes and Reynolds were all up in that little valley, scouting for likely spots to dig. We'd gradually become separated from sight of one another, but we were well within earshot."

"Then what?"

"Then pretty soon we hear a gunshot. That had to be Grimes, I told myself, knowing he was the sort of man who had enough experience but who wasn't afraid to defend himself. We'd been on the lookout for Shoshone ever since we got there, but, by God, they're more of them every time I look around. I bolted up over the low hill between us, and to his right I seen Indians, at least three, hiding behind trees and taking shots at us. From behind, I could hear the fading shots of miners. I felt pinned and shouted for everyone to just stop shooting, for God's sake, lest they hit one of us accidentally. Then I saw him. It was George Grimes."

"Grimes is dead?" Splawn looked at Wilson, who nodded.

"Shot from the front or from behind?" He held the young man pinned to the spot with his gaze.

"Well, I'd guess from the front. That's where the Shoshone was, up ahead, near as I could tell. Mr. Splawn, the woods is crawling with 'em. We got to get out of here."

As the air buzzed with random gunshots, Splawn shouted for his men to hold their fire. "Get Grimes in that prospect hole. Cover him up as best we can, we'll do for him proper when we return."

Splawn, the man who called himself an Indian fighter, looked at the diggings. He hated to leave it now, but they did have enough ore to head to Walla Walla, file their claims, and load up on supplies.

"It's only August ninth. You reckon he'll keep 'til we get back?"

"He'll have to, ain't no choice. And this high up, winter comes quick. Cold'll settle into the ground soon, that should keep him." Splawn glanced back at the men straggling behind him. "Besides," he said, "I don't want to be gone that long from our rich diggings. I expect you all will feel the same."

"What about Grimes?"

"What about him? He's dead."

"But he has a claim here, too."

Splawn closed his eyes and gritted his teeth. He wanted to say that the man's dead, that he would take over the man's claims, that the chips don't always fall in ways we liked. Instead he pulled in a deep breath and let it out. "We'll do right by his widow, sure enough."

◆

As he looked around the snow-dusted woods, William S. Wilson thought that two months was a long time to have been gone. Here we are in the middle of October, trying to find a dead man's temporary grave and get a start on our diggings. But if the claims proved up according to the assayer's estimations, Wilson was glad to have been able to come back at all. Splawn had been right, of course. It was damn cold already up here in the mountains. Had even snowed, just a dusting, but that changed the look of everything.

He was having a devil of a time locating George Grimes's grave. He wondered if Grimes's body was there anymore—maybe Splawn had been right and a bear got to him. They might never find a trace of him, but they had to try. But the trying was getting tiresome. Time and again, just when he thought he'd found the spot where they'd buried him, he turned up nothing. And then he saw it—the toe of a boot sticking up through the earth. So there was George Grimes at last.

"I've found him!" shouted Wilson. "I've found Grimes."

He knelt down and brushed away the sparse scattering of leaves, paltry snow. Just under his sweeping gloved hand, there was the man's forehead.

Wilson recoiled, looked around to see if the men had seen him. Fogus was the closest, followed by three others. All of them were moving with reluctance, and Wilson didn't much blame them. But he also knew that this was no way to leave a man they'd known. They had to make a proper job of it. Had to.

"Here, Fogus, help me scoop away this dirt. It's clumped a bit, but still loose enough that we can unearth him. You other men, start a fire and fetch water. We'll need to clean him up properly."

The other men set to their tasks, but Fogus hesitated, not taking his eyes from the blue, drawn face of George Grimes, perfectly preserved from the day he had been shot two months before.

"I know this is a hard thing, but we have to go through with it, and I need your help. I'll pay you $5 and a bottle of whiskey too if you'll lend a hand." The man stared a moment more, then nodded and resigned himself to the task. He pulled off his coat and hung it on the snapped stub of a branch on a nearby tree.

Both men were surprised at how well preserved Grimes's body was. Once they laid him out on his back on a canvas, Wilson pointed at Grimes. "See here," he said to no one in particular. "I don't see a wound caused from someone shooting him from the front, do you?"

But he didn't wait for Fogus to answer. He knelt beside Grimes and flipped him onto his stomach. Small clods of frozen soil had clumped here and there on the man's jacket. He brushed at them, and as they fell away, he saw something that made him and the other man both groan at the same time—a bullet wound in the man's back.

"You were here that day."

Fogus nodded but said nothing, knowing what Wilson was about to ask him.

"You recall that nobody actually saw Grimes get shot, right? Help me undress him."

"What?"

"Have to. Might be a man was killed by his own men here. Besides, we got to clean him for burial. It's only decent and right."

Minutes later they stared at the puckered bullet wound off-center of the middle of the man's back. "No doubt about it. George Grimes was backshot by one of his own."

"Don't mean he was murdered, though."

"You're right, of course. But it don't mean he wasn't, neither." He turned to face the man. "Grimes was one of the leaders of the group, had grubstaked us all, and so he was entitled to twice the claims that we are. Could be that someone didn't like that."

"You know what you're saying?"

"Yep, and I also know I'll have a devil of a time proving it." He looked down at Grimes's dirt-crusted corpse. "But I have to try."

Owing to the potential richness of the claim, at least two men from the Grimes party were suspected of shooting their leader in the back. It is known that Grimes had a disagreement with one of them, and that man may have concocted the tale of Indians dogging their trail as an excuse to shoot Grimes and blame the Indians. It is also likely that there were Indians shooting at the men and that one of the men, in his haste to return fire, accidentally shot Grimes in the back and killed him.

The claim Grimes helped discover there in Washington Territory, which later became known as the Boise Basin, of the state of Idaho, went on to become the source of $250 million worth of gold within a few decades, more gold than has been found in all of Alaska. Idaho City, the nexus of the Boise Basin mining district, was at one time the largest city in the Northwest. By the mid-1860s, up to forty thousand people lived there. But George Grimes wasn't one of them.

Years later, in November 1916, William Wilson, then ninety-four and still in full possession of his mental faculties, told a reporter that he had suspected a man of the party of killing Grimes but that he had lacked the hard evidence required to file a formal charge. He was told, however, that the man he suspected had struck a deal with Grimes's widow for a share of whatever he might get for her via her power of attorney. Wilson tried to persuade her to go to Idaho and file charges against the suspected murderer. He heard, years later, that Grimes's widow eventually received, as Wilson mentioned to the press, "quite a sum."

19

DOOMED FROM
THE START
(1863)

Early in April 1863 twenty-three men band together under the leadership of James Stuart, with an eye toward discovering "color" along the Yellowstone River drainage. They split into two groups, and soon both are bedeviled by the unrelenting, warring Crow Indians. For many in both parties, the search for gold does not end well.

◆

George Ives scanned the surrounding country without rest, convinced he was about to experience the singular sensation of an arrow through the heart. He had dreamed of such terrible occurrences, and he fully expected to die at an early age. If that was to be the case, he told himself as he lugged wood for the campfire, he would prefer to be seized in his bed by a sudden affliction. Anything but a Crow arrow. And then his worst fears seemed about to materialize.

"Men!" shouted Captain Stuart loud enough for them all to look up from their respective tasks. It was late in the afternoon, and the fifteen men were preparing to eat and settle in for the night. Since they had ridden deep into Crow country, they had begun posting watch. Nothing was as rascally as a Crow Indian, and theft of horses was not only their main source of pride but the horses would also prove useful, since it had been a hard winter for the Crow. So vigilance was all in the roving mining camp the members called the "Yellowstone Expedition."

All fifteen men threw aside their firewood and bedding and drew their sidearms and rifles. Within seconds, and with no warning, thirty Indians swept into camp, shouting and yipping and shaking their arms high above their heads. Stuart's entire group tensed, each man keeping his eye on as many of the intruders as he was able, for each man knew who and what they were: Absaroka to themselves, but Crow to the whites—sneaky and fierce enemies, and cunning horse thieves.

Two men of the expedition ran to the picket line where Stuart's men had stationed their mounts and pack horses. Already a handful of Crow bucks had slipped off their horses' backs and had dropped in among the Stuart party horses.

"Git on, git on outta here! Git!" George Ives jammed a round in the chamber of his rifle and held it before him, ready to drive it into the face of the nearest brave, a youth no older than fifteen. The brave sneered at him and stood his ground.

Several chiefs and one Indian familiar with the Snake language took their time in dismounting, walking forward, and arranging themselves on the ground in a circle. They beckoned to James Stuart, finding that he appeared to be the chief among the men. He took his place in the circle, and they smoked and talked for hours.

Watkins nudged Bostwick in the arm as they stared, guns cradled in their arms, at the Crow braves who took every opportunity to mimic scalping, their long sheath knives flashing, their eyes narrowed and their mouths sneering.

"I can't speak a lick of Crow, but that's all the lingo I need, right there."

"I know what you mean," said Bostwick. "I've had my belly full of Indian fighting—have for years, but I tell you what, I could tuck in right now and kill me some."

The other men felt the same way. Even fair-minded Hauser seemed more perturbed, as the Crow took every opportunity, every slight glance away, to advance closer all the time to the sloppy piles of camp gear.

"They'll pick us blind," said Hauser, not daring to take his eyes off the brave before him. It seemed to him that the brave had been doing the same. Hauser went to the campfire and whispered in Stuart's ear: "The men have about had it. The braves are in amongst the horses, in and out of the tents, and I guess you've heard the blasts from their shotguns. One more of those and Watkins or Bostwick is going to lay right into them."

Stuart's face was flat, as if carved from wood. "Keep them calm, Sam. Only start fighting if I give the order. Remember, we are in their territory, not ours. And Sam? Tell the boys that the main Crow camp is less than twenty miles away. This isn't but a welcome party."

In an effort to extract as much surface gold as possible, hydraulic mining, first used in California in 1853, was introduced to Alaska at the turn of the twentieth century. The destructive practice washes away entire hillsides in a short amount of time, leaving a scarred, rutted landscape still visible today throughout the West and North. *US Geological Survey*

Finally the discussion among the chiefs broke up, but Indians roamed the camp throughout the night, and the men got no reviving sleep. Noises outside their tents proved to be Indians trying to steal something. At three a.m., the Crow pushed once again, en masse, into the crowd of the Stuart party horses and singled out the best, offering their bony, ill-kept nags for the fine horse-flesh the whites had brought. The Indians, it seemed, were also interested in trading horse blankets, which they had draped over their arms.

Stuart's men were kept from shooting only by his insistence that he knew what he was up to. When the transaction was almost complete, Stuart stepped in close, cocked his rifle, and brought it within inches of the old chief's chest.

It was all the indication his men needed, and they brought their arms to bear on the Indians closest to them. And the Indians dropped the horse blankets, revealing weapons concealed beneath.

Finally the chief nodded and his braves backed off, though it took them long minutes. Stuart's men loaded up the rest of their gear and departed.

◆

"What day is it, captain?" George Smith whispered in the dark.

"I happen to know that it's May 12," said James Stuart. "As I wrote in my journal just a short while ago."

As if in response, rifle shots and shotgun blasts filled the drizzly evening air. Horses screamed, and men in their tents howled and snatched up their rifles. But it was dark, the moon was elsewhere. Soon they heard sobbing coming from several spots in the camp.

"How many of ours were killed, James?"

"I don't know yet, Sam. But it's not good. We'll get who we can and crawl to the river. In the morning, when we can see, we'll let them have it."

"Why not now?"

"Because we can't even see our own hands before us, let alone a Crow. And the red devils will see where we are if we fire. Whoever shoots will be dead in seconds."

As light slowly crept into the sky, it became apparent to Stuart that the Crow had retreated, but not far up the ravine before them. He beckoned to the rest of the party, and they crept back to camp to see who had lived through the raid. What they found stilled them in horror.

Watkins had taken a ball through the right temple. It bored a hole downward through his left cheek. Somehow, though it appeared he was oblivious to his surroundings, he was dragging himself around the campsite on his knees and arms. Bostwick fared worse, having sustained five wounds. He lay there, unable to move from the pain surging through his body. One of his shoulders was a blasted-away mess, and his right thigh had been snapped in three places.

H. A. Bell sustained a gut wound that passed out near the top of his hip bone. And a man near him, Underwood, though only shot once, was left with six wounds where the bullet had passed in and out of his body. Another man,

Geery, had an arrow lodged in his shoulder, and another two men sustained flesh wounds. In all, seven of the fifteen men had suffered wounds of some sort, four horses were killed, and five more were wounded. The Yellowstone Expedition was a sorry lot, indeed, thought James Stuart as he surveyed the scene.

Hauser made coffee while Stuart told them how he wanted to proceed home—southward toward the Oregon Trail. It would mean a journey of more than a thousand miles through Sioux lands, but they might avoid more Crow. He decided that they would abandon the bulk of their supplies, so they might travel faster, perhaps up to seventy-five miles in a day or two. He hoped that if they waited until midday, the three most seriously wounded men might die in peace. Then they could bury them and move on. But the men didn't die. Stuart decided to move on with them but not before offering the Crow a fight.

He walked into the clearing before them and bellowed a challenge to the Crow, who had been hiding among the rocks all night and morning. He taunted them, shouted at them, tried everything—including calling them thieves and cowards and murderers—but nothing tempted them down out of their high rocks.

As they loaded up their wounded and what gear they would take, Bostwick decided to stay instead of go through what he perceived as the pointless agony of riding the rough trail. He knew he would only slow them down. Convinced he was sure to die anyway, Bostwick requested his revolver and shot himself in the head.

Several days later, while resting in their makeshift camp, Geery, whose slight arrow wound had begun to ache less and less as they journeyed, dragged his rifle across his blanket, so as to have it closer to him. But the trigger caught somehow, and a shot cracked off. Geery stared at his companions as if he had struck a bonanza, then fell backward. He had shot himself in the chest. The men swore they would stay by him, but he resisted, knowing that those few hours could be precious to them, especially when he knew he would soon die. He cocked his pistol, prayed, then pulled the trigger.

By May 26, through days of privation and thirst and hunger, the ragged remainder of the Yellowstone Expedition descended down out of the rough country. Eventually, in addition to numerous Indian tracks, the little party of haggard men also saw wagon tracks. And those tracks looked better to them than veins of pure gold.

The members of a twin expedition that got turned around at the start fared better in certain respects than did Stuart's group. The other eight, reduced to seven at the outset when one decided at the last minute to stay home, were soon captured by Crow warriors. But with the help of bold action by one member of their party, they were deemed bad medicine enough that the Crow let them go, provided they return to Bannack City.

On their way back, however, they discovered gold at a place downstream from where Stuart's group, weeks before, had also found color. Unlike Stuart's group, this smaller party decided to prospect at the spot for a time and ended up founding Alder Gulch. Their happenstance claim grew to become the single-richest placer mine ever discovered, yielding ten million dollars in its first year.

After months of arduous travel, James Stuart's small band of survivors eventually made it to the Oregon Trail and back to their homes. Several members of Stuart's group would be remembered for a diversity of accomplishments: Samuel Thomas Hauser would go on to become Montana's seventh governor. George Ives would, on a late December day of that same year of 1863, be the first man hung by Virginia City's famous Vigilante Committee.

James Stuart, elected captain of the Yellowstone Expedition, would go on to hold many positions, among them physician of the Fort Peck agency. He died of cancer in 1873. Stuart was also brother and business partner of the equally renowned Granville Stuart, who would in his later years be known as Mister Montana and was named a diplomat to Uruguay and Paraguay.

20

THE LOST ADAMS DIGGINGS
(1864)

In September 1864 two starving prospectors, hunted by Apache warriors in east Arizona's desert country, are found by a US Army patrol. Once revived, the men tell of the massacre of their party at the hands of the Apache chief Nana. They also speak of a hidden canyon bursting with gold nuggets as big as bird eggs.

How you reckon that Mexican's ear got that way, anyhow?" The miner leaned on his pick and squinted up at the high blue sky far above the edges of the hidden canyon. Neither of the two men closest to him answered but instead kept on with scooping and sifting the gold-rich gravel.

Finally, when the man didn't bend back to his task, one of his companions said, "Filkins, you going to worry all day about that boy's chewed-up ear or are you going to get back to work? Remember that we're all pooling the gold we collect, so the labor's got to be equal, too."

"I know all about it, you. I don't need no mother hen." Filkins sighed and bent back to his pan. "Just wondered why they call him Gotch Ear is all."

The two working men exchanged glances, too hot and tired to say any more. But there was no way they were going to stop. Each of the twenty-two men up and down the stream cutting through the bottom of the hidden valley felt the same way. They had only been in the valley for a few days, but already their accumulated wealth was enough to let them each live in comfort for a long time.

"I should think you'd be more worried about them Apaches than that Mexican's ear. Besides, the Mexican did us all a good turn by leading us here."

"Yeah, but where is he?" said the young man.

"He's gone off, headed for Mexico, I expect. That's where he was headed before he hooked up with us, anyway. He got all he asked for—them two horses, saddle, gun with it, and two gold pieces. Plus Foley's red silk bandanna."

"Wouldn't catch me wearing a red bandanna. Them Apaches see you coming from miles away and pick you off soon as look at you."

"You might want to keep your mouth quiet for the time being, Filkins." The man nodded toward the steep, long trail zigzagging down the canyon. "I'll be damned, but I think that's Chief Nana and his boys."

The men waded out of the stream and looked toward the chief, then toward Adams. Adams knew that as their chosen expedition leader, he would be expected to parlay with the Apache chief. He stepped forward, his hand on his pistol butt, as some of the men crowded around him. Before Chief Nana rode close enough to hear, Horsley, one of the older, more experienced members of the crew, said, "Spread out, boys. We cluster and we're easier to pick off that way."

The men did as he bade them, as the Indian and about thirty warriors rode close enough to talk with Adams, who had walked forward beyond the rest of his crew.

The chief regarded them for a few long, tense moments, his dark face creased and unsmiling. "You may graze your horses here and dig below the falls at that end of the canyon." Here he pointed to his right, toward where they all knew a waterfall flowed beyond the far trees. "My people are camped there, above the falls. Never go up there."

With that, Nana and his warriors walked their horses down the valley and worked their way into the trees and rocks toward the falls. After a few long minutes, Filkins said, "Didn't Gotch Ear tell us that there was gold chunks as big as turkey eggs up there? We'll need some way of getting up there."

A few of the men murmured their agreement, but Adams said, "Don't let me catch any of you men up there. He has us outnumbered, and I believe there is enough gold down here to keep us busy for some time. Don't you agree, boys?"

The question met with both anger and agreement. Adams spoke again, "You mean to tell me you'd risk your own neck for a chance at more gold? Shouldn't we be happy with what we've got here at our feet?"

After ten days Adams had sent six men back to Fort Wingate for provisions, well before they became desperate. At the rate they were finding gold, they might be there for quite a spell. He also assigned several men to build a log cabin. In one end they constructed a great fireplace with a large, flat rock that made up the best part of the hearth. Under that, they hid their gold at the end of each day's digging.

Adams looked up from his labors to see Filkins leading back to camp the two horses that had strayed away above the falls. Filkins was smiling as he handed Adams a nugget of gold as big as a bird's egg.

"More where that come from too, Adams." The young man had obviously scouted the forbidden region.

"Filkins, I told you not to go up there. Now I'll hear no more of it. Stay down here, and if we have to retrieve stray horses up there, we do it and get back, no grubbing for gold. You hear me?"

Adams watched the young man stomp away, wondering how much damage this might have done. He hefted the amazing nugget the lad had given him, and when he was sure no one was looking, he secreted it under a stone beneath an old tree stump.

Twice more within the next two days, a few of Adams's men made secret forays into the forbidden region. Without immediate punishment, confidence increased in their abilities to fend off what they guessed were Nana's thirty Apache warriors.

Even with the provisions party a day late, Adams wasn't too worried, as the valley proved abundant in game, and a single man hunting was able to bring in a deer a day to feed the work-weary crew.

Still, Adams kept an eye on the zigzagging trail leading down into the valley, the only trail they were aware of going in or out of the wonderful place. He decided at last to scout for them. Who knows, he thought, I might even meet up with them. He could already taste the coffee and flapjacks.

"Davidson, what say you and me ride up to the top of the trail, see if we can spot the provisions party. Might be they need a hand—lame horse or some such."

It took most of an hour for the two horsemen to reach the stone doorway at the top of the precipitous trail. Once they gained the top and rode through the narrow passage that led out of the gate, they found their way blocked by a mass of gear. Flour sacks were ripped open and trampled, pack saddles and gear sat slashed and strewn about the rocks, and the bodies of several dead horses sprawled in the trail. And amid it all lay the bludgeoned, hacked bodies of five of their men.

Adams and Davidson dropped from their mounts and crept together to inspect. They realized, after a few somber minutes, that they could not find John Brewer, the sixth man.

"Let's drag them into the rocks," said Davidson. "We can't let the animals at them. Then we should return to the camp and get the boys, then light out of here while we all still can."

As they descended the narrow trail, urging the horses forward as fast as they dared, they heard shouts, loud and long, and from many voices—far more than the remaining fourteen men at the camp could make. The two men dismounted, and as they hurried down around the last bend in the trail, their camp by the stream and the open meadows lining it all came into view. Before them was a hellish scene neither man would ever forget.

Three hundred Apache warriors danced and howled in a frenzy of blood-lust. A mass of flame engulfed the cabin, the green logs crackled and popped, and thick, black smoke boiled skyward. And all around lay the dismembered, mutilated bodies of the prospectors, while warriors hacked at the corpses and swung dripping scalps high above their heads, shrieking as if this were their greatest achievement.

Davidson slumped back against a boulder and shook his head, his mouth agape. Adams was the first of the two to recover. "Davidson." The man didn't respond. Adams slapped the man hard across his bearded cheek. "Come on, man. We have to save ourselves."

Davidson nodded, then his eyes seemed to focus.

"We'll have to let the horses go," said Adams. "If they're seen, the Apache might think the horses are just two more from our herd. Here, help me yank the saddles."

When that task was finished, the men crawled into a dense thicket to wait out the daylight hours. As the day wore on and slowly faded into dark, the warriors wandered off and the valley grew quiet. Adams and Davidson crawled out of the thicket and made their way across the near meadow, taking care not to disturb the bodies of their dead friends.

They crawled to the stream and drank their fill, then paused, not far from the still-burning cabin. "Our gold will still be there," said Adams, squinting into the smoke and coals. "Under that mass of charred timbers. If we only had an axe and fifteen minutes, we could clear the way to the hearthstone, lift it free, and—"

"And what?" said Davidson. "How could we ever get that gold anywhere? We have no horses, and even if we did, we need to travel fast, and a horse loaded with that much weight will not gallop far."

Adams stared at the far end of the cabin where the half-crumbled fireplace sat.

"And besides," continued Davidson, "that gold's safer there than anywhere else we could secret it."

"That's a fact," said Adams. "We'll come back for it. Yes, we'll get to safety, then get a new outfit, come back for it."

"It's a deal," said Davidson. "But now we got to find some canteens if we're headed away from the stream."

"Nothing for us here now except what them fellows got." Adams looked into the dark for a few moments, then said, "Right, we best make a start while we still got night on our side. Wouldn't surprise me a bit to find that the Apaches can see in the dark."

After wandering in the desert for two weeks, Adams and Davidson were found by a patrol from Fort Apache, Arizona Territory. They were taken to the fort and nursed back to health. While there, Adams (his given name is unknown) mistook several peaceful Apaches for members of Chief Nana's band. He fired at them with his pistol and killed two. Facing murder charges, he stole a lieutenant's horse in the night and headed to California, where his wife and children awaited him. Davidson was older than Adams and died a short time after leaving Fort Apache. He is said to have left a map and a diary about the affair, but their whereabouts remain unknown.

Over the years, Adams's story was repeatedly corroborated. He tried and failed for decades to locate the lost diggings, using other people's money. Each expedition ended in frustration, not surprising given his inability to recall landmarks and his uncanny ability to get lost. Though numerous expeditions have been launched on behalf of the Lost Adams Diggings, to date no one has found the fertile little canyon, the lost cabin, or the hearth covering the fortune in hard-won gold.

21

SNOWBOUND
AND STARVING
(1865)

During the brutal winter of 1864–65, aka the "Hungry Winter," Virginia City, Montana Territory, rich in gold but poor in provisions, is socked in for months on end under a dumping of seven feet of snow. A much-needed wagon train of flour from Salt Lake City is caught in an early blizzard. It is March before the road is passable.

◆

Ho! Ho there! Ho!" Alex Toponce held up his right arm, waving it back and forth, hoping the boys behind him could see. The last thing he needed was a knot of traces and oxen and harnesses. These poor beasts just couldn't go on. In this one storm, the snow had mounded up to their chests, and it was still coming. He would admit that he'd gotten a late start, but it was still only early November. Too darned early, by his calendar, for a four-foot snowstorm in Idaho.

"By God," he said to no one in particular, watching the steam rise off the backs of the lathered animals, their sides heaving and their tongues sticking out like nubs of pink wood. Fighting to get these beasts through the snow on the flats was one thing, but uphill? He stared at the rising range before him and saw four trains of wagons owned by his freighting competitors, Coe and Carter, but they were near enough to the top that it looked as if they would make it up and over.

Toponce shook his head. "Not a prayer in hell," he said, spitting the last of his chaw to the snow beside the wagon. It had curled up so close beside the seat that he could reach out and touch it.

He looked up at the sky, the branches of the riverside trees veining the raw moon, and closed his eyes for a silent minute. He knew he was about to either make a wise decision or a stupid mistake. He thought back on the previous few days—setting out northbound from Salt Lake City with loads of flour for which he would be paid a respectable profit. If it weren't for the storm, he might already be up and over the Divide.

.He blew out a big breath of air, pluming in the frigid night sky, and brushed the snow from his eyelashes and beard. "Thomas? Let's get these oxen over to that island in the middle of the Snake River. We'll unhitch 'em once they're there."

Thomas, one wagon back, figured he couldn't have heard Toponce right. He sat still for a moment, the last of his boss's words hanging in the air. Finally he said, "What did you say, Mr. Toponce?"

The big man sighed again. "Clean the dung out of your listenin' holes and do what I say, boy. Now that I've made up my mind, I don't like to wait. I need some shut-eye before the morning."

"Yes, sir." Thomas nodded at the back of his boss's head and out of habit, looped the reins around the brake. Then he jumped down into the snow, higher than his waist, and sucked in a breath as if he had plunged into an icy river.

"What's the matter, boy, you got a bit of a chill, did you?"

"Yes, sir. It's a mite cold."

Toponce jumped down from his wagon and said, "Well, hoist your britches high, boy, 'cause it's fixing to get even colder." He nodded toward the silent black river a few dozen yards in front of them. "We're going to be in a world of hurt if we don't get these animals to a place where they can at least try to forage for themselves."

"Yes, sir."

"And stop saying that. Makes it sound as if I'm forever whipping on you or something. You're a good lad, but you must have had a hard mother."

Thomas said nothing.

The burly freighter felt the sting the silence provided. "No need to answer that, Thomas. Wasn't my call to say such things. It's this damnable weather. Got me all worked up so's I don't know what I'm saying half the time, and blathering like a fool the other half. Like now, dammit."

The boy smiled, though he knew he shouldn't.

"You think it's humorous, eh, boy?"

"No, no . . . sir."

"Well, just for ribbing to me, I'm going to make sure you keep that smile as the warmest memory in your bag of tricks for the next little while. See that island?"

"Yes, yes I do."

Toponce looked at the boy, then smiled. "Good, because we have to get these 175 head over there." Then he shifted his attention to the man who had just struggled up to him from the third wagon.

"Hawkins, you're the wagon boss, but we have a situation that I did not expect to be faced with." Toponce held up his hands as if testing for rain. "Namely, this storm. I'll need someone to stay with the wagons, keep an eye on the stock while I go on ahead to Virginia City with the others, see if I can figure out a way to salvage this mess."

The wagon boss, as was his way, said very little. But his usual shrug and casual nod of agreement was commitment enough for Toponce.

Though his supplies were plentiful, had he known it would be March before their cargo would be retrieved, the taciturn wagon boss might have voiced a different opinion.

Early March rolled in before Toponce finally located a freighter who agreed, for a steep price, to venture down from Virginia City and help the flummoxed Toponce to retrieve the flour and other goods that had been locked in by the early and persistent winterlong snows. By the time the last of two round-trips had taken place and the wagons were emptied, other outfits had gotten through to the northern mining camps, so there was an abundance of goods once again, and accordingly, the price of flour had dropped to pre-crisis levels of $20 to $30 per hundred-pound bag. Toponce sighed as he unloaded the last of the flour from his last wagon. His poor wagon boss had spent the winter nursemaiding the now nearly valueless cargo, and now all Toponce could do was smile and shake his head. "You know," he said to O'Linn, the merchant who stood beside him. "I would have done just as well to have left this flour to rot back there on the wagons."

"Why that's a terrible thing to say, Mr. Toponce." The storekeep turned slightly away from him, as if to show his disdain.

"How do you figure that, O'Linn? Not only have I not turned any profit on this damnable flour, but I have lost money on the entire deal."

"You win some, you lose some," said the merchant, as if it had all been a whimsical undertaking.

Toponce pushed his hat back on his head and regarded the aproned man for a moment. He considered popping the smug merchant on the nose but found he suddenly didn't have the strength to bother. He snatched the meager amount of money from the man's hand, climbed aboard the wagon, and rumbled off down Virginia City's muddy main street.

A month later found Toponce and several of his men a-horseback, picking their way through the mud back toward where poor Hawkins had spent the coldest months of the year. They walked their mounts slowly around the last of the wagons. Good, solid wagons, but he would have little chance, at least for a while yet, of retrieving them.

On this April day, though, Toponce had other concerns in mind. As they rode he had wondered how he was going to get feed to the oxen he'd settled on that island in the middle of the Snake River. He knew he'd have some losses. Not all of the beasts would have made it through the winter, certainly not such a tough one. But he was anxious to see what sort of herd he'd have left. Any chance to recoup his losses of this disastrous speculation of flour hauling would be most welcome.

The water was still riding high, but they were bound to find a crossing place. They figured they'd build a fire and thaw out a bit on the island before riding back across once they saw the sort of herd they'd have to feed. They approached the river, and the island slowly came into view. And as Toponce squinted across at it, his cheeks drooped. Nothing moved over there.

When they finally reached the island, his worst fears had been confirmed. "By God," he said, rasping a hand across his stubbled chin. The other men were silent, each seeing the same thing. Before them lay the bloated, half-savaged corpses of what looked like all of his 175 head of oxen.

From what they could tell by walking among the ribby carcasses, all but one of the animals had died. "I hope they froze before they starved," said Toponce, knowing that it was more than likely a combination of the two.

"A chinook wind, I'd guess," he said, staring at the dead beasts' legs. "Melted the ice, then refroze it into a crust, cut their legs all to hell, made it hard to walk and made grazing nigh on impossible. Double dammit-all, anyway! I wish I had never thought to turn a dollar on hauling Salt Lake City flour all the way up here to these heathen hills."

Alexander Toponce is one of the more fascinating men to have heeded the call of adventure and headed out west. And he did so as a ten-year-old runaway. He tried his hand at numerous professions, including logging, mail delivery, cowboying, stagecoach driving, ranching, and prospecting. He also ran a slaughterhouse, was elected mayor of Corinne, Utah, and ended up owner and operator of one of the largest freighting concerns in the entire Northwest. He wrote a wryly funny and readable autobiography of his various ventures called Reminiscences of Alexander Toponce.

In Idaho City, Idaho, in that same "hungry winter" of 1864–65, mobs of flour-deprived folks rioted and looted stores and even their neighbors' homes, so desperate were they for a pinch of flour. In Alder Gulch a man traded his wife for one hundred dollars in gold and two bags of flour. Though most of the mine camps were able to resume their flour-filled meals by March, some remote communities, such as Emigrant Gulch, saw no flour until May.

During that winter in Alder Gulch, three children, the father of whom was a long-gone gambler somewhere in the state of Nevada and the mother a wastrel who could not be located, were found begging for food door to door. The eldest of the children, a twelve-year-old girl, lugged a twelve-month-old babe and led her ten-year-old sister, who clung to her older sister's only winter garment—a ratty slip. Ladies of the town took up a collection and helped feed the wayward waifs, known as the Canary children. The oldest girl, Martha Jane Canary, would later be known as the famed frontier figure, US Army scout, dance-hall girl, and drinking buddy of Wild Bill Hickok better known as "Calamity Jane."

22

FIRE IN THE HOLE!
(1869)

As shifts change on the morning of April 7, 1869, the Yellow Jacket Mine catches fire eight hundred feet down. Timbers collapse, and the fire spreads quickly, killing at least forty men. Some bodies are never recovered.

◈

On the morning of April 7, 1869, in the brief period of maneuvering after one shift ends and before another begins, the cages at the Yellow Jacket Mine in Gold Hill, Nevada, ran up and down the main shaft. They carried begrimed men up and barely rested men back down for their shift. A hissing, rushing sound caused everyone to pause and look toward the shaft and the massive timbered structure at its mouth. The structure bore the weight of the filled cage, where just below its massive crosspiece the shaft's primary entrance gaped, cables taut and pinging as the cage crawled upward.

The sounds that rushed were chased by an invisible cloud of gas. But it wasn't until the miners were hauled up, unconscious and flopped in heaps as if poleaxed, that the other miners and wives, children, and mothers of miners knew this was a bad, bad fire.

Down again plunged the cages, the men operating the cranking mechanisms working their best to raise and lower them, to get them to stop at each depth at which they suspected men were waiting in the heart of the oven the mine was fast becoming.

Far below the surface, Alfred Bigelow felt the glow and saw the heat before he realized what was happening. In an instant it occurred to him that there was a fire in the worst place of all, right where he was—down in the bowels of the Yellow Jacket Mine. And he knew that the thing he dreaded most was happening. His next thought was that wood burns, and the tunnels were filled with wood timbers forming a maze of cribwork veining outward all around him in the dark.

He recalled how on his first day in the mine a few months before, at eight hundred feet down, he had remarked to his shift foreman that even in a forest, a man might be hard-pressed to see so much wood in one place. The foreman had no sense of humor, and Alfred had since given up on getting him to smile.

He rounded the sharp corner that marked the connection from the Yellow Jacket to the Kentuck and, as if by magic, the brightest, hottest sight he had ever seen bore down on him. He knew it would soon roll over him like a train over a man strapped to the track. He knew that if he didn't get the hell out of the path of that thing, whatever it might be, he would never see his boy again, never see his wife.

Alfred spun and bolted back the way he had come, the sound behind him increasing, its heat reaching him first. The light filled the tunnel, and for a slim moment, he saw other men before him ducking low, glancing back at him, seeing him. He saw on their faces the very thing he knew others had seen on his face seconds before, as he too had turned and run up the tunnel, leaving others behind. And then there was a thick, full agony such as he had never known, and Alfred Bigelow knew no more.

"Get those men off that cage, pull them off—get them off!" Corcoran saw his bloodied palm, felt the sting as his skin stripped away, but he didn't care. He had to get that cage back down there. They'd only managed two trips, and he knew other men were down there, though he couldn't be sure of the number since it was changeover. They might not know for days. "And get those women out of there—pull them back!"

He watched as a short, fat woman tried to pull a man from clinging to the outside of the cage—he needed more like her, he thought, as she worked to keep the cage emptied. When she pulled the lolling man free, he saw the skin of the man's hands sizzle and smoke on the bars where it had grafted to the metal of the cage. Dear God, thought Corcoran, what next?

Soon the heat would be too intense to bear. Soon, he knew, the cages could no longer operate. But there's always time for one last try, he thought, and he set a lit lantern in a cage on top of a note that he scribbled in haste:

*We are fast subduing the fire. It is death to attempt to come up
from where you are. We shall get you out soon. . . . Write a word to
us and send it up on the cage and let us know where you are.*

He and the other men carefully lowered the cage at each stop down all of
the long eleven hundred feet and then repeated it all the way up. They could
all tell that the cage was empty, but the raw hope on the faces of the gathered
women spilled over to all of them, even though they knew the vile truth. And
when the cage came up at last, empty of anything save the unlit lantern and the
note he'd sent, charred but otherwise untouched, none of them said a thing.
They stared at the empty cage in silence.

It was all he could do to keep people from going near the shaft mouths.
Several times he watched too far away to help as men, their bodies smoking,
their hair aflame, ran in mad circles before plunging unwittingly headlong
down shafts.

Throughout the day miners fortunate to be on a different shift thronged
to the mine entrance. Along with trained firefighters, many miners descended
to the hellish depths below, looking for survivors. Unsure of what they might
encounter, unsure if they would ever see their own families, but they somehow
knew this must be done. As Corcoran and the others took turns hauling them
up and lowering them down, each time they raised the cage, those he hauled
up were crowded by people desperate to see if their loved one had at long last
made it to the surface.

But the only ones who ended up being hauled out were the firefighters and
miners who all day long volunteered to go down into the Yellow Jacket to look for
survivors. And when these brave souls were hauled up, Corcoran was shocked at
what he saw. Their clothes were nearly all burned away, their skin had bubbled
and welted, beyond red to a throbbing purple. Their hair was mostly singed off,
their eyebrows, beards, and eyelashes curled and matted to their heads in smoking knots and clots as if it were tar stuck on with a thick brush.

Worst of all were the screams of the men as they fell forward out of the
cages, unable to walk, unable to grasp hands extended to them, for their very
flesh had been seared away to the bone. Corcoran saw what looked to him
like white gloves on one man whose face was so bubbled and distended he
had no recollection of the man. But as the man pitched forward, writhing and

In the nineteenth century, hard-rock mining far below the surface was a decidedly dangerous undertaking. Man-made tunnels, shored up with massive amounts of timber, could snake for miles. Cave-ins, explosions, and fires were common and often exacted a high death toll. *Courtesy Library of Congress*

snapping his head back and forth on the ground, Corcoran saw that what he thought were gloves were actually the man's bones.

It was nine at night, and only ten bodies had been brought out of the hole.

Corcoran watched smoke as thick and as gray as solid rock boil and roll upward from the tunnel mouth. Down there, nearly a thousand feet down, he knew, were miles of main shaft and crosscut tunnels filled with millions of feet of rough timbers, extending out into the Crown Point and Kentuck Mines, too. Entire forests of lumber and timber were down there, massive structures of cribbing piled high, shoring ceilings against cave-ins, flooring laid plank on plank. Every six feet, level on level . . .

"You know," said Marta Bigelow, stroking her son's hair. "The tunnels stretch for miles in this direction, under the town."

The boy looked at her, his eyes narrowed.

"It's true. And so I think that your papa . . ." she paused, wiped her eyes, and found her voice again. "Your papa is under us right now looking for a place to climb out. He'll—"

"Stop it!" the old woman shouted. It was Alfred Bigelow's mother. "Stop that talk right now. He is not coming out. He is dead, burned to death like all the rest of them!"

"But . . ."

"No! You saw the smoke, you heard the screaming. Do not be a fool and say things you know to be untrue."

"But Papa . . ."

A strangled cry burst from Marta, and she hid her face in her hands. "No, your grandmother is right, son. Your father is dead. He is dead, and that is all there is to it."

There was quiet for a long time, then the little boy said, "Mama . . . what do we do now?"

The Yellow Jacket Mine continued to burn, and most work on the Comstock shut down so that people could help their fellow miners. By two a.m., thirteen bodies had been recovered. After three days the fury of the subterranean fires increased, and the tops of shafts were covered with layers of planks, blankets, and wet soil. Two days later, when the shafts were uncovered, the fires had redoubled their efforts and now blazed with abandon. The shafts were sealed again and left for another eight days. Alternative means to the tunnels, from adjoining mines, were attempted, and more bodies were recovered,

bringing the total to forty-one dead. In addition, maimed men and men suffering from severe gas inhalation overflowed camp hospitals and makeshift infirmaries. Thirty-nine days brought about the discovery of several more bodies, but at a price—the fresh air introduced reignited the blazes. Various tunnels were then sealed and left alone. After three years some of the drifts were reopened—and the rock inside was still red hot.

In what is considered one of the worst hard-rock mining disasters in United States history, a three-day fire in the primary copper mine shaft two thousand feet beneath Butte, Montana's Granite Mountain, trapped four hundred men, killing 164. Perhaps more than any other mining town in the world, Butte has been through the boom-bust-boom-bust wringer—and lived to tell its amazing tale.

In 1864 placer gold attracted attention at Silver Bow Creek. Within two years Butte City was laid out, and within three years her population hit five thousand. But life in a mining town can be a fickle thing, as is reflected by Butte's population of sixty-one in 1874, one decade after its founding. Fortunately, several events emerged fortuitously to cause a resurrection of Butte: Copper was soon discovered in paying quantities, and the 1876 and 1879 invention of the telephone and electric light, respectively, prompted a massive demand for copper wire.

By 1880 Butte's population had rebounded to a robust three thousand souls. Within two years, and after new copper discoveries, the famed Anaconda Vein was discovered. By 1885 Butte's resident tally hit twenty-two thousand. By the time of the tragic fire known as the North Butte Mining Disaster, on June 8, 1917, the city's population peaked at more than one hundred thousand people. It would be several more years before a snarl of litigation would be sorted out among three enormously wealthy men: William A. Clark, Marcus Daly, and F. Augustus Heinze, known as the Copper Kings, who battled for supremacy in the Butte region for years.

Today Butte's population has settled at around thirty-four thousand. In addition to sporting a fierce civic pride, Butte's residents work hard to preserve the city's rich cultural diversity and a legacy as one of the West's most notorious mining boomtowns, once home to bordellos and saloons numbering in the hundreds.

23

A LIVING HELL
(1872)

The owners of the Ophir Mine, Comstock District, Nevada, imprison four miners for three days at eleven hundred feet down in a sweltering tunnel—to ensure that word of their latest bonanza doesn't leak out prematurely and harm their investors' per-share prices.

<hr/>

McClellan, the shift supervisor of the Ophir Mine, watched Clancy's wife approach. Seemed he'd never seen the woman without a bairn on her breast and another on her hip. Still, despite the toll the mining camp and six children had taken on her, he had to admit ol' Clancy was a lucky man.

He lowered his tablet and slipped the pencil behind his ear. "Well, you finally came to your senses, eh? Here to see me? I guess what they say is true about Irish attracting Irish. . . ."

She came within slapping distance and narrowed her eyes at the chunky foreman. "I'll make like you never said that, Mr. McClellan. And I'll thank ye kindly to not talk like that in front of the children. Now, I've come to find out where my husband is."

McClellan rasped a hand across his red cheeks and stubbled chin. "Your husband, is it?" He smiled. "Mrs. Clancy, if you can't keep tabs on that husband of yours, how the devil do you expect me to?"

"His shift ended two hours ago. He must still be in there. I already checked the bars."

"Then he must be lost, because I don't know where he is and you don't know where he is, and the most important people in his life, the barkeeps, apparently don't know where he is."

The sleeping babe in her arms stirred and cried out once, then slumped back to sleep. She adjusted the thin child on her hip and stared at the shift supervisor.

"Now look, I'm a busy man. I don't know where Clancy's got to, but unless you intend to put them childers to work, you best clear off." He wagged his pencil at her. "I'll not say it again."

She turned and walked off. After a few paces, she spun and caught him staring at her. "You know, Mr. McClellan, there's a bunch of wives who have about had it with the mine making men work too long in the hole. Don't think we don't know what's going on there."

◆

The tall, thin man stood and pushed against the rock wall, stretching his back. "How long you reckon this business is going to last this time? That last time they kept us down here, it was nigh on two days."

"What's it matter to you, McGill? It's a secret shift, plain and simple. They say they're going to pay us pretty good. . . ."

McGill waved a hand at him as if to shoo away Clancy, the speaker. "Hell, I believe that when I see it. I been through secret shift stuff more times than anybody down here. But this ain't a secret shift. On one of them, a man's word was his honor, and if he's lucky he might get better pay and a couple, three shares, too. But here McClellan, the supervisor, is saying that he don't trust us, plain and simple. Now that ain't right."

From his spot in the corner, Borstein, a thick man with dark, stubbly hair, cleared his throat. "Couple of years back I was one of eighteen fellows stuck in the hole for a week. Owners were afraid we'd say something, so they toasted us up with top-shelf vittles, decent bedding, and even booze. And by the beginning of that next week, if we didn't all go back to work as if we'd been on a luxury cruise. No," he stood, stiffly, his hands on his knees. "We are the fools. We deserve this treatment."

"It wouldn't be so bad, but this heat is killing me sure as I'm Irish."

"Clancy," said Merton, the fourth man, "you'd complain if they dipped you in liquid gold. Besides, from what I see, you could stand a night away from your old lady. Give that poor thing a rest!"

Clancy stood his full diminutive height and squared off in a classic pugilistic stance. "I dare say the fair Mrs. Clancy has no complaints!"

Merton shook his head, not rising to the bait. "Course not," he said. "She's exhausted, Clancy."

The little Irishman shuffled closer and rotated his fists in a churning fashion before him, all the while huffing and puffing and working himself into a lather.

"Now men, now men," said McGill, rushing between them, his hands outstretched. "Let's keep this from a fight. We ain't got no way of getting any injured man up eleven hundred feet out of this hole. We've only been down in this tunnel half a day longer than our shifts. Who knows how long we'll be locked down here."

"It's like a prison, I tell you. I can't take it."

McGill nodded. "I know, but I'm telling you, this could go on longer. There's no cave-in. It's all because of this new strike. This here tunnel is a solid thing, and they know it. And they don't want us up there spoiling the news until they're sure they can nudge those stock shares higher and higher."

"And meanwhile . . ."

"And meanwhile we sweat in the near dark. No, if this was an accident or not planned, why, by God, boys, they'd not have laid in these supplies for us. Even some whiskey, which was good of them. Didn't have to."

"Listen to you, already, Merton. You'd think you liked being kept a prisoner in this mine, for no reason other than so a whole passel of rich men stand to get even richer. And all because they force us to keep our mouths shut by keeping us locked away in an underground dungeon."

"You know, it just come to me. This is the opposite of one of them Irish or English fairy tales, eh Clancy?"

"How do you mean, McGill?" Clancy lay on his side on his cot, not moving, staring at the barely lit rock wall inches from his face.

"'Cause instead of being locked away in a big, tall stone tower, like a castle or something, why, we're locked away underground, straight down, in a stone cell, in the very bowels of hell."

"Yes, it is hell. Of that much you are right." Borstein ran his sodden kerchief under his chin, sopping up the steady dripping sweat off his red face and wondering if he would ever again see the light of the sun. He swore to himself that if he did, he would leave this place, this raw, rocky country, and head to the water again, to the coast. He longed to see the ocean, to see nothing but miles and miles of green water slapping and rolling for as far as he could see. He could feel the crisp air, even in high summer, and the wounded cry of the gulls far overhead.

◆

Ophir Mine shift supervisor McClellan glanced out the front window of the shack and nearly looked away, out of habit. But the crowd advancing on the office was the biggest one yet. He groaned loud enough that the one young clerk sitting at the desk in the far back corner looked up. "Sir?"

"Mind your own business, boy." But inside he winced for the hundredth time that day. He wished the owners didn't force him to keep the men locked away down there. It wasn't right, wasn't fair, he'd be the first to admit. And yet it was his job, and if he didn't do it, he knew that the mine owners would find someone who would. He shrugged on his jacket, pulled in a deep breath, then opened the door.

The crowd was twenty strong, at least, and they all began talking at once. Several were men, miners whom he knew and would not forget their faces. The rest were women, harping on him as if they even had the right to visit the diggings.

McClellan put his hands up to quell their mounting rage.

"You can't tell us a thing anymore, Mr. McClellan. We won't listen to it. We got something to say to you, sir." And with that, the crowd parted and a smartly dressed man, at least McClellan's age, stepped forward. And just behind him, two men wearing silver badges. How had he not seen them when the crowd walked up?

The dandy man strode straight to him, bold as brass, and slapped two long sheaves of folded papers against his chest.

"Who are you?"

Mrs. Clancy, two children glommed to her body and a third in tow at her skirts, stepped forward. "He's our lawyer!"

"Well, what's this?" McClellan said, grabbing the papers involuntarily when the man let go of them.

"You, sir," said the lawyer, "have been officially served with writs, on behalf of the families of the four men you have imprisoned illegally for three days now in the Ophir Mine. I also wish to inform you and the owners of said mine that a series of lawsuits for unlawful detention of said four miners are proceeding at once. The mine owners have also been served."

"What . . . what do you expect me to do about this?"

"I suggest, sir, that you bring those men to the surface at once." The lawyer stepped forward and in a low, firm voice, said, "And you had better pray that they are all alive. Or you, sir, may well swing for this."

McClellan's florid face drained, and he shook his head as if refuting the idea. Then he said, "All right, all right. Right away, then."

The appalling practice of intentional imprisonment of men in mine tunnels far below the surface for days and weeks at a time became a widespread problem beginning in 1863. Within a few years there were reports of up to twenty-five men being imprisoned in a mine for several days. And in 1869 eighteen men spent a week in their subterranean jail. All so that mine owners and their superintendents could keep the miners quiet until they could manipulate the stock share price. The practice, though degrading and inhuman, was effective—the stock price of one mine jumped in less than two years from $3 to $1,825 per share.

The mine owners had good reason to suspect that their employees might reveal too much about a poor- or good-paying mine. It was a common, if unspoken, practice for miners to cadge free drinks, money, and trade goods in exchange for potentially useful information about their employers' mine works. Sometimes the buyers of such information were stockholders themselves, who for various reasons had not been kept in the know about their investment's performance.

The miners just as often came out on the short end of the stick in many mine-camp transactions, where most purchases were paid for with raw gold powder. When a man's sack of gold, or poke, was proffered, it was common practice for merchants, bartenders, and even prostitutes to use small scales to measure out their earned payment. Common vendor practices included keeping one's hair greased and then running one's hands through it just after a purchase was made. A quick wash of the hair at the end of the night would yield a few dollars' worth of gold. Another trick was to squeeze pebbles in between sales so that a pinch of someone's poke might yield a slightly larger pay-off in the resultant dents. But this was a two-way street, as many miners also augmented their hard-earned dust with brass shavings.

24

BLACK HILLS BETRAYAL
(1874)

In July 1874, six years after the region was ceded by treaty to the Sioux, Lieutenant Colonel George Armstrong Custer treks into Indian territory, scouting for two months, and discovers gold, resulting in broken treaties and the loss of the six-thousand-square-mile Black Hills region, sacred ground to the Lakota (Teton) Sioux.

❖

He smiled at the thought of what his superior officers must think of the boy general trekking into the Black Hills with a full military band in tow. If General Phil Sheridan was right, there would be gold to find in these hills—had been, in fact, by several previous prospecting parties. Considering the government's coffers were at a low ebb, this just might be a way to fill them back up again. And, thought Custer, this expedition just might help me smooth an admittedly rough path I'd made for myself at times.

But, he'd asked the general, what about the Sioux? The man had intimated that George ought to keep his mind on the expedition and on finding a suitable spot to build a fort.

Fine with me, thought Custer as he sat before his tent in a canvas chair. I can read between lines. He took in the pleasing sight of the tree-clad mountains that surrounded them. But at some point, he thought, the Lakota Sioux are going to be somebody's problem, because they won't take kindly to being told that the US government wants the gold in their sacred ground. Especially not after we signed a damn treaty with them six years ago forcing them to this very region.

What sort of leverage would Sheridan use next with them? Money had proved to be a nearly useless persuader, as had the promise of other tracts of land. Then Custer grimaced—their provisions, of course. Thanks to Sheridan, we've already nearly exterminated the Indians' primary source of food, the buffalo. He had to admit, when Sheridan had said, "Let them kill, skin, and sell until the buffalo is exterminated," he'd thought the tactic harsh. But it had been effective. Now, he didn't doubt that if the United States government wanted the Black Hills region bad enough, it would strike the Sioux a crippling blow. And where could it do the most damage? Why, in their stomachs, of course.

Threaten to withhold their winter provisions, supplies the Sioux depended on to survive now that they had been evicted from the broad range of their hunting grounds. He shook his head, not at all sure he approved of the notion. It might prove effective, but at what cost?

He sighed and puffed on his cigar. The more he thought about the idea of balking on the treaty, the more Custer shook his head.

"Sir?"

"Yes, sergeant."

"Those two prospectors are here, sir."

"Fine, fine. Oh, and Patterson, I want the usual precautions taken. Just because we've been camped in this spot for a few days without molestation does not mean we should lessen our vigilance. We may number above one thousand, but the Sioux are wily. Our superior firepower may keep us from the brink of death, but I'd rather not have to be driven to the brink—not good for us or the Sioux, I'd say."

"Yes, sir. I've already posted the usual double sentries, and the scouts are due back any time now. I'll have them report to you."

"Excellent, Patterson. Make no mistake, they know of our presence here, and I daresay they are not nearly as impressed with us as we are with ourselves. No sir, never underestimate the Sioux," he claimed, almost as if talking to himself as the two men he'd requested were brought before him.

"Well, my trusty Indian guides tell me this is French Creek. You've been panning it for a few days now, so I assume you know why I've called you here, don't you, boys?"

The two prospectors nodded, smiling.

Custer blew out a plume of cigar smoke. "And from the looks on your faces, I'd say you have something to tell me."

"Yes, sir. To be blunt about it, we've found color all throughout the place." The man warmed to his topic and rubbed his calloused hands together as if he were trying to kindle flame. "It's not a lode by any stretch, but I daresay there's more, and since the region is largely of the same rock, I'd guess we're looking at a potential strike that could . . . ah, solve a few headaches, sir." Both men offered excited, indulgent smiles.

Custer smoked, rocking back in his chair, his boots heel to toe in front of him. Then he smiled and nodded at them. "Fine news, men. Fine, indeed. Perhaps tomorrow morning, over breakfast, you can show me exactly what it is we're dealing with, and then I might arrange a chat with that journalist fellow I invited along on this expedition."

He kicked forward suddenly and, still seated, pointed the glowing tip of his cigar at them. He lowered his voice. "As with all the other spots you've been asked to pan, and especially now that you have found decent color in this French Creek, you are to tell no one but me, do you understand? I repeat, no one. Or I'll see to it that Patterson has your hides stretched and nailed. It's a matter of national security, among other things. Beyond that, I am not at liberty to say." He looked askance for a moment, as if to verify that perhaps he'd said too much.

The prospectors stiffened with the weight of his words. "Yes, sir," they said in tandem.

He nodded to them and they left. He watched them depart and marveled not for the last time how the son of a blacksmith could rise to the position of having men his father's age address him as "sir." He didn't question it, he just liked it.

After a few silent moments finishing his cigar, Custer stood, ground the stub hard into the gravelly soil, then stretched his thin frame. "Anybody up for a swim in that creek? I surely am ready to swap the day's dust for another sort." He winked at the closest officer to him and headed for the riverbank, humming and thinking of the words he would use later in his tent when he wrote that letter to General Sheridan.

Even though the United States government magnanimously ceded the Black Hills in 1868 to the Sioux in the form of the Treaty of Fort Laramie, in 1874 the United States War Department commissioned Lieutenant Colonel George Armstrong Custer to rove the Black Hills, seeking an ideal location for a military post. It was hoped that such a strategic positioning might

This Black Hills, South Dakota, Wells-Fargo "treasure wagon," carrying $250,000 in bullion, was one of many such heavily armed transports hauling hard-dug ore from mine camps to banks. *Courtesy Library of Congress*

provide assistance to the multitudes of Argonauts on their way to Montana's famed gold fields. The army also hoped that the fort would provide an ideal location from which to keep an eye on the Sioux.

Knowing that his ordered incursion into the Black Hills was unlawful and breaking a treaty with the Sioux, and yet sanctioned by the US Army, Custer led nearly one thousand soldiers, 1,900 mules and horses, three Gatling guns, 110 wagons, 61 Indian scouts, and a sixteen-man military band into the Black Hills.

Two of his party happened to be prospectors, and soon after his party's arrival, Custer, ever a man with optimistic flair, reported to his superiors that the Black Hills offered "gold in paying quantities" and that a man could "reasonably expect . . . to realize from every panful of earth a handsome return for his labor."

Word leaked out, and soon the general populace streamed into the Black Hills. The US government, in a desperate attempt to save face and prevent all-out bloodshed, tried to bargain with the Sioux by offering six million dollars for what the Sioux considered a sacred abode of the spirits, and thus not for sale. By the fall of 1876, threatened by the US Army with no provisions for the winter, the Sioux were forced to surrender their hold on the Black Hills.

Earlier, in the spring of 1876, and well before the final negotiations between the government and the Sioux, approximately ten thousand people had flooded to the northern hills region to prospect. In April 1876 brothers Moses and Fred Manuel formally established the Homestake Mine, located near the current town of Lead. Little more than a year later, tycoon George Hearst bought the mine from the brothers for seventy thousand dollars. Considered one of the most lucrative mines in the world, the Homestake was also one of the longest lived. It yielded one billion dollars in 126 years of continuous operation before it was shut down in 2002 due to increased operational costs.

In July 1980 the US Supreme Court ruled in favor of the Lakota Sioux and stated that the Black Hills were indeed illegally taken from them. A settlement was offered, consisting of the initial offer of six million dollars, plus interest accrued over the century—approximately $106 million. The Lakota said no thanks and instead wanted the Black Hills returned to their people. The money, now topping three-quarters of a billion dollars, sits quietly bearing interest. The Lakota staunchly refuse the cash, as they say this would condone the theft of their sacred space.

25

TRESPASSERS REMOVED!
(1875)

By early 1875 the Gordon Party of prospectors secretly builds a fortified stockade in the Black Hills near French Creek, the site of the Custer expedition's gold discovery. Though the US Army evicts the Gordon Party by April, there is little that it can do to prevent thousands of prospectors from streaming into the Black Hills soon after.

◆

The voice of Annie Tallent's husband sounded tight, his teeth on the verge of chattering, as he whispered into her ear. "I wish to God I had made you and the boy stay back in Iowa, Annie. This is no place for a woman and child." He closed his eyes and waited for the fiery woman he married to turn on him and give him a good tongue-lashing.

But she didn't. She squeezed closer to him under the layers of heavy bedding. She was thankful they had taken the time to build the stockade in December, when they trekked into the Black Hills. It hadn't been easy, evading army patrols, but they felt as though French Creek, where water flowed well, might yield their fortunes.

By now it was nearing the end of January, and Annie knew that her husband's concerns were not ill-founded. It had been a difficult few months. There was little in the way of privacy in the company of twenty-six men. And being the only woman had its drawbacks, as they all regarded her as their mother and confessor and seamstress and cook. The others seemed to forget that she had her own son and husband to look after. And yet she liked the land, the treed hills, the icy flow of French Creek. If she could change anything, it might be that they find more gold, or "color" as the men called it. Thus far, they'd found precious little of the stuff.

They had been so convinced of imminent wealth back in Sioux City when they'd first set out, and even long after they arrived. Gordon, the expedition's leader, had had dealings with several men who were in Custer's expedition from earlier in the year, who had told him the region was brimming with gold.

"David, how much have you found so far?"

Her husband sighed. "Less than thirty dollars' worth. But it's tough this time of year. Wait until spring, Annie. It will be different then."

She was silent a few moments, then she said, "Don't you think the army will try to find us? They must know we're here."

"How could they know? We're from so far away, no one who misses us will accidentally tell them. And by the time they send patrols this far into the territory, they'll see how much work we have put into this place."

In early April, on the heels of a spring blizzard that scattered their cattle, the members of the Gordon Party were visited by four soldiers who indicated that they were sent as emissaries from the main camp twelve miles away. They were instructed to retrieve the trespassers.

"You have twenty-four hours to make ready and vacate with us."

"But we have set up our lives here," said David Tallent. "We have built the stockade, furnished it with cabins, and set about gold mining and other pursuits."

The senior soldier looked at the man as if he were speaking French. He finally said, "I repeat: You have twenty-four hours to pack up yourselves. You will take only what is necessary, and only what can be carried on your own backs. The rest, I suggest, you cache hereabouts in the unlikely event that you be allowed to return to retrieve your goods, tools, and the like."

"But—"

"You will all be fortunate, the lady included," he glanced at Annie, "if you are not put under arrest and transported to Cheyenne in irons."

"What?"

"Come now, sir, don't act surprised. You knew when you and your party ventured into these Black Hills that you did so in violation of the treaty the US government has with the Sioux."

"What's different about us or Custer coming in here last July, making a big hue and cry about gold, and with a brass band, no less?" Annie's husband stood defiant, his arms crossed in front of his chest.

"Sir, I have no argument with you, nor with the Sioux, but if you don't do as I say, the Sioux, who are fixing to stir themselves up into a rampage any day now, well, the Sioux can be . . ." He looked again at the lone lady in the camp. "They can be unpleasant. Let's just leave it at that. Now, the government is the government, and being as that's the case, and being that I have no desire to go against it, and being that it is my employer, you are in violation of the law and I have been ordered to remove you from said premises and bring you back— drag you back, if necessary."

"That won't be necessary. The dragging, anyway. We shall do as you say."

"But—"

"Relax, Annie. I dare say we all could use a meal that ain't bacon and beans, eh, officer?"

"Your presence here has also emboldened the populace in general for miles, and the news is, as we speak, rippling across the country in newspapers. There are rumors that you have found much gold."

Annie laughed, "Now those are rumors, soldier."

The man, still seated on his horse, slammed a gloved hand hard on the pommel of his saddle, emphasizing his words and the fire in his eyes. "Do not make light of what you people have done! An earlier company of soldiers was sent after you, but they were trapped in severe cold and nearly died. Many of them were my friends."

The gathered Gordon Party members said nothing, their faces belying realization of their impending punishment.

"You have broken laws and caused untold hardship and headache. You have also helped speed a war with the Sioux that, though it may have been coming, might well have had a different outcome had you and others like you not sneaked onto these Sioux lands. It is a mighty poor example you have set."

There was a drawn-out silence, then Tallent said, "I am sorry to hear of the hardships your fellows have suffered, and if we have any guilt in the matter, then we will no doubt pay for it dearly. And perhaps justifiably, but I will not stand by and take the blame for crimes which the United States government has committed before me."

The soldier stared at the speaker for a few cold seconds, then said, "You are wasting time."

Earlier in the winter an army expedition from Camp Robinson, under the captaincy of Brevet Brigadier General Guy V. Henry, ventured out to retrieve the Gordon Party members. But the soldiers timed their foray into the Black Hills poorly. They were caught in the teeth of a vicious midwinter cold snap some thirty miles from the Gordon Party's stockade, of which they did not know the exact location.

Several soldiers had begun to bleed from their noses and ears, and still others dropped from their mounts, so cold were they. With as much vigor as he could muster, Henry urged them all into one last surge of action. "Mount up!"

Those men whose horses had not wandered off remounted into their stiff leather saddles and kicked weakly at their horses' heaving ribs. The animals seemed to sense the urgency, and though the soldiers were still some miles from their post, they nonetheless all seemed to realize, man and beast, that a last mad dash was at least preferable to expiring while sitting still, out in the open, in the bitter cold.

"Praise God," cried one man presently, and those nearest him looked up and squinted into the near-darkness. No, it could not be true. But it was—a ranch house, humble yes, but salvation, nonetheless.

Soon a door opened and closed, revealing for the briefest of moments a slice of golden light, and with it the promise of warmth and succor to the ravaged company. The rancher, a white man, and his Indian wife came out to help the afflicted men from their mounts. He corralled the horses, fed them from his own stores, and helped his wife usher the men into their humble abode.

"I had heard of a squaw ranch somewhere in these hills, but never would I have guessed we were so near it," said Henry. He tried to offer a hand in grateful friendship, but the man patted him on the arm.

"Stay seated, sir. No ceremony here. We're just glad we could be where you needed us to be." The rancher's face grew more serious as he packed wood into the hearth. "Sir, I won't candy the situation. You and the men are in bad shape. Some of the worst cases of frostbite I've seen. By rights, some of you should be dead. And once you warm up, some of you are going to wish you was dead. You got me?"

The commander nodded and looked at his men, who sat on the floor, leaning against one another, huddling and shivering despite the increasing warmth of the little cabin.

"Some of these men have been through cold, sir, but nothing on the order of this night. Would that we had never gone after the trespassers."

"You mean that group went in back in December?"

Henry looked at the rancher. "You know them?"

The man shook his head. "No, sir, but I heard of 'em. You ain't the only army folk come around these parts, you know. I'm surprised you don't leave them fools well enough alone until spring. Ain't worth it chasing them in these cold months."

"I can't say I disagree with you, sir. But right now, we have other worries." He looked down at his own hands and saw the telltale signs of deadening flesh.

None of his men would ever forget this night because they wouldn't be allowed to forget—most of them, if not all of them, would lose fingers, toes, or worse. Of that he was sure. And even if they didn't, he had seen enough old-timers gimped and crab walking to know that the rheumatism would be near crippling. For the rest of their days.

The men from that early failed retrieval expedition suffered horribly soon thereafter. In a firsthand account, published years later, the patrol's leader, Brevet Brigadier General Guy V. Henry, wrote: "To this day many are suffering from the effects of this march by the loss of members. Even where there is no physical disability, freezing leaves a nervous prostration, from which one never recovers. . . . I was not recognized, owing to my blackened swollen face. All my fingers were frozen to their second joints; the flesh sloughed off, exposing the bones. . . . The joints of my left hand are so stiffened . . . I am unable to bend or close my fingers."

A quarter century after the Gordon Party's ignominious ouster, after having collected barely forty dollars in gold from December through April, Annie D. Tallent, the only woman on the expedition, wrote a book, The Black Hills, or, The Last Hunting Ground of the Dakotahs, a Complete

History of the Black Hills of Dakota, from Their First Invasion in 1874 to the Present Time. *The highly readable work is in part a memoir of her long but memorable months as a young wife and mother in the stockade in the Black Hills.*

Mrs. Tallent had apparently developed a fondness for the region, for her family later moved back to the Black Hills, where she became a teacher and later superintendent of schools.

SNOW ANGEL
(1875)

Businesswoman Nellie Cashman hears of twenty-six miners stranded in a snowstorm in the nearby Cassiar Mountains. The Canadian Army refuses to mount an expedition, so she sets off with six men and pack animals carrying fifteen hundred pounds of supplies. Humiliated, the army tries to retrieve her. She refuses and spends seventy-seven days trudging through ten-foot snows.

◈

From across the cookfire, deep in the snowed-in campsite close by the Stickeen River, Nellie Cashman saw the Canadian Army soldiers before her men saw them. Good thing, too, she thought. The soldiers were a lively bunch, to be sure, but she wasn't really surprised to see them and knew exactly why they were there. She continued singing the Irish song, "Keg of Brandy," one of her mother's favorites. Soon enough, her men saw the soldiers as well and fell into a nearly closed circle around Nellie.

The young woman continued to prod the sizzling venison she had been preparing. "May I interest you gentlemen in tea and a shared repast?"

An officer at the fore of their small contingent nodded. "Yes, ma'am. I speak for the group of us when I say that we would very much like that."

Over their meal, Nellie listened to the officer in charge and did her best to suppress a smile.

"Surely, sir, it's not enough that I am forced to do your job as well, but now it appears as if you want me to curtail my expedition to save the twenty-six men we all heard about back in Victoria."

"Ma'am, please," said the tired Canadian officer. "You must know that this is no place for a company of Canadian Army soldiers, let alone a woman and a handful of miners." No one said anything, so he continued. "My commander explained to us that he firmly believes you are insane, ma'am, to even consider trekking all the way to Dease Lake in the middle of the winter and in the grip of such a series of snowstorms. Even the old-timers say they've rarely seen the equal of this winter's snowfall." He sat up straighter and brushed snow from his wool coat's sleeves. "Our orders are to rescue you and bring you back."

This time Nellie did laugh, long and loud, her voice echoing down the snow-laden river valley. "If I need rescuing, you can be assured that I will do that myself. There are rumored to be twenty-six men in dire need of medicines and vegetables, else they may die of the effects of scurvy. I suspect the number is higher, as there are about two hundred men up there now. I can help them, but only if we get to Dease Lake in a timely manner."

She eyed him for a moment, then continued. "You can see for yourselves that we are making every effort to reach them. In this case, unfortunately, that does not mean speedy. But it is quicker than if you were to take us back with you, for then I should be compelled to set out again, and that time, there would surely be deaths at hand once we reached the diggings. Are you qualified, young sir, to personally take on the responsibilities of all those deaths?"

Other than the odd snap and sparks spiraling upward as a chunk of wood surrendered to flame in the fire, silence once again descended on the group. Only the snow moved, continuing its interminable drop downward, and the flames danced, reveling in their own heat.

Soon it was too much for one of Nellie's six trail companions to bear, and laughter burst from him. "You are a corker, Nellie Cashman," he said, slapping his leg and shaking his head. It seemed as if all the time on the trail helped pull the mirth up and out of him. Soon the other men joined him. Even the soldiers—including their commanding officer—surrendered to the laughter, too. They all spent a restful night in camp, and in the morning the Canadian Army patrol wished the Cashman expedition well and parted ways, heading back to Victoria without her.

A week later the men set up Nellie's tent on a hillside and anchored it securely in the ten-foot-deep snow. During the night the hillside became a snowslide, and she, along with her tent and all her gear, slid a quarter mile down the hill. When one of her men brought her coffee in the morning, he was shocked to

Restaurateur, boardinghouse owner, and merchant Nellie Cashman (1845–1925) was famous in mine camps throughout the West for her selfless acts of kindness. Often called "Saint of the Sourdoughs" and "Miner's Angel," her love of mining and miners took her from California to Arizona to the Yukon. She worked her own claims wherever she went. *Courtesy Alaska State Library*

find no trace of her. She was far below, having spent the better part of the night digging herself out of the deep raft of snow.

She soon righted her gear and, after a brief breakfast, continued on with the journey, pulling one of the sleds they used to transport the lifesaving goods. I just pray we're not too late, she told herself. Then she shook her head and worked harder at trudging through the snow that seemed to grow deeper with each step. The entire time she was oblivious to the fact that her men were awestruck by her unstoppable spirit.

"That would have killed a normal man," said one fellow.

The miner next to him winked. "Nellie Cashman is no normal man."

By midafternoon on their seventy-seventh day on the trail, Nellie and her six enlisted men, knowing they would soon arrive at Dease Lake after so much time and under such strenuous conditions, staggered to a stop at the low rise that overlooked the camp. They saw more of what they had become accustomed to seeing on the trail, a snowy landscape, but this one was dotted with snowed-in cabins and slow-rising smoke from several chimneys.

"Something's wrong," she said. "It's cold enough that there should be more chimneys smoking."

The men struggled to get down the slope, but Nellie stayed just ahead of them, lighter and swifter in the snow as she was. Soon she abandoned her sled and shouted for the men to take it. And she ran, falling once on her snowshoes but righting herself immediately and stomping forward. Soon she reached the little village. Her shouts of "Hello, hello!" rose in the clear afternoon air.

Soon several slow-moving men emerged from the cabins, then a few more. "Nellie? Is that you, Nellie? You come back in the middle of the winter?"

"Hello, Pete!" Nellie pasted on a smile over her worried features and held the thin, swaying man's bearded face in her hands. The friends stared at each other a moment, then he led her toward the cabin that she'd had built as her boardinghouse.

"I told you I could watch your place for you, but we've had to use it as a sort of hospital. Some of the boys have got the scurvy bad, Nellie."

"That's just what it should be, Pete. But me and the boys have brought supplies that will soon have everyone on their feet in no time, you wait and see."

As she entered the low-ceilinged room, the close smells and moans and coughs greeted her. The smell of unwashed bodies and the thick indefinable stink of sickness clouded her, made her eyes water. "For the love of God, Pete, open the window and keep that door open."

She peered closely at several of the men who were lined up side by side in makeshift beds along the walls. They all had dried and fresh blood trailing from their noses and mouths, their eyes wept pus, and when she lifted the begrimed wool blankets, she saw lesions on their limbs. Most of the men had slipped too deep into their sickness to know they had a visitor.

Nellie peeled off her thick traveling coat and rolled up her sleeves. Soon she heard voices outside and her trail companions filled the doorway. They ferried in the fifteen hundred pounds of supplies, which included lime juice and potatoes, both of which would be useful in defeating the scurvy that had afflicted the miners.

On her arrival at Dease Lake, Nellie Cashman found that the sick numbered seventy-five, far more than the twenty-six she had heard about. Most everyone in camp was suffering the death-dealing effects of scurvy, a foul disease that arises due to a lack of vitamin C, found most readily in fresh fruits and vegetables. Miners, who subsisted largely on meats and grains, were frequent victims of scurvy, especially in winter.

With experience gained from years of nursing ill and wounded miners, Nellie was able to save the lives of all the afflicted men. This and many other such episodes throughout her life earned her the sobriquets "Frontier Angel," the "Angel of Tombstone," "Miner's Angel," "Saint of the Sourdoughs," and others.

An Irish native who came to the United States as a young girl, Nellie Cashman was a born entrepreneur. While working as a bellhop in a Boston hotel, she was told by General Ulysses S. Grant, who saw the flame of adventure in her, that she should head west, so she did. She hired out as a cook and by 1872 had opened her first business, the Miner's Boarding House in Panaca Flat, Nevada.

Stories of her selfless acts abound: After a Tombstone miner fell down his own shaft and broke both his legs, Nellie raised five hundred dollars for him and then nursed him back to health. A devout Catholic, she is also well remembered in Arizona for dismantling a freshly built wooden grandstand erected specially for the hanging of five murderers in Bisbee in 1884. She did not believe the hanging should be a public spectacle and especially not one for which the grandstand's carpenter should charge admission.

In 1898 the shouts of "Gold!" echoing southward from Alaska and the Yukon proved too tempting to the Irish do-gooder, so she headed north to the diggings. At last, it seems, she found where she truly wanted to be. Over the next few decades, Nellie Cashman would start a number of successful businesses and own a variety of claims, which she worked to varying degrees of success. Just before she died, in 1925, she traveled 750 miles alone by dogsled to work her latest claim.

27

DEADWOOD'S BADMAN
(1877)

With promises of safe, well-paying jobs in hotels and as stage performers in his famous Gem Theater, Al Swearengen lures dozens of women to the mining town of Deadwood, Dakota Territory—and forces them into lives of slavery as prostitutes.

But that can't be right—I've been working, doing what you said. I . . . I expected to be paid by now."

"You took my money, didn't you?"

"No, no, I never took no money from you . . ."

"I paid for your trip out here from Iowa City, didn't I?"

The girl nodded slowly.

"Therefore, you took my money."

"But I been working . . ."

"You may call that working, Flora, but you have cost me more money so far than you have earned. And that, you little simp, is bad business. And I do not run a bad business. I run a profitable business."

Flora stared at him but said nothing. "You promised me I could clean rooms until another position on the stage opened up. I been practicing my dancing and all."

The man relaxed, stepped back, and looked the girl up and down. "I'm sure you have, my dear. I'm sure you have." His eyes traveled slowly up her body, resting halfway, before continuing to her face. "OK then. You will probably have to show me your . . . dances so that I can tell whether you're ready for the stage or not."

From behind him, a woman's voice said, "Pardon me."

Al Swearengen turned around. Silhouetted in the midmorning light of the Gem Theater's open front door, a woman stood, wearing a hat and traveling clothes and clutching the straps of a carpetbag.

"Who are you? And how long have you been standing there?"

She walked toward him. "I am Inez Sexton. I'm a singer. I am looking for Mr. Swearengen."

"You found him," said Al, leaning an elbow on the bar and offering her a smile.

What she saw was an average-height man with a dark, low brow and thick features. "I wrote to you with my credentials," she continued. "You replied four weeks ago and told me to show up, that you had need of a singer."

He nodded slowly. "I remember now. You're the one who didn't want me to pay your way out here. A man doesn't forget a thing like that." His smile dropped.

"I'm pleased to hear I made an impression." She smiled.

Swearengen took his time looking her up and down, his eyes trailing from the toes of her muddy boots to the top of her hat.

From the dark corner, a small cry quickly stifled.

Swearengen turned around. "You're still here? Stop sniveling and go finish the bedding. Then come see me in my room. We'll discuss your debut."

Flora nodded and turned to go.

"Wait a minute." He turned to Inez. "Follow the weeping willow here. She'll show you where you'll be staying."

"That would be most welcome. I'd like to rest. It's been a long journey."

"I'm sure it has, but we have rooms to clean, floors to wash, cuspidors to empty."

"But I'm a singer . . ."

"And I am a wizard of high finance." He grabbed a grimy rag and mopped the bar top with exaggerated circular strokes. "And yet I still have to cook, clean, and sew, don't ya know."

She stared at him.

"Let me tell you a little story, Miss Inez Sexton. When I arrived here in May 1876, it was a Monday. By Saturday I had my first dance hall up, and I have not stopped to 'rest' since then."

Flora tugged the new girl by the wrist. "Come on, Inez. Sooner we get to it, the sooner it will get done."

"Ten minutes, Inez. Then come see me. Top floor, in the back. Can't miss it."

"Don't you want to hear me sing?"

Swearengen looked at her as if she had told a bad joke. "No, not particularly. Save it for the miners. And take that thing off. Wear something that shows more of your body—you look like you're wearing a buffalo robe."

For the first time since she walked in, Swearengen thought Inez looked scared. Good. Now I'll know how to keep her heeled. Maybe her dear old mother made the hideous coat especially for her big trip out west. We'll see how long before we can get her out of it and helping the miners out of their pokes.

"Oh, Miss Sexton." He smiled. "One more thing. Once your songs are over with, I want you to work the boxes." Swearengen dropped the stub of his cigar into a drained beer mug. It hissed and smoke curled upward. He looked at her again. "Now you're going to tell me you don't know what I mean by 'working the boxes.' Right?"

Inez Sexton slowly shook her head. "I am a singer, Mr. Swearengen. My voice is for sale. Nothing else." She turned and followed Flora up the back stairs.

He sighed, drummed his fingers on the bar top, and stared at the empty doorway. "We'll just see how long you can go without food or sleep, Miss Inez Sexton."

Every bang on his door was like a blacksmith's hammer-blow to the forehead.

"Mr. Swearengen! Mr. Swearengen—open up! There's been a terrible tragedy."

He forced his eyes open and groaned. Other than his Gem burning down, or perhaps his own death, there was little in Al Swearengen's world that he might consider a tragedy.

"It's Flora, Mr. Swearengen. It was the laudanum, I think. We have to do something . . ."

He groaned. The girls, always the girls. Why couldn't he just serve liquor and call it even? Why did these damn miners need girls? He smiled. Same reason I do, he thought, as he heaved himself upright. He staggered to the door as Inez embarked on a fresh round of pounding.

"Enough on my door!" He whipped it open and stared at Inez. He had to admit that even in his aching morning torpor, she still proved a fetching sight. "Inez, what is all this?"

She grabbed his wrist and led him down the hall, talking the whole way. "It's Flora, Mr. Swearengen. I think she's done something stupid."

"Again? When will that fool learn that what she's here for isn't the cleaning. Well, not at night, anyway."

She led him to Flora's room, before which were clustered his other girls. She pushed her way through the little crowd and nodded toward the bed. The room was a filthy mess. The girl lay naked before him on the bed, two empty brown glass bottles on the bedding beside her head.

"Well?" he looked at Inez.

"I've already called the doctor."

"You did what?" He shook his head. "No, no, no. I do that sort of thing."

"Then why didn't you?"

"A bit obvious, isn't it?" He nodded toward the girl. "She's dead."

He turned and walked out the door. "And if she ain't quite there yet, she will be soon enough." He stopped and looked at her. "And Inez, never bother me again like that. Especially not for a dead girl."

◆

Ellis Albert "Al" Swearengen, an Iowa native, arrived in Deadwood in May 1876 on a wagon with his first wife and a team of oxen. He did indeed have his first establishment set up within days of his arrival, a wood and canvas affair, and shortly thereafter he built a small bar, the Cricket Saloon, in which he staged prizefights. Less than a year later, he opened the doors of his Gem Variety Theater.

Though the establishment featured full bars, gambling, prizefights, and various variety acts, as well as theater performances, it was the girls, some of them doubling as performers, and whom he had lured from far and wide with promises of work as actresses and singers and waitresses in his theater, who were the primary attractions. But it was under false pretenses that he lured them to Deadwood, for they were all soon to become prostitutes.

Swearengen entrapped them into lives of indentured servitude and forced them to work all manner of menial tasks and long hours. In exchange he controlled their wages so that they became hopelessly indebted to him with little chance of ever paying him back. He also addicted many of them to drugs and alcohol, and the girls often became riddled with disease. In desperation many committed suicide. If they did not submit to his demands, he and his henchmen beat them severely, sometimes killing them, and then covered up the beatings to make it look like a suicide or a tragic brawl between two girls.

The singer Inez Sexton was one of the few women, if not the only one, to escape relatively unscathed from Swearengen's clutches. Like so many before her, Sexton was lured to Deadwood by Swearengen's advertisements in Eastern publications, claiming the need for stage performers and offering high wages. Most arrived with no money, and he paid the way west for many of them. Sexton worked for him for a couple of months, and then, in a final act of defiance, walked out the door, penniless, and up the street to a respectable hotel. She told her story, and the "proper" ladies of the town collected enough money to send her on her way, presumably crooning back east.

Famed sheriff Seth Bullock was not even a match for Swearengen in his prime. Bullock is credited with almost single-handedly cleaning up the streets of Deadwood from its raw, violent, lawless start and helping it become the largely lawful, prosperous town it would become within a few years. And yet with Swearengen, whose establishment brought in five thousand to ten thousand dollars in a single night (the modern equivalent is about one hundred thousand dollars-plus per night), Bullock had to be satisfied, though not happy, with agreeing to a "deadline"—an unseen boundary separating the red-light district from more "respectable" businesses, and across which Bullock's power of exercising laws was greatly diminished.

The Gem was damaged by fire in 1879 and refurbished. Later that year, on September 29, a large fire swept through Deadwood and razed many of the stick-built structures to the ground. Swearengen rebuilt and spared no expense in the task. The result was a grand three-story establishment that lasted nearly two decades, burning again in 1899. Swearengen by then must have had his fill of dealing with drunks and enemies, for he left Deadwood shortly thereafter, having spent more than twenty years as one of the town's leading figures. On November 15, 1904, he was found dead of a head wound on a street in Denver, an apparent murder victim. He was not killed, as has been the popular story for a century, by (poorly) trying to hop a freight train.

Seth Bullock went on to become an even more-famous lawman and best friend of Teddy Roosevelt. Among many other achievements, in 1894 Bullock built Deadwood's first hotel, a three-story, sixty-three-room establishment with steam heat and indoor bathrooms. The Gem is but a fascinating memory, while the Bullock Hotel is still in operation today—and is said to be haunted by the kindly ghost of Seth Bullock.

28

HEART OF A
SOURDOUGH
(1877)

Though a millionaire from his share of the diggings at Tombstone, Ed Schieffelin, founder of that famed Arizona town, is happiest prospecting. Years after the Tombstone strike, he is found in his Oregon cabin, age forty-nine, flopped dead over ore samples flecked with gold. Nearby, his journal reads: "Struck it rich, again, by God!"

❖

The soldier at Camp Huachuca shook his head at the tall, thin character who'd just returned near dark from the surrounding hills. "You keep on heading out there with them Apaches about, and the only rock you'll find will be your tombstone."

Ed now thought about that remark as he made a cold camp well after dark out among the hills, too far to head back to Camp Huachuca. He found a spot for himself and his burro that looked to be well protected and hidden from Apaches. It was farther up the gully than he had been before and seemed to him as if the Indians would have to be right on top of him before they saw him. Even so, on this particular night it was small comfort that in months of roaming these hills, he'd not seen any Apache close enough to cause him grief.

Night came quickly, as it always did in the arid hills of Arizona Territory, and though Schieffelin was exhausted from his day's labors, he slept little. Every piercing cry, every shift of his burro's feet, every dry skittering sound as some nocturnal creature clawed across a rock face tensed the twenty-nine-year-old miner. He pulled his blanket tighter around himself and leaned back against the unforgiving rock.

His thoughts turned to lots of things that night, but never once did he consider abandoning his quest for gold. He had thought of it for so long, had lived it for years, that the very act of prospecting was to him as vital as eating and drinking. The quest for a bonanza was all-consuming. With those comforting thoughts, Ed Schieffelin dozed, finally, just before the sun rose and warmed the very rocks he sought.

After a cold breakfast of water, bread, and jerky, he fed and watered his burro, then loaded his gear onto the beast's back and decided to explore farther up the wash and into the hills. It was one direction he'd not yet been in. As he trudged up the wash, as was his habit, he kept his eyes on the gritty earth beneath his worn boots. And what he saw there caught his breath and stopped his feet. Silver float. Small hunks of it scattered about the gravelly wash.

The pieces became more numerous as he walked, faster and faster, until he was almost running. The trail led to a massive outcropping of black and red rock. And struck straight through it was the telltale blackened vein of pure silver. The visible run looked to be fifty feet long and a foot wide. As he climbed up to it, he didn't even breathe, so stunned was he. Could it really be what he knew it to be? Would it be, once he reached it? Would it just disappear? Could he really have found a vein of pure silver?

He had spent so long roaming hills just like these all over the Southwest with nary a decent strike to his name. But now this! Deep in Apache country, just under the gaze of the Dragoon Mountains. He trembled as he reached for it—it felt real, felt solid. He drove his pick into it. It left a deep dent—that's good, Ed nodded as if in conversation with himself. Silver is a soft metal, especially if it's pure. Within a few nervous, frenzied minutes, Ed Schieffelin was sure of what he had. And he hoped it was the start of something big and long-lasting.

It would be months before Schieffelin could return to his find. He had but a few cents in his pocket, and he needed to get to Tucson to show his ore samples to a fellow named William Griffith, who promised to record claims for Ed in exchange for a share in whatever it might be that the young man had discovered. Ed made it to Tucson, and on September 3, 1877, Griffith recorded the name Ed had given his new find: The Tombstone. Schieffelin couldn't help but feel just a pinch smug and prideful at the thought that all his labors would soon pay off.

Then he would show those who had laughed at him. No longer would he have to console himself with the thought that they didn't understand the life of a miner.

To heck with them, he thought. For here I am, on the verge of great success. He stepped into the street, headed left, to the mercantile for some tobacco. And it took all his money—all thirty cents of it. Before he could track down his brother, Al, who he found out was at the McCracken Mine in Silver City, he had to earn money for the trip. So he rolled up his sleeves and tucked into work as an overnight crank operator at a local mine.

As soon as he had built up a bit of a stake, he outfitted himself again for the road and tracked down his brother. In the process, the two men picked up a third partner, an assayer by trade, named Richard Gird. He deemed the stone worth two thousand dollars to the ton. Gird was rewarded with a third-stake in the new findings, and the trio set off through Apache country. Over the next few weeks, disappointments outweighed successes, and Ed's partners nearly chucked it in, disgusted that they had quit good-paying jobs at mines for this wild-goose chase.

Soon, though, Ed found an even bigger strike. His shouts brought his brother and Gird running. By the time they clambered up the graveled slope to his spot, they were out of breath. But then again, so was Ed, though his heavy breathing came from the discovery he'd made—another raw vein of silver. All he could do was smile and nod toward it as his two partners stared, their mouths dropping open wide.

"You have some kind of magic touch, brother!"

Ed Schieffelin set the canvas sack full of ore samples down on the little table that served as his desk and purposefully kept himself from looking at them. Soon, but not yet. He stirred the coals to life in the little stove, just enough to warm up the cooled coffee in the enamel pot. He could scarcely believe his luck—and yet he knew it was not because of luck but dogged determination that he had once again found a most-promising silver strike. He knew he didn't have any particular knack for it. Heck, he reasoned, if he had a skill for finding rich strikes, he certainly wouldn't have waited twenty years since the strike at Tombstone to hit another one!

This old, time-worn sourdough has paused in his travels, perhaps regretting selling for a song claims that later "proved up" for the new owners. Most often, though, old sourdoughs were in it for the chase, not the capture, and in the end, as was the case with Tombstone founder Ed Schieffelin, wanderlust proved more tempting than gold. *Courtesy National Park Service*

He didn't feel different from anyone else, certainly not special, and yet, as he gazed at the ore samples on his table, his breath caught in his throat again. This was what it was all about—the thrill of the hunt, the moments of discovery, the private feeling of satisfaction of a job well done. But tinged with the elation he felt, there was a whiff of sadness, too. For this discovery would no doubt force others to this pretty spot on Day's Creek in Oregon. And hadn't he chosen this spot for his cabin in order to get away from other people? It might also mean he would have to return to the city sooner than he wanted. His wife would be waiting, and while he couldn't really blame her, he had warned her before they married that he was happiest when he was out and about in the hills, with a canteen over one shoulder, a pick and shovel over the other. He knew, even if he lived to be one hundred, that he would never lose that feeling.

He poured a tin cup full of coffee, sat down at the table, then opened his battered journal. He rolled down the top of the sack to reveal the ore samples, and there they were, laced with silver traces. Yes, indeed, he was sure of it—they were as promising as he'd suspected in the field. This was it! Another strike as big as Tombstone? Maybe so, maybe so. Ed Schieffelin licked the tip of his rough pencil, and at the top of the next blank page in the journal, he wrote the date: May 12, 1897. He glanced at the samples again, felt a fluttery feeling in his chest that he took as deserved excitement. He then wrote: "Struck it rich, again, by God! Found it at last! Richer than Tombstone ever hoped to be!"

The fluttery feeling spread through his chest, felt as though it was about to crawl up his throat, and as he gazed on the little mound of ore, the inside of the small cabin seemed to fill with a brightness he'd only experienced outdoors, on a sunny spring day, full of warmth and beauty and promise. . . .

In many ways Ed Schieffelin personified the heart and soul of the Old West prospector, and his visual appearance fit the bill. The writer James McClintock, in a Tucson newspaper, described Schieffelin thusly: ". . . the queerest specimen of humanity ever seen in Tucson. His clothing was worn and covered with patches of deerskins, corduroy, and flannel, and his old slouch hat, too, was so pieced with rabbit skin that very little of the original felt remained. Although only twenty-nine years of age he looked at least forty.

His black hair hung down below his shoulders, and his full beard, a tangle of knots, was almost as long and he appeared to be a fur-bearing animal."

Soon after his Tombstone discovery, other mines were dug, but because Schieffelin and his partners were there first, they ended up owning shares in several mines in which ore ran a rich fifteen thousand dollars per ton. From that point on, it didn't take long for Tombstone to establish itself. By March 1879 her bare bones were laid out, consisting at first of tents and ramshackle lean-tos built of scraps. Within a few short years, tens of millions of dollars in silver ore were worked out of nearby mines. By 1882 Tombstone's population crept up to fifteen thousand, and the town offered such modern conveniences as running water, refrigeration (in part for its skating rink), and telegraph and telephone service.

With a haircut, clean clothes, and his new fortune, Schieffelin toured the country. By 1883 he'd grown weary of people, so he sailed to Alaska and prospected in the Yukon. Not finding promising ore, he headed south. In San Francisco he met Mary Brown. They married, but city life soon wore on him, so he set up a cabin in Douglas County, Oregon, overlooking Day's Creek, near a ranch owned by two of his brothers. It was here that he was found dead, slumped over his desk, ore samples at hand and his journal opened. He was four months shy of his fiftieth birthday. An inquest performed at the cabin found that his heart gave out from the excitement. He didn't leave any maps to his newest bonanza, though the ore that so excited him tested out at two thousand dollars per ton, another hearty strike.

His will had requested that he be buried at the spot where he discovered the Tombstone silver. He was buried on May 23, 1897. All his relatives and everyone in the town threw him a massive send-off. And he was buried as he had requested, in his old miner's clothes—his faded red flannel shirt and ragged prospector togs—and with the pick, shovel, and canteen he'd had with him when he'd discovered the Tombstone strike.

29

LOST AND FOUND . . . TOO LATE
(1878)

Prospector Joshua Ward, his wife, and their two little daughters strike it rich in silver. But no one will know for thirty years, when their arrow-riddled corpses are found in their hidden cabin—along with a fortune in gold coins stashed in the fireplace.

◆

Joshua Ward eased back on the reins, and the oxen pulling his over-loaded ore wagon slowed. It had taken a good hour longer than usual to return home from his diggings, but it was worth it. Abby would be so pleased. A couple more loads and they'd be able to buy a team of horses. Then the trip to Eureka to cash in the ore would take at least two days less than the six it took with the bull team.

"Whoa, whoa there . . ." Joshua looked around for the girls, Phoebe and Sarah, and his wife, Abby. But he saw no sign of them. He also noticed there were no flutterings and cheeps from the meadow birds in the field he kept for the oxen, no shrieks from the girls, no shouts from Abby. He guided the ore wagon to a halt halfway between the well and the back corner of their little home at the bottom of the draw. Something was off. He set the brake, then jumped down, his worn boots raising dust clouds where he landed.

"Abby—Abigail! Sarah? Phoebe?" He looked around the dooryard. He raised his hands to his mouth to call them once again, when he saw a flutter of blue just past the corner of the house. So, one of the girls was playing hide-and-seek with him, he bet. That was why they were so quiet. Well, he thought, Papa can play at that game, too. Joshua bent low and walked silently forward. He parted the dried grass and saw her head surrounded by a puddle, like a wet, red halo. And then his eyes flicked toward the front of the house. His wife lay half in, half out of the door, reaching forward with both hands. . . .

Quick as a gunshot, he knew his life had changed forever, and for the worse. Joshua bent low and lifted little Phoebe, her body a ragged doll in one of his brawny, sweat-streaked arms. In the doorway, with his other arm he scooped up his wife, her head a bashed-in thing of blood and bone too awful to think about. And that's when he saw two arrows sunk deep into the logs beside the door. Who? His mind would not work, try as he might to quell the gagging wad of emotions boiling up his throat.

And Sarah? What of his Sarah? He dragged his wife to their bed by the fireplace and laid Phoebe on the floor nearby her mother. "Sarah!" his ragged cries burst out of the little cabin with him, and he didn't have to race but ten feet from the door to see his sweet girl, Sarah, quiet as ever, in her pink flowered dress, never to smile and saunter over to him again as if she hadn't a care in the world.

The unexpected punch of the first arrow slammed into the center of his back and drove him forward, sprawling on top of his dead daughter. Joshua looked up then and saw the advancing ragged line of Indians, too far to tell who they were. But he bet some of them were the same men he had given water to in the past. He'd always been so careful to make sure that Abby and the girls were out of sight, tucked in the house.

His eyes filmed with stinging sweat as he rose to one knee and lifted Sarah, her head flopped back just like her sister's. He would be safe inside, just bolt the door and then he could fight them. If he could hold them off. . . .

The second arrow sunk into his back inches from the first. This time it poked through to his front. He could see its glistening red tip forced through the rough, striped fabric of his work shirt. This cannot be, he thought as he staggered across the threshold. This is not how they had planned their lives.

Joshua heard the whistle of the third and fourth arrows, and they sent him sprawling forward into the cabin. Sarah tumbled out of his arms and flopped on her side like a dropped doll. Joshua tried to shout, to tell the Indians they had made a mistake, but even as he thought this, he heard their garbled voices drawing closer, shouts rising above his own choking sounds.

He staggered on his knees toward the door and caught a glimpse of dark skin, dirty cloth, arms wrapped in some sort of cord, a bow, the dead-cold black steel of a rifle barrel, then he slammed the door closed. Protect your family, he told himself. Protect them at all costs, that's been your job from the very moment you said, "I do," in that little church back home.

Home, he thought as he coughed. A bubble of blood rose from his mouth, popped against the door he dragged himself upright against. He could not prevent the blood from pumping as if he were vomiting. It gouted out of his mouth, down his shirtfront, the shirt Abby had made for him. Such a good woman. He fumbled for the first bar, dragged it across and rammed it in place. The second, yes, in place. He tried to do the same with the third bar, but it was too low and he dizzied as he bent to retrieve it from its cradle beside the door. He finally dragged it across and settled it in place.

Joshua Ward sighed, safe at last, girls. He tried to say it and heard nothing but a gurgling sound. He slumped to his left side hard, then fell to his back. Pain, for the first time, washed over him like a landslide. The last thing he saw were three arrows poking from his gut and chest. The last thing he thought, as pain and grief warred in his mind, was that he was home at last, home with his three girls. Then Joshua Ward died.

No one would enter the cabin for thirty years.

◆

In 1908, miner and mine-country gadfly Frank Crampton and a partner were asked by a prominent lawyer from Boston to look into the disappearance of long-ago relations who had left for the West in the spring of 1876 and had faithfully written to family members for two years, detailing their new homestead's location near Cherry Creek, Nevada, and how it was laid out. They'd even included sample chunks of silver ore to verify that they indeed were doing well. The last letter from them, dated August 12, 1878, bore a Cherry Creek postmark. No letters followed, and the back-east relations never heard from the Wards again.

Crampton was dubious that he might find a trace of the family, let alone the lost silver mine that sounded so incredibly lucrative for the young family. But he and his partner outfitted themselves with gear, supplies, guns, and as many maps of the region as they could locate, hopped in their rugged Ford, and headed out from Cherry Creek late in the year.

Within a few days of searching, they found a set of old, overgrown but still visible tracks, the sort that might be made by a heavily laden ore wagon cutting into the dry earth. Soon they had to abandon their vehicle. They packed lightly and trekked in on foot, following the tracks for twenty miles. They followed these to the top of a small valley, and a half mile below them, they saw the cabin, plain as day.

It was nearly nightfall, so they camped by the well, which sat just where Abigail Ward had described it in her letters home. In the morning the two men explored the area surrounding the forgotten little homestead. It was so accurately described by Abigail that Crampton felt as though he had been there before.

Halfway between the well and the house, they found the remnants of an ore wagon, the wooden sides having long since collapsed, spilling its full load of silver ore to the ground. What remained of the wheels had sunk into the ground. The men moved to the front of the wagon and found the bleached bone remains of two oxen, still in the rotted remnants of the traces. Their skulls had been neatly cleaved as if by an axe.

The men felt a grimness growing, though neither said much about it. They moved to the house, tried the front door, but found it would not budge. A loose board hung from the top of the door. With a little effort, they were able to peer into the room and spied an overturned table and four chairs. They worked at the old wood until they were able to break part of the door enough to wrench it open.

Dim light filled the interior of the cabin, and a thick layer of dust covered everything inside. Off to the right, against the wall, sat an organ. There were bookshelves, a desk, and across from the door sat two beds. A body lay prone on the floor to one side of the door. Another lay on the bed closest to the fireplace, and two smaller bodies lay on the floor between the bed and fireplace.

The men knew then with instant and awful clarity what had happened to the Ward family. The bodies of Abigail and her two daughters each had crushed skulls. The men presumed by the same instrument that had been used on the oxen. The body by the door didn't appear to have been treated in the same way. The men saw the spiky remnants of arrows bristling from the dead man's chest and gut.

The same thoughts occurred to each man: Why didn't the Indians loot the cabin? Why didn't they burn it? Why didn't they steal the oxen for meat? Unless they butchered them where they fell.

The two men carefully laid all four family members beside each other on one bed and covered them with what remained of the Wards' bedding. They then took all the papers from the desk and newspapers from 1878 from the bookshelf. They left the cabin, repaired the door, locked it tight, and hiked back out to their vehicle. A storm had commenced while they were busy in the cabin, the first of the season, and snow was piling up. They vowed they would return in the spring, but at the present there was little more they could do. Neither man spoke for a long time as they trudged away.

◈

The two men did return in the spring. They were accompanied by several other people and a team that made the road in more passable, allowing them to bring caskets for the family's remains. The bodies were shipped back to Boston. In tidying the cabin, Crampton found a loose rock in the fireplace that revealed a hiding spot with five thousand dollars in gold coins—the squirreled earnings, no doubt, of the Ward family's silver strike.

In addition, the ore from the wagon outside was analyzed and found to assay at one thousand dollars per ton, a promising and sizable quality ore. Concerted efforts over the next few years were made to locate Joshua's mine, but to date it has not been found. Years later, Frank Crampton recounted this gripping saga, along with many others, in his excellent book, Deep Enough, *about his life as a "working stiff" in the mine country of the West.*

30

QUIT WHILE YOU'RE DRUNK
(1878)

A prospector with a penchant for boozing it up, Crazy Bob Womack digs for twelve years around Cripple Creek, Colorado, beginning in 1878. By 1890, he establishes the El Paso Mine. Though it would earn three million dollars in the coming years, he sells it while drunk one night for a modest three hundred dollars.

◆

She's called Cripple Creek because she's mighty hard for them strays to cross, being so knobbed up with rocks."

"Rocks . . . I'd venture to say they're boulders."

Crazy Bob Womack looked down the gulch, regarded the streambed a moment, considering the eastern journalist's estimation, and nodded. "I guess you're probably right at that."

"And you've been at this how long, Bob?" The young man's pencil hovered just off the notebook's page. "It looks as though a giant prairie dog has had his way with this place."

"It's true. I dug all over this here country," Womack waved a lanky arm wide to indicate the entire surrounding region, then he fixed the stranger with a red-eyed stare. "For twelve years I dug all over this here place. Then I struck her, back in 1890. Sank a shaft, called her the El Paso Mine."

The stranger thought back. "That would make it 1878 when you first began here."

"Yep, about then I found my first piece of float down yonder near the creek. I was rounding up strays."

"Float? What is that, Mr. Womack?" The reporter held his pencil poised above his notebook. "Does it have something to do with water?"

"Naw, naw, you greenhorn pup," Womack shook his head and wheezed out a laugh. "Float's a hunk worked off the mother vein by time and the weather. Drifted on down there, I knew, from up above somewheres."

"And that's why you chose to do your digging up in that region, then?"

"Why, I should think that would be plain, yessir."

The young man cleared his throat and pushed his spectacles higher up on his nose. "Could you describe your piece of float, then?"

"Sure I can. It was as long as my hand and two, three fingers wide. But the odd thing was that she was lighter than a rock like that has any right being. But that's what ore will do." He rocked back on his heels, proud of his ability to educate the youngster in the ways of the prospector.

"How did you know its potential worth, then?"

"Oh, I sent her to a friend in Denver who give it to an assayer to analyze. Turns out she was worth about two hundred dollars a ton. So I knew then that if I could just find that mother vein, I'd be in tall cotton."

"But it took you twelve years to locate it?"

"Yep, and thank the Lord, too. I'm not sure I would have lasted much longer." Bob leaned forward and, in a lowered voice, said, "A man's patience can only wear so thin, you know."

The journalist nodded and tried to suppress a smile as he chewed the end of his pencil. "So, I understand you had trouble attracting investors to help you develop the El Paso."

"Ain't that the truth." Womack licked his lips and rubbed his hand across his bearded face as if he were considering some deep question.

"Why was that?"

"They all thought I was off the beam." He tapped his temple with a long, shaking finger. "But they come around."

"Yes, because those other men near your mine struck it rich."

"Could be the reason, yes." Womack stretched and yawned. "Could also be because they finally figured out I'm a man of my word. I say there's gold there, by gum, there's gold there."

Womack carefully lifted out of his pocket a clear glass bottle stoppered with a cork. He uncorked it, smiled at the *punking* sound, then upended it and pulled in several long swallows. He caught the young man watching him from the corner of his eye and said, "You like a snort?"

Old-time hard-rock mining was a dicey business at best. Lone miners were often found crushed to death in their diggings from a collapsed tunnel. Some were never found, and their bodies remain sealed in their long-lost mines today. *Courtesy Library of Congress*

"No, no thank you, Mr. Womack. Ah, never while I'm working."

"Funny, I found the best time to drink was when I was working. Helps make the time go by faster. Course, I'll allow as how there have been times when I could maybe have gotten more work done had I not had so much to sip of a morning. But I'll be jiggered if I'm going to play with any regrets just now."

"Speaking of regrets, sir."

"Sir? By God, boy, ain't we been jawing for an hour or more? You'd think by now you'd know enough to call me 'Crazy Bob.' I ain't really off my bean, just something the locals took to calling me 'cause I didn't never give up. Even when they said this here area was played out, I kept on going."

"But surely, er, Crazy Bob, you must regret selling, as you did, your mine, the El Paso, the first and largest at Cripple Creek. And for the pittance you did . . . ," the journalist smiled.

"You think that's funny, boy? You get some livin' down your gullet, then come back and work me over. Maybe by then a little something like booze will have you by the tail, then you'll see if three hundred dollars don't look like a good deal."

"But sir, you were paid three hundred dollars for a mine that to date has earned millions of dollars. Surely your dozen years of backbreaking labor deserves more than three hundred dollars?"

"Maybe so, maybe not. I didn't really consider it that way. More like I recall it seeming like a fair trade at the time. I tell you what, mister pencil man, I had me one whale of a time with that money. What I remember of it, of course." Womack winked at the young man, then looked off over the journalist's shoulder, still smiling at the memory of it all.

For every man like Crazy Bob Womack who told everyone he knew that he'd struck a rich vein, and yet for the longest time could get no one to believe him, there are hundreds of cases of people going to great lengths and taking great pains to conceal their strikes.

So quiet and skittish were prospectors who had found what they believed was a tremendous strike that they were quite often at odds as to what to do with their sample ore. Should it prove to be indicative of a rich strike, word often leaked from an assayer's office (even though these men were under a moral obligation to keep their clients' business confidential). Soon the otherwise secretive miner would find himself followed by dozens, sometimes hundreds, of people just waiting for a chance to set up a claim directly adjacent to the potentially winning claim.

Crazy Bob Womack died bedridden and flat broke in 1909, his health shot from years of alcohol abuse. The entire Cripple Creek gold rush, for which Womack is largely responsible, would go on to yield eighteen million dollars in gold in the coming years. His own mine, the El Paso, would change hands several times, and each time would make subsequent owners wealthy. It would eventually earn more than three million dollars.

31 RAGS TO RICHES TO RAGS
(1878)

Horace Tabor, a Leadville, Colorado, merchant, grubstakes two prospectors to the tune of seventeen dollars—and a year later reaps one million dollars for selling his share in their diggings. Tabor also leaves his devoted wife for Baby Doe, a much younger woman. Years later, poverty plays them false.

◆

Augusta Tabor folded the lawyer's letter and closed her eyes. Here it was, 1883, and she'd been abandoned by her husband a year before, with no more to her name than the massive Denver house she hadn't wanted a thing to do with and a handful of servants she had to figure a way to take care of. She'd even been forced to take in boarders to bring in a meager income. Meanwhile, she knew because he had told her, his income from his various investments totaled more than one hundred thousand dollars per month. And she had been made a fool of for two years by that young thing, half her age, Baby Doe. Now he planned to marry that child who was not much older than their son, Maxey. It was all too much to bear.

She thought back to twenty-six years earlier in 1857, when she and "Haw" Tabor had set off for the West from New England, bound and determined to strike it rich. They had settled in Colorado and worked hard—though Horace could most often be found playing poker. Which, she had to admit, didn't gall her as much as it should have, but only because he was a good gambler.

The beginning of the end came when those two Germans staggered into the store. August Rische and George Hook. Lord but they were a hard pair to look upon. She had told Horace to get rid of them.

"Now, now Augusta, these men are probably looking for a stake. I can at least let them eat their fill of crackers and listen to their tales of woe."

"You mark my words, Horace, one day your naïveté will be the death of you."

"Augusta, where's your charitable side?" He'd smiled at her, then turned to the two haggard prospectors. "Now, gentlemen, what can I do for you?"

Within a few hours Horace had given in to them, as she knew he would, and had loaned them seventeen dollars. They had even filched a bottle of whiskey. Horace later tried to tell her that was part of the deal, but she could tell that at the time he hadn't known a thing about it.

"You gave them seventeen dollars *and* a bottle of whiskey, all for one-third of their mine, eh?" Augusta looked at him over the top of her blue-lensed pince-nez. "I call that one-third of nothing."

Well, remembered Augusta, no one was more surprised than she. That one-third stake in the Little Pittsburg Mine had not been worthless. In fact, and she still hated to admit it, it had been a most exciting time for them. That following year had been a blur, as she recalled. She could finally afford a decent parlor stove and the best cookstove on the market. At the end of a year, Horace and she had sold his share for a million dollars. Neither of them knew quite what to say.

Then the real trouble began. For the next few years, Horace did well with the money. "I'm using the same tricks that help me win at cards, dear Augusta," he'd say, touching the side of his long nose and winking at her, that ridiculous walrus mustache rising up on one side in a smile.

She loved him then, just as she loved him now. That's what made this latest news so difficult to take. The public would soon find out what she had been experiencing for two years. She looked down at the letter on the table beside her. It was from his lawyer, and it demanded that she grant him a divorce or he would see her penniless. In exchange for her quick and silent acceptance of his terms, he would grant her three hundred thousand dollars.

"All this so he can marry that child," Augusta said this aloud, knowing she was alone in her kitchen. And knowing that she had little choice in the matter. She would never get her Horace back. Yes, indeed, thought Augusta Tabor, this life is sometimes too much to bear.

Horace A. Tabor lay on his deathbed, smiling slightly at the fact that, though it was 1899, he would not be alive to usher in the brand-new century, the bold century of promise, as so many of the country's finest journalists had been calling it for several years now. He had, however, been up and down and seen as much of the grand life as any man had a right to see. He'd also had his share of misfortunes and regrets. He wished somehow that life could have been different with Augusta, could have ended on a happier note. She had always been so very practical, and so very bitter, never wanting to enjoy their wealth.

What was money for, after all, he'd told her, if not to enjoy? Baby Doe had understood that. That had been one of the things that had attracted him to her.

Never had there been a happier man than H. A. W. Tabor. Not even the dour, pleading letters from Augusta had soured his mood back then. For he had married Baby Doe in a fancy ceremony in Washington, D.C. Hers was a seven-thousand-dollar dress adorned with a necklace of diamonds valued at ninety thousand dollars. Love had bloomed between them, and for that he was eternally grateful. And for the two beautiful daughters they had together. Those were heady years, indeed.

He only wished he was not leaving them in such dire circumstances. But the silver ran out—and with it, the money. Even now, on his deathbed, the shame of what he had to put his dear Baby Doe and daughters through flushed his cheeks, and he felt his throat tighten against it. Should have been a better poker player. But somewhere along the way, he had lost his knack for winning a hand. Or maybe he never had it? Maybe he had only had extended periods of luck, had hit a few hands at the right time?

The turning point had come in 1893, when a dozen Denver banks closed within three days. From then on their lives changed drastically. They'd had to hock their jewelry and home. The public shame was one thing, but Baby Doe's hot tears on his cheek were too much. And yet he had to bear up under the shame. For it was he who had done this to them.

He'd had to leave them then, living in one room in a hotel, with Baby Doe rationing the last of their money, while he wandered into the hills prospecting. But he had spent far too many years dining well and had lost his taste for hard labor. That had been two years ago, he recalled from his deathbed. And then, in a gesture of kindness, he'd been rewarded with the position of postmaster of Denver. They were able to buy food, but they still lived in the one room in the hotel. And now here he was, dying in that same room, his wife and two young daughters by his side.

But there was one thing that he could still give her. The one thing he had held onto, had held out all hope for—and that was the Matchless Mine in Leadville. By God, if ever there was a mine that still had promise, it was the Matchless. He could feel it just as he'd felt those winning hands in poker all those years ago when he simply could not lose. He smiled at the memory of the Matchless in her heyday—bringing forth a thousand dollars every day. Tabor forced his eyelids open with a flutter and beckoned to his wife. She bent her tear-stained face close over him. So pretty, so very young and pretty was his Baby Doe. "Hang on to the Matchless, it will make millions."

She nodded and tried to smile.

Elizabeth McCourt "Baby Doe" Tabor sat hunched in the one chair in the little cabin at the Matchless Mine. She had become so confused lately. Sometimes she knew it was 1935, but other times her memory played tricks on her, and it was those times she enjoyed the most, because then she was still young and beautiful and rich beyond imagining. Just as she used to be, before this. She looked around at the little cabin, newspapers piled high, the only thing she could burn now that she had no money for wood or coal.

It grew so cold in the cabin at the mine, the mine that she remembered her husband had told her never to sell. But he didn't know what it had been like. Once he died in 1899, she lived in Denver for a time, raising their two girls, but then after a few years, she moved to the only place she didn't have to pay rent to anyone. But by 1927 she'd had to sell even the mine, for debt trailed her like a starving wolf. She sold the Matchless and wept for days. The new owners allowed her to stay there in her little cabin.

Their eldest daughter, Elizabeth Bonduel Lillie, left her to live with Baby Doe's Wisconsin family. She never heard from her anymore. I think perhaps she is ashamed of me, thought Baby Doe, pulling her threadworn blankets tighter about her shoulders. She wished she had a sip of hot coffee with sugar and cream. Oh, those were the days, drinking hot coffee with sugar and cream from solid silver. She closed her eyes and tried not to think about the past, but it would not let her be.

Between those old memories and the increasing whistle of the wind from yet another Colorado snowstorm, Baby Doe felt as though she might not live to see spring. I wouldn't care if I didn't, she thought, if I could only see my youngest baby once again. Rose Mary Echo Silver Dollar Tabor—why won't she visit me? And then there was something—a slip of a memory with a tinge of sadness to it? What was that?

With fleeting clarity, she recalled that Silver Dollar had been found dead in her room in Chicago, scalded to death, they said. No one knew how or why. And she had even changed her name to Ruth Norman. She too had been ashamed of the Tabor name. But Baby Doe was too tired and too worn out for tears.

Soon she felt sleep gripping her. She fought it for a time but finally gave in and dreamed of a life lived long ago. During the night she slipped to the floor, prone, as if grasping for something just out of reach.

◆

After a particularly bitter stretch of cold, snowy Colorado weather, Baby Doe Tabor was found dead, frozen on the floor of the cabin at the Matchless Mine. It is believed she had been dead for at least a week. The year was 1935, and she was eighty-one years old. Her few remaining possessions were auctioned for seven hundred dollars to help defray debt. She was buried beside her husband at Mount Olivet Cemetery in Wheat Ridge, Colorado. Her fascinating life and death have been the subject of countless books, songs, films, an opera, and even a chain of restaurants.

H. A. W. Tabor's first wife, Augusta, died wealthy in Pasadena, California, in 1895. She is buried in Denver's Riverside Pioneer Cemetery.

32

WRONG PLACE, WRONG TIME
(1882)

Vigilantes mistakenly lynch young James Williams for a horse theft he didn't commit. When his body is cut down, in his pockets are found ore samples and a partial map—to the Lost Spanish Silver Mine of St. Marie's River, in Benewah County, Idaho.

As soon as he squeezed the trigger of his shotgun, James Williams knew he would be eating well that night. He couldn't have happened on the grouse at a better time. It had been days since he'd had a good, hot meal of meat roasted over a fire. As he tracked the still-thrashing bird into the brush, he licked his lips and thanked whatever bit of luck gave him the bird.

This treasure hunting had turned out to be long days filled with hard work as he followed the precisely laid out directions to the mine. Though it was not too much work for a young man with a map, a canoe, prospecting supplies, and boundless ambition. And so he had spent weeks following the trail to Lake Coeur d'Alene. From there he had to follow the St. Joe River to the St. Marie's River tributary.

His uncle, for whom he was named, had promised him on his deathbed that the map was genuine, given to him for favors he did for a priest. The uncle swore it would lead to a lost mine of the Spaniards from hundreds of years before, back when the Spanish were known to have ventured all over the West.

Young Williams poked the thick, low mountain willows with his gun barrel. The bird had to be close by. The branches grew at the base of a rock outcropping, and when he parted them, he saw a hole in the ground nearly five feet in diameter. His mouth suddenly felt dry and his throat tight. Could it be? Even as he stared at the hole partially overgrown with brush, his mind tallied through the directions to and descriptions of the mine, and this matched most of them.

With shaking hands Williams secured two ropes to jutting rocks, lit a candle, and lowered himself into the hole. A few feet into the dark cave, he found his grouse and smiled as he tucked its limp form into a sack. As he crawled deeper into the hole, it became more evident that this was no mere animals' cave but had been a mine, and that it had not been worked for some time. He passed several small piles of ore chunks that even in the near dark felt and hefted of promise. And then, a few feet beyond one of the piles, he found what looked like a broken pick. And the discovery made his heart hammer in his chest. This was proving almost too good to be true.

He half expected to find old Spanish chest plates and a helmet or two. "Later," he said in the dark. "There will be time later."

He wanted to explore the branching tunnels further, but he knew he had best head back to the surface and think things through. Excitement was one thing, but he didn't relish jeopardizing his future because he had been foolish while alone in the wilderness. On his way back to the opening, he half-filled two sacks with the most promising of the ore. It was difficult in the near dark, the candle melted onto the brim of his hat throwing barely sufficient light to inch forward by.

That night in camp, he made his plan. Each moment seemed to him to carry extra significance. He was now, he felt sure, a man of impending wealth. He would take the samples back to Spokane, have them assayed, and then hire a team of professionals to open up the mine. He packed his pipe and told himself, as he drew on it to get it glowing, I will sit back and wait for the riches to favor me.

He spent all of the next day making detailed notes about the countryside, then set off for Spokane. Days later he reached Rockford, Washington, and decided to rest for a day or so in an abandoned cabin near town. He had pushed himself hard to get back, and his health had suffered because of it. He rested for two days and decided he would leave the next morning. But in the middle of the dark hours, he was roughly awakened by the kicking boot of a man holding a torch.

"Get up, vagrant. Wake up, I say."

Williams looked up to see several more men flanking this one. "What is the matter? Who are you?"

"We're asking you that very question, boy."

They dragged him to his feet and, still fatigued from his heavy trek and from the effects of sleep, James Williams stood swaying before the men.

"Nobody knows who you are here, mister. But I tell you what, a local man name of John Wallace—a respected man in these parts, though someone such as yourself might not appreciate that—he had himself a pinto pony in a pasture not far from here. And do you know what?"

Williams could only shake his head, his mind racing, wondering what it was these men were going on about.

"Well, that pinto has disappeared. Right about the same time you showed up in our town."

"Now, now men, wait a minute. I have no horse—"

"You mean you didn't have a horse, until you stole his! A man afoot is a useless thing in this country. You show me a man afoot, and I'll show you a man who wishes he had a horse." He turned to his cohorts. "Am I right?"

The murmured assents chilled young Williams's guts. "What? Where would it be?" Williams threw his arms wide. "I tell you, this is all I have, right here, in this pack. I am traveling through, nothing more."

The men said nothing but stared at him, seemingly unconvinced but still not speaking. Williams decided to play his one last card that should convince them fully he was not their suspected horse thief. He explained the map his uncle had given him and the prospecting trip that brought him to the region.

"A Spanish mine. In this part of the country." The leader of the vigilante group held the lamp closer to Williams's face and said, "Boy, you had better think up a better story and quick. We'll give you the benefit of the doubt, but we'll be back."

As soon as he heard their boots recede on the gravelly path that led to the lane out front, Williams let out a stuttering breath. This would not do at all. This was not something he had planned for. A horse thief? He'd been called a lot of things in his life so far—a rogue, a practical joker, a dreamer, but never a horse thief. No, these were coarse men who wanted nothing more than to seek revenge for their friend's lost pinto. And then a thought stopped him cold.

What had he done? He had told them all about his mine. In his desperation to make them see logic, he had told them all about the promising mine. And he had said that he had a map to it. Williams pulled on his clothes, stomped into his boots, and in short minutes had shouldered his pack and headed down the road, determined to put as much distance between himself and these fools as possible.

He'd barely gone a mile when he heard horses thunder at him from out of nowhere. He had not had time to leave the wagon trail before they were on him, sidearms drawn and oaths of "thief" and "scoundrel" and worse filling the air. They would not listen to reason and instead bound his hands behind his back and led him back to the abandoned cabin, where they guarded him through the night.

The next morning the burly man from the previous night stood before him outside the cabin. A thin Indian stood nearby. "This the white man you saw, Baptiste Louie?"

The Indian nodded and looked back down at his holey boots.

The big man looked at Williams. "Seems that Baptiste Louie here seen you selling a horse to some Nez Perce who, unfortunately for Wallace, are far south of here, though we may get to them yet."

Williams shook his head, now more angry than afraid. "Look here, I've never seen this man before in my life. I've never seen the pinto you're going on and on about, and I certainly have never sold any horse to any Indians, Nez Perce or otherwise."

The big man stood still, his arms folded across his chest. Finally he spoke. "You about through . . . horse thief?"

Williams could scarcely believe his ears. "What?"

The big man nodded, and the next instant, James Williams felt a rope pass over his head and cinch about his neck. He shouted a blue streak then, but all it did was fire up the vigilantes until they were all cursing him for being a horse thief.

They drove him in the back of their wagon to the very pasture from which the horse had been stolen. All the while Williams pleaded with them. Between weeping and shouting, he told them to only look at his pack; in his coat pockets they would find the maps, the ore samples. All to no avail. It seemed to him they wanted to hang a man more than they wanted to get rich. They had laughed at him when he shouted this to them. They pulled the wagon up under a thick, low branch off a big pine in the pasture and slung the rope over the branch.

They gave him a minute to make peace, and he used part of it to try to convince them of their mistake. But sensing they were uninterested in hearing the truth, he grew quiet, closed his eyes, and prayed in a fervent whisper.

The last thing he heard were men's hands whacking down hard on the rumps of the horses pulling the wagon on which he stood. He saw a flash of blue sky through the branches fingering out above him, and then a hot flash of pain flowered up the side of his head, and James Williams's dreams of grand wealth were no more.

The next day the vigilantes cut down the body of young James Williams, and in rummaging through his pockets and his pack, they did indeed find all the materials of which he spoke. It is believed that on hearing his story the night before, and learning that he not only had directions and maps but also ore that had the look of promise about it, the men decided that they could use the excuse that Williams may have been the horse thief they sought. And if he happened to have a map and directions to a promising mine on his person, well, to the victor go the spoils.

If, on the other hand, they weren't that nefarious and had truly believed that Williams was the horse thief, despite the holes in their own story of the events, then they must surely have felt deep remorse when the renegade Pend Oreille Indian, Baptiste Louie, later admitted that he was the one who stole the horse and sold it to the roving band of Nez Perce.

Whatever scenario was true, James Williams had apparently been sketchy about the location of his newly found Spanish mine, at least in the details that he committed to paper. For neither the vigilantes nor anyone else ever found the mine.

33

RICH AND UNGRATEFUL
(1885)

The jackass of down-on-his-luck miner Noah Kellogg wanders off one morning, lost in the hills near Coeur d'Alene, Idaho. The exasperated miner and his partners follow—and come upon the beast staring at a silver lode that will yield three hundred million dollars in the next sixty years. But the little animal's braying is too much for the mine camp, and extreme measures are taken to silence it.

He's too far down the creek." Noah Kellogg stood, rubbing his sweaty forehead with a kerchief. "Besides, it's near dark. Thank the Lord we unpacked his load when we did. I'm in no mood to chase that blasted beast again today."

He balled the sodden cloth and stuffed it in his breast pocket, then readjusted his hat. "We'll just have to leave him be for the night and hope that a grizzly kills him."

His companions, Con Sullivan and Phil O'Rourke, snickered as they busied themselves with camp cookery. Con stirred the sizzling bacon in the fry pan and nodded, squinting through the smoke that seemed to follow him no matter what side of the fire he chose to squat on. "If a grizz don't kill that jackass, I will."

Kellogg used his kerchief to grip the handle of the coffeepot. He poured a cup of strong, black coffee, pleased that he'd been able to get even a slight grubstake in the form of $18.75 worth of beans, flour, and his favorite, bacon, plus the loan of that ornery donkey, which, he had to admit, had so far been a heck of a pack animal, able of footing and steadfast in its pursuit of a trail where none existed. But Con was right, the cursed jack wandered off every time it got the chance, no matter the hobbles he put on the thing. He blew across the top of the steaming coffee. "A more exasperating animal you'll not find, boys."

Phil stood up and stretched his back. It had been a long day, and the coming night's rest was most welcome. "Where did you ever get that ten-cent word?"

Kellogg smiled. "I guess I have a few things in my bag of tricks you haven't heard yet."

"'Exasperated.' Whew. Word like that might be enough to put a man off'n his feed."

Kellogg reached for the bacon. "Good, then I'll just help myself to yours, too."

Con snatched the fry pan from the coals with a whoop. "Not likely, Mr. Kellogg! I tell you, I'm so hungry I could just about eat a . . . jackass!"

Kellogg laughed. "You may have to, Con, if we don't strike something soon."

"We will, Mr. Kellogg." Con dished up the biscuits, beans, and bacon. "Mark my words, I have a feeling we'll be onto something soon."

The three men ate in silence, the only sounds to be heard were the irregular clank of their spoons against their tin plates, the occasional belch, and the gurgle of the water in the creek alongside their meager camp.

Con was busy fingering up the last of the bean and bacon juice when Kellogg spoke. "I surely hope you're right, Con." He sipped his coffee and rummaged in his coat pocket for his cigarette makings. "About striking something soon, I mean."

The other man nodded and wiped his hands on his trousers. "Wait and see, Mr. Kellogg. We'll be swimming in rich ore."

Early the next morning, the men packed up their camp, bundled what they didn't want to carry with them, and lashed it tight. "We'll come back for the rest once we find that blasted jackass."

The men said nothing but nodded and took off walking downstream in the direction they'd heard the jack head the night before. After a few minutes, the men paused, unsure how the little animal could have gotten through the tangle of downed trees and boulder rubble that lay before them.

Burros and mules were considered the "ships of the desert" and were indispensable in hauling heavy loads of ore across scorching deserts and treacherous mountain terrain. Despite their usefulness, many were subject to abuse and treated as little more than expendable commodities by their owners. *Courtesy Library of Congress*

"Well, he must have gone this way," said Phil. "Only way he could have gone, Mr. Kellogg, or we'd have heard him."

Twenty yards ahead they saw the tufts of hair the donkey had lost in dragging himself over the downed timber.

"A more determined beast you'll not find in this part of the country, I'm sure of it." Kellogg shook his head in amazement, despite his growing anger with the creature.

"He's headed down into the canyon. We'll have a devil of a time getting him back up to camp."

They hiked another ten minutes until they reached the bottom of the small canyon, the creek flowing before them. "There he is," said Con, pointing across the creek and up the hill.

Sure enough, Kellogg too saw the beast. "What's he doing, standing there like that?"

All three men regarded the jackass for a moment.

"Looks like he's staring at something." Phil lowered his voice. "You think it could be a bear?"

Kellogg shrugged. He didn't care at this point. He had a rifle and had wasted half the morning, once again, looking for the wandering jack. "You two go that way, and I'll stay upstream of him, might be one of us can grab hold of his halter should he bolt."

But as they drew nearer, the little donkey, though obviously worse for the wear from his journey, never shifted. Kellogg closed the last bit of distance between them, wondering with each passing second when the little brute was going to bolt. But it stayed put, ears cocked forward, and stared across the little canyon at something. Kellogg allowed himself a peek in that direction.

Kellogg looked at Con and Phil, but they were staring at the rocky surface on which the donkey stood. It was a thickly veined outcropping, from the looks of it, worth sampling. Kellogg's eyes wandered again to where the donkey was so intently staring. And he saw a great chute of what looked for all the world like new tin, reflecting the sunlight. He'd never seen the like.

The men exchanged glances and wasted no time in tethering the jack down by the creek. Then they set to work, marking out the corners of their new claims.

"What do you think it is, O'Rourke?" said Kellogg.

Phil O'Rourke, the most seasoned prospector among them, visored his eyes with a calloused hand. "She looks to be galena—that's a good mix of silver and lead." He smiled at Kellogg. "There's bound to be money in it."

Kellogg stared at the bustle of activity before him. Scarcely a few months have passed since our discovery, he thought, and already a raw town has taken shape. Where will it end? He watched two men dropping planks across a mud patch. This could be but the very top of the greatest strike the world has ever known. Despite his hangover, he smiled to himself, allowing the indulgence to soak in, like a snort of good whiskey after a long, dry spell.

Then he heard the rasping braying of the damned donkey. The sound hacked through Kellogg's head like a crosscut saw. He knew he should feel grateful to the beast for its unintentional discovery, but lordy, it was the single most annoying sound he'd ever heard. All this time and he'd never gotten used to it.

He held a shaking hand up to his temples and rubbed. "I'd about give anything if that nasty-sounding beast was shut up for good, no questions asked." It was then that he saw movement out of the corner of his eye. Two miners were walking by, looking back at him, then at each other. They must have heard him talking, he thought. Still, lots of men talk to themselves, didn't they?

It was but a few days later, after numerous and continued midnight brayings and wanderings, that the noise of the donkey drove some men of the camp to drastic measures. Knowing full well its importance in the discovery of the strike, there were few men in the camp who were pleased with the fact that the jackass brayed at all hours. It seemed especially keen on going full-throat in the dead of the night when they all desperately needed their sleep.

A group of them trailed after the beast, led by two miners who had related to the group what Kellogg had said about the donkey. Since they had been aware of its nightly urge for freedom from its tether and its ability to escape from most knots used in containing it, the men arranged to make its escape easier that night. They followed at a safe distance, lugging the wooden box between them. They shooed the donkey up into the higher reaches and soon grabbed its tether.

A couple of the men felt bad about their impending deed and turned heel for camp. But the rest set about their tasks with excited backslaps. Within minutes, they had arranged the donkey's load of dynamite strapped to its back, and without any further ceremony, they drove it off a steep mountainside. The resultant blast ensured that no one would ever again lose sleep due to that donkey's untimely braying.

Two men named Peck and Cooper grubstaked Kellogg with $18.75 worth of beans, bacon, flour, and the loan of the jackass. But Kellogg initially tried to keep his find separate from his dealings with the two men who grubstaked him. The case went to court, and Judge Norman Buck, Idaho District Court, decided later that year that since the Bunker Hill and Sullivan Mines were discovered in part by the jackass, and since the curious creature belonged to Peck and Cooper at the time, they were entitled to half-interest in the Bunker Hill claim and quarter-interest in the Sullivan. The ruling earned the jack the sobriquet of "The Four-Million-Dollar Donkey." So famous was the story that in concert halls across the West, a popular jingle included the ditty: "When you talk about the Coeur d'Alenes/And all their wealth untold/ Don't fail to mention Kellogg's jack/Who did that wealth unfold!"

The Bunker Hill and Sullivan ended up yielding more than three hundred million dollars in the ensuing sixty years. Though the donkey, as its discoverer, would not be around to see it.

In a similar story, Jim Butler found gold in Tonopah, Nevada, in 1900 while pursuing his burro, which had huddled behind a rocky outcropping. He caught up with it, and while he waited for a storm to blow itself out, Butler scraped at the mass of jutting rock with his knife. He ended up discovering the second-richest silver strike in Nevada's history, eventually generating more than $150 million in ore.

Donkeys and their smaller cousins, burros, were referred to as the "ships of the desert" because they were unusually hardy creatures renowned for their ability to travel long distances. They toted great burdens of ore and gear in heavily laden panniers filled with "giant" powder (an early version of dynamite), nitroglycerin, jugs of whiskey, pots and fry pans, picks, shovels, axes, ropes, foodstuffs, and much more.

But never was a beast of burden asked to do more than in Kerbyville, Oregon, in the 1860s, when a man tried to transport an entire pool table on his mule. It worked for a while, until the exhausted creature collapsed, then expired. Unable to shift the table elsewhere, the man let it stand on the spot, erected a bar beside it, and soon a mining town emerged around it.

34

BEYOND ENDURANCE
(1886)

Prospector Tom Williams and an Indian boy named Bob travel through severe winter weather to tell the outside world of a fresh gold strike on the Yukon's Fortymile River. Forty-four days later they reach Chilkoot Pass and build a snow hut three miles below the summit. After five days without food or fire, they try to walk onward. Then the going gets tough.

They had been at it for a month, leaving Arthur Harper's trading post near the Fortymile River. Tom Williams and eighteen-year-old Bob, an Indian boy, had departed on December 1, and it was now January 3. The pair was charged with getting to a place where they could wire Harper's partner, McQuesten, who was in San Francisco, buying goods for the coming year. And the word was good—gold had been found in the Yukon. It was not yet a tremendous strike but was promising enough that the masses would find out—via Tom's message—and soon the rush would be on.

In that month they'd only managed a few hundred miles, with most days spent advancing about ten miles through a heavy ice pack. The worst came on days when they broke through the ice and had to drag themselves out of the numbing water. It had taken its toll on the men, to be sure, but the dogs, hardy as they were, were beginning to show the strain of this hellish journey. Tom knew signing on that it would not be an easy task. They had to trek upriver, then cross mountains and glaciers before heading down to the Panhandle and open water. What sounded easy, he'd known at the outset, was a trail fraught with all the dangers subzero weather in such northern climes will bring with it.

In his weaker moments, at night with the silent Bob across the campfire from him, Tom Williams wished the trip had come at any time of the year but the dead of winter—even though he knew that travel by sled, under ideal conditions, was the best way to go. And then the day came when he had to leave one of his dogs behind. The poor beast simply could not carry on, could not keep up with the rest of the team. It had been the repeated dunkings in the damnable rivers. And though he knew the dog was too exhausted to follow them, it pained him a great deal to think of the beast—especially when he and Bob and the other dogs could only make two miles before having to once again pitch camp.

The next day a blizzard hit them on the trail.

"Bob!" He had to repeat his shouts several times, until the young Indian finally heard him. Bob's endurance and dedication to breaking trail for the team with his snowshoes seemed never to waver. The younger man loped back to him. "We'll camp here!" Williams waved his arm at the wind-whipped frenzy of snow about them.

At the start Williams had had serious misgivings about the wisdom of taking on the trip, and he was now wholly convinced that he had made the biggest and perhaps last mistake of his life. And he had the dead sled dog team to prove it. One by one over the past weeks, the dogs had died off, too weak and starved to crawl forward. He'd had to put several of them out of their misery, so acute was their pain. He could see it in their eyes, as if pleading to make it stop.

"Williams," said Bob, pointing his furred mitten ahead. "Chilkoot."

Williams looked up. Sure enough, Bob was right. Chilkoot Pass stood before them. And so did another blizzard. "You feel what I do?"

Bob nodded, held up a mitten as if testing for rain. "Big one," he said.

Lucky us, thought Tom. It was a fool's errand even on the clearest of days, but today such a climb would be sheer suicide, given the coming weather.

He and Bob dug with frozen hands, stiffened and formed into claws. They managed a snug-enough snow shelter but had no idea that the blizzard would last for five days. They shared the last of their jerky on the first night and lacked any means of kindling a fire. Williams had never felt so low. Even Bob seemed a shrunken figure of the robust eighteen-year-old he had been just two months before, keen on making a heroic journey through impossible terrain and against impossible odds. And his family could surely use the payment he would receive.

But now there was nothing to heat themselves with, no food, and only ice-cold snow chunks to gnaw on for sustenance.

"You hear that?" whispered Tom in a low, throaty croak, opening his eyes in the near dark of the snow shelter.

"No," said Bob, still huddled down in his parka, not daring to open even one eye.

"That's . . . just it," said Tom, nearly unable to raise his head for very long. "The storm . . . it stopped."

Bob opened his eyes and nodded, then closed them again. "We have to dig ourselves out."

As they dragged themselves into the harsh sunlight and almighty blue sky above, it was easy for Tom to leave behind his journal and the other materials in the little dugout snow cave. He'd had no food for nearly a week, so he didn't care about the rest of it, and now they were faced with a harsh trek. The odds of finding anyone who might help them were slim, indeed. Counting himself, he guessed there weren't a dozen whites in the whole of the Yukon. Unless they came upon an Indian encampment, they might well die.

Williams tried to rise to his feet and managed to stagger forward a few yards before collapsing face-first in the snow. He was conscious but somehow could not figure out how to push himself up out of the snow. The most energy he could muster was to wag his head from side to side and moan. Soon he felt himself being lifted and realized that Bob had hefted him. Slowly they were making their way upward, toward the pass.

Bob carried Tom Williams for five days, staggering through deep snow, tripping over his own snowshoes, collapsing out of exhaustion, but always rising again, sometimes after as little as a few minutes' rest. He knew, from what Williams had told him, that they had to get the message from Harper to someone who could get it to McQuesten.

This must be important business, he thought, if Tom Williams has risked his life for it. And so the devoted young man pressed on, carrying Williams even in the teeth of driving winds that pelted them with stinging snow and threatened to turn him from the trail with every step.

Despite the whimsical pose of these three Alaska prospectors in sixty-two-degree-below-zero weather, they were sure to treat the fickle and brutal elements with the utmost respect. One careless moment could mean a lost ear, hand—or worse. *Courtesy Library of Congress*

The strong smell of cooking meat tickled Williams's nostrils. Someone drizzled hot broth on his cracked, dried lips, and this roused him from his stupor. It stung, burned, but it tasted so good. Some time later, when Williams could open his eyes, he saw Bob sitting beside him. "How long?"

"Five days to get here. Now we go to Healy's Post."

Tom recognized the Chilkat Indians. So Bob had carried him for five days, then found them help. And now the Chilkats were going to assist further by helping them get to Taiya Inlet. He had a feeling they were still far from their destination. And with that thought, Williams drifted from consciousness, feeling as if he had gone far beyond making the worst mistake of his life. As if he were near some sort of end to it all.

The Chilkats stayed with them the entire trip to Healy's Post at the Taiya Inlet. As they drew closer, Bob felt a relief threaten to ease his mind before he should let it. I must get Williams to a safe place, get the doctor for him. Then I can rest, he told himself. And before he knew it, he was surrounded by men, mostly whites, all asking too many questions.

"Get Williams inside," he said, bending to lift his trail mate. But Williams's eyes opened, and he pushed himself up onto his elbows, looking up from the sled at the faces peering down at him. He blinked hard a few times, his thin face trembling with the effort, with fatigue as he tried to speak. His voice came out in a thin croak. He licked his lips and tried again. "Gold, gold at Fortymile. My letter from Harper . . . explains it all. . . ." The effort was the last Tom Williams would ever offer. He collapsed back to the disheveled mess of furs on the sled and died.

Bob stared at Williams for a moment, the spell only broken when all the whites began jabbering at once, poking him, grabbing his shoulders, and asking about the gold, gold, gold, that's all the whites wanted to know about. But Williams was dead, Bob could see that. And that made no sense to him. Not after he came all this way, risked everything for the man and his news for these whites.

The more they poked and prodded and grabbed at him, the more he understood that it truly was all for the gold, nothing more than that.

"Where's this letter, boy? Hey!" A paunchy man with a cigar protruding from his brown teeth and a funny round hat on his head stared close into Bob's face. The fat man's cheeks were red, as were his eyes. The cigar and the man's breath smelled bad. Worse than anything Bob had smelled in a long time. Bob closed his eyes. More than ever, he wished for sleep and food.

"I said, where's that letter?"

"The letter is at the base of Chilkoot, back in the pass."

"Take me to it."

Bob shook his head. Someone else clamped a big hand on Bob's shoulder and said, "Leave the boy alone. Can't you see he's had a rough time of it? He risked his life to get that news to us, and Tom there, he risked it all—and lost it all. You need anything, boy?"

"You go find the letter. In our snow shelter, from the storm."

The miners did indeed form a search party that retraced the unfortunate duo's steps and recovered the letter but a few days later. Shortly, Fortymile began receiving the first of hundreds of midwinter travelers. Back at Healy's Post, prospectors who knew Tom Williams and who appreciated Bob's mighty efforts on their friend's behalf took up a collection of $102.25. They gave Bob that and a sled worth $8. They buried Williams and passed along the news of the gold strike to McQuesten, who was able to buy the additional supplies that his partner rightfully suspected they would need in the ensuing frenzy for gold.

The gold strike for which Tom Williams lost his sled-dog team and his life proved young Bob the Indian's mettle as a man among men and a true unsung hero with stamina, the likes of which few people have displayed. The strike also proved to be but one of a series of smaller strikes that seemed to be hors d'oeuvres for the main course: the 1897 Klondike strike, which eventually drew one hundred thousand desperate gold-hounds to pound their way across Alaska. And nearly all of them had to ascend the unforgiving, twenty-five-mile-long Chilkoot Pass.

35

HELLS CANYON
MASSACRE
(1887)

In May 1887 dry gulchers massacre thirty-four Chinese men prospecting for gold in Oregon's Hells Canyon. The whites who do it are brought to trial but are never convicted.

◆

Kong Mun Kow paused in shoveling gravel into the flimsy rocker. Not for the last time did he scold himself for secretly wishing that he was working for himself instead of as a hired miner for the Sam Yup Company, a San Francisco–based outfit. But still, he told himself, this was so much better than China. Too crowded there.

He stood up, stretching his back and wiping his forehead as he looked up at the slight slope lining the Deep Creek section of the Snake River. Two of his friends had also paused and were talking, he bet, of what they would do if all the gold they had found so far was theirs to keep. He almost smiled, for he had been thinking much the same thing.

It had been a long eight months since they'd poled their flat-bottom boats upstream in the big Snake River the entire sixty-five miles from Lewiston, Idaho. So much work. Some of them had toiled on the railroad before this and had commented in their camps along the river at night how the railroad work was a walk in the park compared with poling the boats up the deep, swift river every day to reach the spot they now found themselves in—Hells Canyon. It was a mighty place, steep with treacherous footing along much of the river, and it was filled with large boulders. But those same boulders helped provide some sort of cover from the wind and rain and snow, which at times could be painful and biting.

Mostly, though, they stayed by the gravel bar along this stretch of the river. There was gold here, too. Flour gold, because the flakes of it were so fine, and there were little nuggets. To date, he guessed they had about four or five thousand dollars in gold gathered. The thought brought a weary smile to his face. Perhaps they wouldn't have to stay here forever. Sure, it was nice, but. . . . He heard far-off cracking sounds. What could that be? It sounded like stones slamming together—a rockslide, perhaps?

Then Kong Mun Kow heard shrieks from his fellow miners, saw one man drop face first into the river and saw another tumbling down the hillside from where he'd climbed above the gravel bar, checking rocks for signs of gold. But now he was pinwheeling toward the bottom of the valley. Another man, Yip, had been panning but now ran toward the nearest rocker. Suddenly he pitched forward, his body slamming over the apparatus, his head snapping forward with tremendous force. Kong heard Yip's forehead hit the wet, swollen wood with a hard smack.

"Hey, boy, over here! Watch this one—see him there, looking around like he don't know what all to do? I'm about to make up his mind for him." The thin man with the drooping mustache snugged his high-powered rifle tight to his shoulder and squeezed the trigger. The rifle cracked loud. Across the valley a white, sweat-stained shirt burst open in a spray of red, and the man wearing it flopped backward between two sizable boulders.

The young man with the shooter, a youth of fifteen, quivered in a welter of confusion and excitement. This is not exactly what he expected would happen, but he knew it wouldn't be easy, no way was it going to be as easy as the men had said. Nothing ever was. Even in his few young years, he had managed to figure out that harsh fact.

He saw the shooter staring at him, the man's smile fading as he scrutinized the boy's face. "You want a cake, boy, you got to break a few eggs." Then he smiled again and said, "Especially if them eggs is Chinese. Ain't like they're people, right?" He jumped to his feet from his kneeling position behind the gray boulder. "Come on, we got us some gold to tend to."

The boy nodded and followed, telling himself over and over that there was nothing for it. It had to be this way, as he'd heard the men saying all week as they rode into Hells Canyon. Otherwise the Celestials, as everybody referred to the Chinese, would be sure to take away everything of value, if given the time to multiply.

As he descended down the last of the bank, he made his way toward the cluster of six other men, all the ones he'd come in with. He picked his way through the tumbledown mess of the craggy riverbank. It looked as though they were headed to the gravel bar that curved halfway out into the river. There seemed to be bodies of Chinese everywhere, most flopped and still, though some were twitching, legs pedaling at the wet gravel. And everywhere, there was blood. Bright red on their light clothes, darker, at times almost black, where it had splashed across the face of the bigger boulders.

They had nearly reached the gravel bar where the other men were rummaging and ransacking the sagging canvas tents and fortified caves dug into the riverbank just behind the diggings, when he heard a shout. He looked up from picking his way through the maze of rocks to see several men pointing downstream.

He followed the pointing arms and saw a Chinaman running from them, trying to remain hidden behind the boulders and dashing from boulder to boulder. Even from his distance upstream, the boy could hear the man grunting and squealing to get away from them. It would be of little use, thought the boy, for the attackers were faster than the Chinaman, and they had leather-sole boots and he did not.

The first rock sailed past his head, and Kong Mun Kow bent lower as he ran downstream. The bank skinnied until he was forced to run in the water. Something slammed into his back, and something else clipped his head. He was thrown forward onto a rock, his hands in the water. He felt odd, decided perhaps he had broken a rib on the rock. Again, he rose, and saw the blood spattering his clothes. He heard the shouts behind him but drawing closer. Something felt wrong with his vision. Then something punched him in his lower back. Another something knocked his legs out from under him, and he looked up into the far-off blue sky.

For some reason he could not hear a thing, but he could still see the sky. And then dark shadows crowded over him, looked down at him. They were the shooters, the cowboys he had seen with the rifles, shooting his friends. They had blocked out most of his light, but he was too exhausted to rise once again.

The shadows drew back. Kong felt himself breathing hard, could see through a wavering red gauze before his eyes. Then, in a flash, he saw the faces of the six men surrounding him grow more serious. He tried to rise, tried to speak, raise an arm, anything, but found he could not. Perhaps they realized their mistake and would now help him and his friends. If he could only show them that he was alive, that he needed their help.

"Someone finish him off."

"Can't—I'm out of shells."

"Me too, but we can still use rocks. He's about done, I'd say. . . ."

Something hit Kong. Something hard and painful—it felt as if it broke his arm. He couldn't even raise it to protect himself. What he thought might be birds were the shadows of rocks. The whites were throwing rocks at him. Kong Mun Kow tried to cover his head, but the pain, oh, the pain! He wished for China, for help, for anything, but all his friends were dead now, that much he guessed. Why us? he thought. Why do they hate us so? For the gold? He would trade all the gold and all the golden dreams they each had talked of as they poled their boats upstream those long months before. But something told him it was more than gold that made the whites hate him so. As the rocks drove down on him, he knew it really didn't matter anymore. But the pain went on for a long, long time after they stopped.

The whites pushed his body into the current, along with the rest, and sent them spinning and bumping downstream.

In the weeks following the two-day massacre, the bodies of thirty-four slaughtered Chinese miners were eventually recovered, most of them floating in the river. Their savaged, hacked bodies snagged on deadfalls and bobbed and eddied in the current. Many of them floated the sixty-five miles downstream back to Lewiston, Idaho, where the ill-fated miners began their journey eight months before.

The killers were seven horse thieves who, as it turns out, were known men and boys from local families in the Wallowa region of Oregon. The reasons for their savage behavior appears to have been twofold: to rid the region of the hated Chinese and to make money. To those ends their attacks were quite successful. Over two days the killers ambushed and savagely cut down what most reports agree were thirty-four Chinese miners. The dry gulchers also stole four thousand to five thousand dollars in gold. The first day's attack resulted in ten deaths. A subsequent attack arose when friends visited the miners the following day. The visitors, also Chinese miners, never made it to Deep Creek. When the shooters ran out of ammunition, they finished the job with rocks.

Of the seven attackers, four disappeared. The remaining three, one of whom was a lad of fifteen, were brought to trial on September 1, 1888. Even though one of the three men confessed to the crime, no one was convicted.

The American West became home to 150,000 Chinese who emigrated there in the nineteenth century. The Hells Canyon Massacre is one of the worst atrocities ever committed against Chinese immigrants in the United States, but it was hardly the only one. On September 2, 1885, in Rock Springs, Wyoming, anti-Chinese sentiment among whites spilled out beyond the mining camps, resulting in the deaths of twenty-eight Chinese miners. Fifteen more were injured, and seventy-five Chinese homes were burned. Anti-Chinese sentiment rose to such fevered heights that in 1882, the US Congress passed the Chinese Exclusion Act, which barred all emigration from China for a decade and prevented Chinese from becoming Americans.

36

DON'T MESS WITH
A SOURDOUGH
(1888)

A young Indian kills a much-loved old sourdough for a bit of food and his meager poke. The prospector's chums find out and hang the boy, then leave the corpse swinging in the breeze as a message to other would-be killers and thieves.

The old medicine man smelled the smoke first. He stopped, pressed a hand to the younger man's chest, and sniffed the air as a dog might. "There is a campfire close by," he said. "Probably down by the water. Come." He motioned with an old claw of a hand, and the pair trudged through the thick riverside undergrowth.

They emerged not far from a bearded white prospector kneeling by a campfire. The man saw them and stared for a few long moments. He had few provisions, but his fry pan smoked and crackled, and the scent of frying pork seemed to hang in the air and waft over to them. Their guts growled. The white man's face softened, and a smile cracked through his thick beard. He lifted the pan and nodded toward them.

"Come," said the old man again, and the pair walked toward the man at the fire.

The white man stood and rubbed his greasy hands on his trousers. "I am John Bremner," he said. "You're welcome to share my noon meal. It's not much, I'm afraid." He continued to smile.

The younger Indian, who Bremner guessed was about twenty-five, smiled, then glanced at the old man, who scowled at him. The young man's smile faded. They both approached the fire, and the white man carved up the fried meat into three equal portions. He retrieved two more tin cups from his grub box and, balancing them on river rocks, he poured strong black coffee into them. He speared one of the hunks of pork with the knife he'd been prodding the cooking meat with, then he set the hot pan on the rocks before the two squatting Indians. They each tweezered meat with their fingers, and the three men shared the meal, chewing in silence.

Finally, when the meat had been eaten, the younger man nodded toward the white man's boat drawn up on the gravel bar behind him and said, "Gold?"

"Yes," said Bremner, with a nod and a smile. "I pan for gold. I know, it seems as if that's all people do here. But I swear there is a fortune just around the next bend in the river." His smile was met with a nod from the young man and a scowl from the old man.

Bremner knew enough about the local native tribes to realize this old man was probably an elder, perhaps a medicine man. He asked him if this were so, but the old man just scowled and sipped his coffee. Bremner glanced at the young man, who seemed to have been waiting for the white man to look his way. The young man nodded, then stopped when the old man stared him into submission.

"Well," said Bremner, rising to his feet and rubbing his knees. "I have to get along now. Let me just pack up my grub box and lug it to the boat. I'll be right back." He smiled as he bent to his task.

As he walked to the boat, the Indians stood. The old man poked the younger man in the ribs and nodded toward Bremner's rifle, leaning against a boulder on the other side of the smoking fire.

"Shoot him," he said in a low voice. "Shoot him now and we can take his boat, the gun, and we will have his grub, too. No one will ever know. We Indians will always outnumber the whites here. Shoot him. Do as I tell you." The old man's wrinkled face widened into a sneer, and he lifted a hand to strike the younger man.

The young man snatched up the rifle and raised it to his shoulder. Bremner was almost to his boat, the talking voices muffled by the increasingly louder sounds of the stream. The rifle cracked twice, and Bremner spun where he stood, the grub box crashing down just inside the boat. He staggered, groped at the side of the wobbling boat, and turned a surprised, haggard look on the young man. "What have you . . . why?"

Bremner lay there, gripping his side where the bullets had punched into him. But it was obvious to the younger man that Bremner was not in danger of dying soon. The young man trembled and was about to throw the rifle to the rocks when the old man grabbed it from him and strode toward the bleeding white man. He came within a couple of paces of Bremner, who looked up at him and raised a hand as if to deflect the inevitable. The rifle cracked and slammed three times more.

The old man toed the white's flopped body, then motioned to the young man. "Sink him in the river." He indicated the boat with his chin, "then we go."

◆

"There's about eighty of them. That's what this Indian girl tells me. I reckon we got the upper hand, what with our weapons and all." The man who spoke sluiced a stream of tobacco juice at a low, stunty pine, then wiped his mouth on his cuff. "Let's go."

The twenty-two men who followed talked low among themselves, all in hard agreement that these Indian attacks against whites had to stop. It was fast becoming a disease that none of them cared to endure any longer.

"You recall what they did to Mrs. Bean, up in Tanana?" one man said to another. His listener nodded, a grim set to his mouth. He offered his own example: "And before that, there was that Russian fellow. I didn't know him, but to kill a man for his goods? Ain't right, and that's the truth of it."

"Well, we'll make it right. Teach them a lesson, by God. And anyway, who'd go and kill John Bremner? A kinder sourdough you'll not find, by God. ..." The man left off with a shake of his head and a wipe of his nose. Every man within earshot knew how he felt.

Taking the entire camp of eighty souls by surprise hadn't entered into their minds, except as a hope. But it happened just the same. And then good fortune really smiled on them. Two men broke into a run. One was old. The other, much younger and more fleet of foot. It was but the work of a few minutes to round them up, and soon it was determined, because they ran, that these two men had killed John Bremner.

"You wanted to what?" said Peder Johnson, a robust prospector and long-time friend of Bremner's who had shared many campfires and meals with the

Among the vast number of mining partnerships formed, relatively few ended in violence between partners. Despite the promising glint of gold, the value of having a trusted, work-sharing, lifesaving partner outweighed personal greed. *Courtesy Library of Congress*

dead sourdough, from Mexico to Alaska. But Alaska is where it had ended. His bitterness rose to a fever pitch as he questioned the quivering youth. The old man, however, remained infuriatingly stone-faced.

The young man glanced briefly at the old medicine man, who scowled at him and seemed to shower sparks from his dark eyes at the boy. The younger man licked his lips and, in a rush of words, said, "I wanted to get outside, away from here. Need money."

"So you kill a good man because you need money?" Peder's eyes flashed between the two men, who would not meet his hardened stare. "String these bastards up high."

After hemming, hawing, and much lowered gazes, it was determined that because of his age, the old man didn't deserve to hang, and so they set him free. Then the men lashed a pole, ten feet off the ground, between two trees about six feet apart. They tossed a rope up and over the pole and forced the young man up on a chunk of wood. One of the men fashioned a noose. They secured it around the young man's neck and watched as he muttered to himself, his head shaking, his body shivering as if it were midwinter.

When his lips ceased their mutterings and his face, for a moment, appeared calm, as if he had just received some snatch of good news, one of the men kicked away the stump. The young man's body dropped several feet, bounced, and for some minutes he kicked and spun, his feet twitching and his tied hands grasping at nothing.

Peder Johnson stood before the finally limp form and said, "We'll not cut him down but leave him here as a warning to any other would-be killers that a prospector's life is a good and sacred thing."

The gathered men nodded in grim agreement.

When the old medicine man returned to his village, the angry relatives of the now-dead young man attacked him with knives. Somehow the old rascal escaped and healed enough to live another two years, far up the Yukon River, well away from his enraged tribesmen. His family and the young man's family feuded for several years, during which time six more tribesmen were killed.

John Bremner was in many ways a typical sourdough, in that he was a man with a varied past that eventually led him to prospect for gold in Alaska. Of Scottish birth, he made his way to the United States and settled as a farmer in Iowa. Some time later, when he was in his early thirties, he left his family behind and booked passage on ships, working his way to foreign lands. It is known that he visited Africa and Australia. He was gone for twenty years and next showed up, age fifty-two, in Alaska. While there he became the first and only white man of the time to live with the Copper

Indians. The waterway on which Bremner frequently prospected, and on which he was murdered, is today called the Bremner River.

Sourdoughs were a breed apart, and one could only be considered a true sourdough through spending time and gaining experience vital to survival in the far north. In a practice that would be frowned upon "back in the States," it was not uncommon for lonely prospectors to take an Indian wife and raise a family, sometimes living with the tribe, sometimes living on their own. One old sourdough ended up marrying two Indian women, outliving them both. He is quoted as saying, "They were fine pardners, good workers, good fish cutters, and I got used to the fish smell and loved them both very much. I busted up when they went to another happy hunting ground."

Everyday survival in the far north depended much more on self-reliance, resourcefulness, and the vital ability to adapt to new and demanding situations. One toothless old sourdough, Paddy Meehan, grew tired of gumming his meat, so he crafted dental plates out of tin kitchen utensils, then used the front teeth from a mountain sheep's skull and found serviceable molars in the jaw of a grizzly he'd recently killed. It was said that he ended up eating the bear with its own teeth.

Another story that has about it the whiff of a tall tale says that sourdough Lynn Smith once survived freezing to death by killing a moose, gutting it, and climbing inside. Unfortunately the hide then shrank. He would have died if it hadn't been for the wolves that chewed him out of it. . . .

37

LUCK OF THE IRISH
(1890)

Three Irishmen secure an overlooked one-sixth-acre claim smack-dab between two mammoth mines in Colorado's gold-rich Cripple Creek. They mine at night under their cabin and in short order dig up ninety thousand dollars in ore—enough to fight the expected legal battles their wealthy neighbors soon wage. After twenty-seven lawsuits, they get more than they bargain for.

I tell you, boys, it will be the making of us." James Doyle rocked back on his heels, his hands stuffed into his trouser pockets.

"Making, you say? Have you seen yourself lately? I'm not so sure you'll want to. The look on your face is quite enough to make me wonder what it is you're thinking."

"Ah, hush yourself and get back to work, Burns. Harnan, you sneak back outside and circle the shack. Keep a sharp eye for any light leaking out between the boards."

"Sure they know we're living here, James." Harnan handed his canvas bucket to Doyle.

"They may well know that, Harnan, but that doesn't mean we need to post advertisements to all and sundry that we're busy doing something all night long," said Doyle, ignoring the rolled eyes of his two partners. They knew he liked to talk, and he knew he liked to talk. And as senior partner, he liked to indulge in a little extra chatter—even if he was merely repeating what they already knew. "Why, who else in these parts do you know who can afford to keep the lamps alight straight through the wee hours? And who else do you know who can afford to sleep all day?"

Harnan smiled. "Right, so . . . " He nodded toward the oil lamp. "Turn that low so I can lift the blanket blocking the door."

As soon as he ducked outside, Harnan paused, his head cocked to one side, searching for any sound that shouldn't be there—anything other than the irregular far-off whoops of drunken miners, the occasional shriek of a less-than-fair lass receiving a bit of a love pinch, or the closer sounds of a high breeze soughing through the sparse trees that tapered to a stunted height this far up.

The trio's hastily built cabin sat in the midst of a wedge-shaped one-sixth-acre claim deemed worthless by the two hulking, close-by claims to either side of them. The trio had never imagined the paltry claim would yield much more of anything than a place to hang their hats and rest their weary, impoverished bodies for a time. It had been a long and rough run of it before they settled here. No strikes worth the price of a beer and a bean. Their provisions had been lean for some time, and less-than-half rations had been the order of the day for far too long. But that had begun to change not long after they set up on the claim.

It hadn't taken long to dig into that vein, though it surprised them all when they did. And a good one it was, too. It had assayed at a respectable $640 to the ton!

As if to underscore the thought of food, Harnan's stomach growled like the echo of a wildcat's call. He ignored it, and hearing no boot-on-gravel crunch that he swore he'd heard the previous night, he stepped forward. He knew the two flanking mines were bitter rivals. He also knew that being caught between the two eastern-owned giants made for a thick layer of worry in and outside the cabin.

Only Doyle managed to keep it pushed down to the point where he actually seemed to think they'd make out all right. Harnan shook his head in the dark. Sure, they were a bit confident—they were Irishmen, after all. But that Doyle, to hear him talk, you'd think they were millionaires already.

Why, to look at the three of them, you'd never know they spent most of their time pulling ore from a tight and deepening shaft in the middle of their cabin. So far, it was a small but promising fortune in gold.

It was daring and it was brazen, and with each day that passed, it was proving to be definitely dangerous. So much so that they had good reason to fear for their lives. The men who regularly patrolled the perimeter of the two flanking mines fairly bristled with guns and sheath knives.

Harnan walked the outside of the shack, each foot placed carefully before the next. Scanning for any light leaks. But there were none. Satisfied that no one other than himself was snooping around outside the shack, Harnan checked on their mules in the little paddock they'd rigged up. He forked more hay to them and watched them nose it for a few moments. One of the men would be out later to harness the mules to the wagon so they could haul out another load of ore. Every load was that much more money closer to being able to fight the inevitable lawsuits they would soon stir up.

Doyle had told them that it was the only way. If the big mines knew that they had struck gold so close to them, they could claim the lot under the thing Doyle had called the "apex law." Harnan didn't like to admit it, but it still made his head swim to think about it. Something to do with the fact that a judge would rule in favor of the larger claim, saying that the vein probably started on that property and not their paltry little claim.

No matter how you looked at it, as Doyle had said, the only way they stood any chance at all was to accumulate enough money to fight them in court. And that, Doyle had said, was definitely coming—not if, but when. . . .

Harnan scratched the top of the nearest mule's head, the beast's big ears wagging as it chewed the hay. He sighed and pushed himself up off the top rail of the paddock. When he ducked back into the shack, he saw only Doyle. Jimmy Burns, he knew, was below them in the hole, chunking away at the quartz veined with gold.

"What are we up to now, Doyle?" said Harnan, hefting an ore-filled bucket.

"With this load, as good as it's looking, I'd say at about ninety thousand dollars."

"And would that be enough?" Harnan didn't need to finish the question, Doyle knew what he was driving at.

Doyle nodded. And smiled. "I'd say so, yeh. Enough to wage a pretty good fight in court. But I'll gladly take more, just in case." He touched his finger to the side of his nose and winked.

The next day, late in the afternoon, Doyle and Burns returned from town, rolling to a squeaking stop before the cabin. Both men couldn't help but smile.

Burns jumped down and hefted a box of provisions from the bed of the wagon. "More coffee," he said. "And a few extras tonight—to celebrate all our good fortune."

Then both men noticed that Harnan wasn't smiling, unusual for him.

"What's happened, John?" Doyle set the brake on the wagon and jumped down.

"A few hours after you two left," he looked at his partners, feeling guilty in the telling of it, though he knew that was silly. "A couple of armed men from the big mine over yonder," he jerked his head backward toward the south side of their lot. "They say someone noticed the ruts our wagon's been making. Said only a heavy wagon could make such ruts. So they checked up on us in town."

"And?" said Burns, still holding the box of supplies.

"Someone told them we've been hauling in good ore." Harnan stood before the cabin, his long, thin arms hugging himself, as he stared at his worn boots.

Burns stared at the ground, shaking his head as if he'd just received bad news from home.

But Doyle laughed and clapped his hands together. "This is grand, boys."

They looked at him as if he were crazy.

"Don't you see? Now we can fight them for it." He waved a hand at the entire mountainside before him. "With what we've put in the bank, we now stand at least a fighting chance." He rubbed his hands together. "I'll put the mules up for the night, you two get the stove hot. I feel like biscuits and a drop of that whiskey."

Both men still stared at him, but their eyes were beginning to shine a bit.

"Look, lads, we've a long, hard road ahead. But at least we're on the road, eh? Now let's get to that supper. Can't fight on an empty stomach, can we?" With that, he let out a whoop and urged the mules to the corral.

Burns and Harnan looked at each other and smiled. "That Doyle," said Harnan, shaking his head.

"Confident is too weak a word to describe the man, I'd say." Burns kicked open the cabin door and began whistling as he set out the whiskey.

The three Irishmen were shortly thereafter taken to court by their power-ful neighbors. A seemingly unrelenting stream of subpoenas and injunctions showered at them, but by then they had retained good legal counsel. Over the ensuing months, Messrs. Doyle, Burns, and Harnan took the upper hand in twenty-seven lawsuits, securing their own meager chunk of land. In counter-suits, their lawyers knocked holes in their opponents' defenses and picked apart their claims. In the end the three formerly penniless Irishmen managed

to accumulate 183 acres of prime Cripple Creek real estate that eventually earned them sixty-five million dollars.

It seems that the Irish had a particular knack for turning a buck in the gold fields. Thomas Francis Walsh, of County Tipperary, made several fortunes by recognizing what others failed to discern, namely gold where others had sought silver, and vice versa. Indeed, he was scoffed at when he bought a played-out silver mine. But his eyes hadn't deceived him, and the samples he'd dug from an ugly and overlooked streak assayed at three thousand dollars to the ton, which eventually earned him seven million dollars and enabled his daughter to indulge her passion for buying shiny baubles, one of which was the Hope Diamond.

38

CURSE OF THE DUTCHMAN'S LOST MINE
(1891)

For saving the life of an elderly Mexican, Jacob Waltz is given the secret to hidden gold lodes deep in the snake-ridden Superstition Mountains, east of Phoenix, Arizona. He mines them for years but keeps his secret. On his death, he passes the location on to one person. In the intervening century-plus, hundreds have died searching for the Dutchman's lost mine.

◆

You have been good to me, so good to me, dear Julia, nursing me these past few years in my decline. I—" The old man broke off, staring at the trembling hand he held before himself, then the other one. These hands, he thought, used to such hard work, and now look at them, long, pointed fingers like a kept woman's, and the skin, so pink and soft, no calluses, as if I'd never swung a pick, never gripped a shovel and worked it hard around a thorny root or stubborn, hard-case rock. Oh, but we had some times, didn't we, hands? He smiled at them, his rheumy eyes red-rimmed and watering.

"Jacob, you should rest now."

He looked up. Of course, it was Julia Thomas. Dear Julia. "What would I have done without you these last few years?" He smiled at her.

"You would have found some other girl to take care of you, you old devil. Now get some sleep. You've tired yourself out."

But as he felt her hand on his chest, he remembered what he had to do! "No, no," he rose up onto his elbows. "There is no time. I'm dying, a dying old man. I must tell you, Julia, for if I do not, then the secret will die with me. And you above all others deserve to know what I could not tell anyone, ever. Do you understand?"

She tilted her head and regarded him a moment. "What is it then, Jacob? This seems very important to you, though I can assure you, you will be feeling right as rain again in the morning. I will make you a fine break—"

"No, please, do not interrupt me. You know how my mind gets these days ... forgive me, but this is very important. And I have to make sure my mind is clear for you." He motioned toward the little table at the bedside. "You write this down now, write down what I tell you."

And as old Jacob Waltz told Julia Thomas of his terrible, wonderful, long-held secret, he lapsed into reverie. His memory of thirty-one years before colored the long intervening years. It had been 1860, in a small mining town in California, the name of which was long lost in the cobwebbed corners of his dusty mind. But there he was, in a bar, taking his time drinking a warm beer, thinking of what he was going to do next. He had had no luck for years placer mining all over California and Nevada.

He heard raised voices and turned to see a drunken gambler had attacked an old, bent Mexican over some scuffle or other. He still winced seeing in the eye of his memory that thin, little blade going into the old man's gut. Jacob wasn't sure what had driven him to the old man's rescue, but the next thing he knew, he found himself there, by the man's side, pulling the drunken gambler off him. He lifted the old Mexican from the floor and carried him to his room. Over the next weeks he nursed the man, Don Miguel Peralta II, back to health. To thank him, Peralta shared with Waltz the fascinating story and the location of a tremendous vein of gold deep in the heart of the Superstition Mountains.

It had taken Waltz several years, but he finally found the gold. He knew it was the lode Peralta had mentioned by the various landmarks—ruins of old stone huts, the covered-over shafts of previous mining efforts. Most of all, there, to the south, like an upthrust arm defying the very heavens, stood the Weaver's Needle, a peak of pure visual power. Over the first few days of his discovery, Waltz found ore left behind by previous mining parties—those of Peralta's family before they were chased off by the Apache long years ago.

Peralta had warned him of a curse on the mountains. But Waltz, who regarded himself as a German who needed more than hearsay and knock-kneed rumor to convince him that he was in danger, nonetheless slept armed and wary. The Apache were still very much about, and now, after all these years of searching for gold, he had no desire to lose his life to a bloodthirsty savage when he was so close to becoming a rich man.

Then came the bittersweet years. Sweet because he had more money than he knew what to do with, but bitter because he had to use the most caution he had ever had to exercise in his infrequent visits to Phoenix. Periodically he would need supplies and little indulgences—booze, tobacco, food items that he would not ordinarily have bought, the most rugged tools and clothes and weapons, of course, always the weapons. Somehow, though, he found that instead of it being a burden, he was suited to this life of constant planning and staying one step ahead of the scoundrels who would do him in for a quick snatch at the gold.

He was followed back toward the mines many times by rapscallions who were so very foolish, so very clumsy, and who he knew were intent on causing him harm. He had paid for his goods in town with the purest of gold that he himself had pared and hewed from the brutal, unyielding rock of the Superstition Mountains. But somehow they found out about his gold, found out about him, and like the desert ticks that feed off the flesh of the recently deceased, like the buzzards with their hideous bald heads, circling slowly downward to feast, so the foolish followers had tried him.

But he was not weak or unsuspecting or dead; he was very much alive and very much willing to wage war to protect himself and his cache of gold. And wage war, he did. Their clumsy efforts at following him had often produced comical results, just before he killed the followers, that is. And he always made sure to do so far from his precious mine, lest the feasting buzzards attract unwanted attention too close to him.

He had lived this way for a long, long time—nearly twenty years, by his reckoning—and in that time he had defended what he knew to be his and his alone. And he knew that many vulturous men who followed him out of Phoenix never returned. What a shame.

Waltz had died six months before, and now she was here in the mountains, trailing behind the prospector she'd hired to help her find old Jacob's gold. If there *was* gold. She wanted to believe Jacob's story, she really did, but he had been feebleminded at the end. I must be crazy, too, she thought. But she kept on hiking up the steep trail, the burro behind her, following the wiry form of the seasoned prospector before her.

"You sure this is the spot?" he said over his shoulder.

"No. I'm not sure of anything. But you knew that before you agreed to come out here with me."

She saw his shoulder scrunch in that peculiar silent laugh of his, saw his head nod. "I know, I know," he said, then peered over his shoulder at her and winked. "No, ma'am, I say we ought to just call it the Lost Dutchman's Mine and be done with it."

Julia Thomas stopped her slow, trudging walk up the gravel path and stared at him. She was tired. It was nearly sundown, and this old prospector she had hired, normally the most optimistic person she'd ever encountered— he'd have to be, as a prospector—even he was beginning to doubt Jacob's story. Maybe he was right, maybe they were all right, and this was nothing but the ramblings of an addled old man on his deathbed. And here she was, spending her summer chasing his phantom fortune and she had, to date, nothing to show for it but a hole in her savings.

Even as she stood there, sweaty and begrimed, her hands on her hips, overlooking the vista of the mountain range before her to the south, stretching away in its jagged purple spires and half-sunned heights, even then, with a stack of bills waiting for her on her return to Phoenix . . . even then she pulled in a deep breath and wondered just how long it would take her to save up for another go at it next summer.

"He was German," she said. "Not Dutch."

The old prospector nodded and said, "Same thing. In heaven it don't make no never mind."

Perhaps more than any other treasure tale, the story of the Superstition Mountains and the Lost Dutchman's Mine has quickened the pulses and set the grim lips of conviction of more would-be treasure hunters than any other. Certainly it has spawned plenty of articles, books, documentaries, and movies. Every year dozens, if not hundreds, of gold seekers set off toward the

Superstition Mountains, thirty-five miles east of Phoenix, in search of what they are sure is still a vast and mighty hoard of treasure awaiting them. If only they can locate it.

Over time, the details left by Jacob Waltz regarding his lode's location have been so altered by treasure hunters intending to throw others off the trail that no one quite knows where any of Waltz's supposed landmarks reside. That they did exist at one time seems to be of little dispute. For the man had been real enough, as was Julia Thomas, his caretaker in his final years.

And after his death in 1891, she did endeavor to find his rich mother lode using the clues he gave her. But she never discovered it, and after several fruitless seasons, she gave up the search. It seems Waltz had covered up his mines too well. And then there are the distinct possibilities of landslides and other weather-related and man-made events that might have conspired unwittingly to further obscure the location of the Lost Dutchman's Mine. Will this rich vein of gold, exploited by the Spanish, the Mexicans, the Apache, and a lone German, ever be found again? Only time will tell. . . .

Another man whose mine and legend have grown to near-mythic proportions is one-legged mountain man Thomas "Pegleg" Smith. After years of prospecting in the Santa Rosa Mountains, hostile Indians forced Smith to flee a claim he said was filled with vast amounts of gold-bearing quartz. He didn't dare return, but he sold maps and claim shares to what he called the "Lost Pegleg Mine." Several parties in recent decades claim to have found significant ore where Pegleg swore vast wealth resides. Still others argue that the Lost Pegleg Mine remains that way because it never existed in the first place, except in the particularly fertile mind of one of the West's greatest hucksters, ol' Pegleg himself.

39

PEGLEG ANNIE'S ORDEAL
(1896)

Idaho businesswoman Annie Morrow and her friend, Dutch Em, are caught in a late-season blizzard. Three days later, a rescue party finds Annie in agony, half-naked and crawling on her belly through the snow. Her frostbitten feet are soon amputated.

It was the silence that finally awakened Annie. For a moment she wasn't sure she was alive, didn't believe it could have been possible, given what she and Em had endured. But it seemed the three-day blizzard had stopped. It felt as though someone were prying her eyelids open with a dull steel blade. Frozen shut, just like everything else, she thought. Her jaw barely moved, even with the greatest effort, and before she began she abandoned the idea of unwrapping herself from her friend's cold body.

And that sudden thought stopped her: Em was cold. Surely that couldn't mean that she . . . died? Sometime the night before, Annie had given Dutch Em her own jacket, blouse, scarf, hat, skirt—nearly all her clothes, just before she herself succumbed to the sickly allure of sleep, huddled there between the two coarse, gray boulders. The great lumps had barely offered protection from the slicing wind. By the time she finally forced one of her eyes open, she wished she hadn't made the trip, wished all over again that she could take it back.

Annie finally managed to slide her arms from around Em. She leaned back and looked at her friend's face in the bright glare of the snow-reflected light. A peeling breeze, sharp as a skinning knife, cut straight through her. *I was foolish to think we could traipse up here with nothing but light woolens and snowshoes. And all for what, Annie? All for money.*

She'd been eager to check on her other "house" and her girls. And Em, or Dutch Em as most folks called her, had wanted a change of scenery. Wanted to set to work over the hill, as they called it. "Should have told her no, should have left her there." She spoke the words between the stuttery jabs of wind and the shivers wracking her voice. Nothing mattered now. She knew she would soon join Em in death.

The blizzard had blown out days before, leaving behind crusted, drifted remnants, as with so many spring storms. It made the going fairly smooth for the search party. But soon, what the men saw stopped them from venturing higher up the pass. The man in the lead shook his head and squinted upslope. The wind whipping the snow had played a mind trick on them. Surely the body before them hadn't moved. It had been more than three days since anyone had heard from the ladies, so they never expected to see either of them alive. Especially not after that late-season blizzard. And yet something was there, just ten yards off, crawling side-slope. It moved again—they clambered forward.

"By God, it's Annie Morrow! She's alive!" The man in the lead dropped to his knees and bent low to lift the clawing, prone form from the snow. The other men crowded close. It was not possible that anyone could have survived such vicious weather, and yet here she was.

They busied themselves with building a fire and swaddling her with extra clothing. She was clad in nothing more than a slip, a pair of flimsy undergarments hardly worth the fabric it took to make them, and little else. Not even socks.

"Annie, Annie, can you hear me? What's happened? Where are your clothes, girl? Where's Em? Annie, where's Dutch Em?"

She made no response.

"Hold her down, she's out of her mind. And hurry up with that fire."

A short while later, as they warmed Annie by the fire, she revived enough to tell them that Em had died. The rescuers decided that several of them would head back to town with Annie, three others would stay behind to look for Dutch Em.

One of the men bent low, speaking quietly to a companion. "Did you see Annie's feet before we bundled her up?"

The other man nodded and kept his eyes on Annie's sleeping face. She had severe frostbite. They had all seen enough of such things, living as they did in the high mountains of Idaho, but never had any of them seen such a bad case. They'd wrapped her feet well in layers of socks and someone's sweater but then

Confident-looking "prospector and social leader" Clara Dunwoody pauses in her labors for a photograph at her variscite claim in May 1910. As mine-camp businesswoman Annie Morrow proved, women played a major role in the history of America's precious mineral rushes. *Courtesy US Geological Survey*

had packed the feet in snow in hopes of slowing the damage. When they found her, howling and dragging herself along the snow-crusted ground, Annie's feet had been swollen, blackening things.

"I don't get why she would give nearly all her clothes to Dutch Em?" the youngest of the group asked.

"You have to ask that, boy, then you probably ain't got too much in the way of friends, I'd wager."

"Huh?"

The older man smiled and sighed. "It's what you do for a friend, you dippus."

"I reckon," said the young man.

It took another day of heavy, hard work to get Annie back to Rocky Bar, the mine camp she'd lived in since she was four, when she'd been carried into it in her father's pack basket. Now she was carried back to that town by men. The other members of the search crew would also soon return to town, carrying Dutch Em's dead, frozen body, pulled from her crevice in the rocks.

"I'll need more whiskey than that! And you all had best take good care of my kids. If I die, I want them well tended. You hear me?"

The few men and women who had gathered to lend a hand during the operation wore fearful looks. Annie was doing her best to keep it light, but she knew there was a good chance she'd not make it through this operation— being as there was no doctor in attendance. She upended the whiskey bottle again, glugged back a few pulls, as some of it leaked down her cheeks and trickled along her chin and around the back of her neck.

"This is for you, Dutch Em, a better woman I never knew." Her lips began to quiver, and tears coursed out of her eye corners. "I only wish it could have been me and not you, girl." She wept and whispered inaudibly a moment more, then her head slipped to the side.

Someone grabbed the nearly empty bottle before it dropped from her loosened grasp.

The man charged with the operation was the best butcher in town. He was also the one who owned the best meat saw. Someone else had sharpened an array of hunting knives and joint boning knifes. Beyond him, on the dresser, stood three full bottles of whiskey, to help prevent more infection.

He checked to make sure Annie was unconscious before flipping back the blanket covering her legs. There were two stout men on either side whose job it was to hold the legs still so he could get a good purchase. Cutting through the flesh would pose no problem, but the bone, thick as it was between the knee and ankle, would be slower going. He also wanted to leave enough flesh to help the nub heal over on itself. It would be a tricky task, to be sure. Butchering was easier, as you didn't have to worry about such things.

The flesh had blackened even farther up the legs than they expected. Instead of taking them off at the ankle, they had to go well above the blackened skin to healthy flesh, in hopes that the decay wouldn't continue to travel upward and kill her with an infection. Which could still happen, anyway.

"Right," said the butcher. "Nothing ventured. . . ." He bit his bottom lip and nodded to the men who clamped tight to the poor woman's leg. Several more men were at the ready and held Annie down by her shoulders, should she awaken in the midst of the gruesome task. He used the sharpest, thinnest knife blade first, dumping whiskey on it as he went, to clear the blood from the clean, new wound and to keep the infection from taking hold.

Once the flesh was sliced through all around, he wasted no time and set to work on the bone with the meat saw. He had sharpened it earlier that morning, and the keen blade and sure, tight strokes made quick work of Annie's leg bones. The rotted feet were put in a canvas gunnysack and tied off. They would be buried later. Two women, one a midwife, helped bandage the poor woman's stumps.

"Keep the whiskey handy," said the butcher. "She's going to need all that and more. The pain ahead of her isn't something a human body should have to endure."

Though it has been reported that the operation to remove Annie Morrow's feet was performed in the maw of the storm, atop a mountain, with nothing more than a hunting knife and a bottle of whiskey, other sources state the more realistic claim that Annie was carried down the mountain to the mining town of Rocky Bar, where she was then operated on. Her feet and lower legs were removed, between the knees and ankles, and she was thereafter known as Pegleg Annie.

Born Annie McIntyre, she arrived at the new gold camp of Rocky Bar on July 4, 1864, as a four-year-old in her father's pack. She grew up in the gold camp and later married, raised children, and owned her own mining claims and several "houses of entertainment" in Rocky Bar and over the mountain at another mine camp called Atlanta.

Annie was thirty-six years old when her life-changing journey with Dutch Em took place in the late spring of 1896. Unstoppable despite a new nickname and a distinct lack of feet, the irrepressibly vigorous Annie "Pegleg"

Morrow continued with her career as a successful businesswoman. She raised five children and wore a pistol while crawling around her popular restaurant and boardinghouse. Various friends crafted artificial limbs for her, but she preferred crawling. Annie lived another thirty-eight years after her ordeal and died of cancer in 1934 at St. Al's Hospital in Boise. She was seventy-five years old.

In her later years she had taken up with an Italian who ran a saloon next door to her restaurant. He planned a trip for himself back to Italy to visit his family, so Annie gave him her life savings, to be deposited in a bank in San Francisco before his departure. She never saw or heard from the man again, nor did she ever receive word that her money had been deposited. Despite this unfortunate turn of events, and ever the optimist, Annie continued to tell people that he had most likely been waylaid by bandits and killed.

40

UP AND DOWN
WITH THE EARPS
(1897)

In 1897 Wyatt and Josie Earp join the Alaska Gold Rush. Within a couple of years, they open a saloon in Nome, then pan throughout the Yukon—and come up with eighty thousand dollars in diggings. In 1901 they find veins of copper and gold in the Mojave Desert. Other Earp brothers aren't so lucky.

◆

I know he's Wyatt Earp and all, and I know he's famous. And I know he's a prickly pear. But the only thing that keeps him out of the hoosegow, I think, has been his way with a gun. Other than that, the man's a hoodlum."

The tall man behind the bar flipped the towel over his shoulder and leaned close to the stranger. "I was you, I'd be careful who you say that to."

"Why's that?" said the man as he lifted the glass of whiskey to his mouth.

Just then, a pretty middle-aged woman with dark hair leaned against the end of the bar just a few feet away. She looked at the two men, her brow furrowed, then said, "Wyatt, you're not scaring the customers again, are you?"

The bartender smiled and straightened, not taking his eyes off the man with the poised glass. "No, dear. He was just telling me what a prickly pear I am. Isn't that the phrase you used, sir?"

The man's glass never made it to his mouth. In fact, his hand shook so much that at least half the amber liquid in the glass puddled on the bar top. "I, ah, I didn't . . . mean to—"

Wyatt slipped the towel from his shoulder, and his hands disappeared behind the bar for a moment.

"Oh God!" shouted the man, his hands clapped to the sides of his wool hat. "Don't shoot me! God, don't kill me. I didn't mean nothing by it."

The few other people in the place that early in the afternoon fell silent, though they knew enough to keep their eyes from straying to the scene unfolding at the bar. The man continued to utter fearful oaths as he backed toward the door. He clunked into it, shrieked while his hands scrabbled and clawed for the handle, then he whipped it open and dashed outside without a backward glance.

Wyatt watched the door for a moment, then leaned on the bar top and laughed. The rest of the patrons uttered nervous laughs, too.

"Wyatt, go out there and find him and apologize."

Wyatt looked at his wife as if she'd just suggested he drink from a spittoon. "Like hell I will. You hear what he was saying about me?"

She folded her arms and regarded him. "Was he wrong?"

"Well, no. But he ain't welcome back in here."

Josie stared at him a few moments more, then a slow smile spread on her face. Wyatt winked at her and poured them each a drink.

"I been thinking, Josie. We got ourselves a poke here now, what with our claims, our earnings from panning in the Yukon, and the saloon and all. What say we pull up stakes at the end of the season?"

"We did that last year. I'm all for it—head back to where it's warm for the winter."

He shook his head. "This time, I mean for good."

Her smile faded. "Wyatt . . . what's gone wrong?"

"You meant to ask, 'What have you done this time,' right?" He scowled and resumed wiping the bar.

"No . . . well you have to admit, we do our fair share of jumping around."

"You tired of that, Josie?"

She nodded, played with her glass.

"Well," he resumed. "I think it's time we go somewhere warmer than Nome, and full time."

"Where'd you have in mind, Wyatt?"

He leaned toward her and in a quiet voice, said, "Tonopah, Nevada. With our poke, we could open a saloon and stake a few claims. It's the next big strike."

"How do you know that, Wyatt?"

He sighed and closed his eyes. "Look, Josie, was I wrong about Alaska?"

"No."

"OK, then. Trust me?"

She nodded. "Don't I always?" and they clinked glasses.

He kept looking at her.

"OK, Wyatt. What else?"

"I have been given promising information about diggings in the Mojave Desert. People are pulling out copper and gold by the fistful, Josie."

"By the fistful. Hmm." Josie looked at Wyatt, knocked back the last of her drink, and set down her glass on the bar top. "Then we best get down there and fill our fists, hmm?"

He smiled at her. "Yes, ma'am."

The two men faced each other over the table in Brown's Saloon in Willcox, Arizona. Each was red-eyed and working to maintain a focus on the other.

Finally, Warren Earp pushed his chair back from the table. "I tell you what, Boyett. I have grown weary of this half-ass card game in this half-ass mine camp and even wearier of your somber face and foul mouth. For the last time, will you admit that you have no claim on her? She is fonder of me by far than she could ever be of a range boss like you."

Johnnie Boyett stood, gripping the edge of the torn baize games table to steady himself. "I've about had enough of you, Warren Earp. You two-bit prospecting stage-driver, think you are a king bee, what with all the hoopla your murderous clan gets up to. Strutting around here like you're cock of the walk."

"Boyett, get your gun and we will settle this affair here and now." Warren Earp waved a hand at his sidearm. "I've got mine. Now go and get yours."

The steamed Boyett clumped out of the bar. Earp and the others heard his boots on the steps outside, then the sound of his boots on the gravel receded.

The man behind the bar shook his head and looked at his resolute patron. "Let it go, Warren. It ain't worth it."

"But it is, you see. Family honor is all," said Warren, winking. Earp stood up and entered the adjoining room.

As if in answer to Earp's comment, Boyett returned. "Warren Earp, you get yourself in here, boy. We have something to get down to!"

"Right here, Johnnie."

Boyett spun, faced Earp, and pulled two shots, one from each of the twin .45 Colts he wielded. Both shots punched into the adobe wall beyond Earp.

Earp turned his back on Boyett and stepped into the street. A handful of gawkers on both sides of the door parted as if he had pushed them back. He unbuckled his gun belt and let it drop to the ground at his feet and turned to face Boyett.

From the doorway, the enraged man fired two more rounds, missing his mark again.

Earp walked back into the bar, his hands holding open his coat and vest. "I am not armed, Johnnie. You have the best of this deal."

Boyett backed up a couple of steps as Earp advanced on him. "Damn you, Earp. Leave it be. Halt in your tracks, I tell you!"

Warren Earp did no such thing. So Boyett unleashed a fifth round that slammed into Earp's chest and sent him sprawling backward to the floor, his last breaths leaking out of him, even as the gouting blood pumped slower from the single wound to his heart. He lay spread-eagled on the floor. He indeed wore no guns, but his fingers slowly uncurled, revealing an open pocketknife in one hand.

"Allie, it's Goldfield, Nevada, or nothin', girl. I've been given word that they need a deputy sheriff. And I hear it's a decent town. Could be a house comes with it and all."

"Oh, Virg. I thought we were going to stay here in Colton. It's where your family lives, it's where I feel most at home. I want to stay here, Virgil."

The man closed his eyes and unconsciously rubbed his arm. "Allie, truth is, I don't think the town's going to change its mind. This is a dry town, and there's too many old biddies with too much sway over their old men looking to keep it that way. I can't operate a saloon here. Being a lawman's the only thing I've ever been good at."

She wouldn't look at him; somehow she knew that he would win. Curse the Earps; they were the most persuasive bunch of talkers she'd ever encountered.

"I have one damn arm, Allie. I need to make the most of it."

"In Tombstone, when you were shot, you said you still had a good arm to hold me with. That's all you need it for now, Virg." She bit down hard, forcing the hot tears to stay put. She hated to show weakness before him.

Virgil Earp leaned toward his wife and pulled her close. "Shh, we'll get squared away there, build up a little savings. Invest in a claim or two. We can dig at 'em together. There's money to be made there, girl. You mark my words." He hugged her tighter with his one good arm.

◆

Baxter Warren Earp was one of the Earp brothers who was not with his brothers in Tombstone at the time of the famous OK Corral shoot-out. He did, however, join Wyatt, Doc Holliday, and the other men on Wyatt Earp's famous Vendetta Ride, in which the small group of angry men tracked down and killed a number of the men suspected of having a hand in the wounding of Virgil Earp and the murder of Morgan Earp.

Though he was not arrested for shooting forty-five-year-old Warren Earp in 1900, it having been legally decided that the fight was the result of drunken provocations, Johnnie Boyett assumed correctly that the close Earp family might send emissaries to avenge their brother's death. Virgil Earp showed up in Willcox, using a false name. He investigated, and though he concluded it was a case of murder, nothing came of it, and Boyett lived out his days in California and Texas.

Virgil, the second-oldest Earp brother, was the most experienced gunman of all the brothers, having served in the army for three years before becoming a lawman out west. He held law-officer positions for much of his life, and at the time of his death in 1905, at age sixty-two, he was deputy sheriff for Esmeralda County, based in the town of Goldfield, Nevada.

In an intrepid life that seemed to contain more adventure than any three men had a right to, Wyatt Berry Stapp Earp in his eighty years managed to straddle the line of the law many times, while staying somewhat beloved in the eyes of the public. At various times, Earp was arrested for horse theft, pimping, and a variety of minor offenses. It is alleged that he claim-jumped at least twice at two Washington mine camps, and though it was not proven in court, it is said that as referee in a high-profile bout of pugilism in San Francisco, Earp fixed the fight and awarded the substantial purse to the obvious loser. He ran gambling houses and saloons, was a lawman all over the West, and had three wives, the last of whom, Josephine Marcus, he was with for forty-six years. In his dotage Wyatt Earp befriended Hollywood stars, including a young John Wayne, who would later use his conversations with the famed Old West lawdog as inspiration for his on-screen characters.

After his death in 1929, to help make ends meet, Wyatt Earp's widow, Josephine, bought old pistols at pawn shops, claimed they belonged to her famous gunman husband, then sold them to collectors for a tidy profit. She also wrote her memoir, I Married Wyatt Earp, an account of fascinating lives led with gusto.

41

DEAD HORSE GULCH
(1897–98)

During the brutal winter of 1897–98, on the Skagway Trail across White Pass to Lake Bennett, three thousand ill-used horses, mules, oxen, and donkeys, dead and dying, are dumped into corpse-choked ravines by rushers eager to get to the Klondike. More than a century later, racks of bones are still visible.

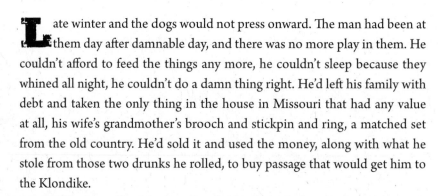

Late winter and the dogs would not press onward. The man had been at them day after damnable day, and there was no more play in them. He couldn't afford to feed the things any more, he couldn't sleep because they whined all night, he couldn't do a damn thing right. He'd left his family with debt and taken the only thing in the house in Missouri that had any value at all, his wife's grandmother's brooch and stickpin and ring, a matched set from the old country. He'd sold it and used the money, along with what he stole from those two drunks he rolled, to buy passage that would get him to the Klondike.

He'd had to roll a few more, but he finally had enough of a poke to outfit himself to suit the Canadian government's demands—a ton of food and supplies—and he'd had the foresight, thanks to that old sourdough, to buy a sled and dog team. At the time he'd felt sure they would be just the thing to get him to the Yukon quickly. After all, he'd reasoned, that seemed to be how everyone else was getting to the gold fields. But it had been harder than he thought. The dogs didn't like him, he knew it from the start. The way to treat a dog, as his father always said, was to beat them from day one, show them who's boss. Otherwise, they will take over and you'll be doing their bidding.

He thought it would be easier to shoot game, thought he would be able to feed the damned dogs all the raw meat they might want. He hadn't reckoned on this much snow. Nor this many people. He'd gone off-trail for a few days, looking for game, hoping to avoid the people who watched him with the dogs.

Same damn people who had bone racks for horses were looking at him as if he were some sort of criminal for whipping on his dogs—*his* dogs. How dare they even give him those looks! He'd told one man so, then pointed out that the man's nag looked half dead. Hell, he could see the blood running out from under the pack blanket where it had chafed the beast's hide clean off, down to the bone. Three of its four hooves were ringed with boils, and the beast stunk if you got within three feet of it. Smelled of death. Hell, the horse was dead, it just didn't know it yet. But the rascal had the gall to tell him to keep his mouth shut and stop abusing his dogs.

Finally, the dogs had just stopped. He wearily slashed the air with the whip, streaking their clumping, matted fur with fresh blood. But this time he barely roused a whimper from any of them. With each passing second, a rage writhed and twisted bigger and bigger inside him like a sickness, like a tight rope being bunched tighter all the time. Soon he couldn't stand it, could barely see what he was doing, could barely sense anything about him other than snow and the river down the embankment to his right.

He ripped into his packs, flinging goods left and right, and he yanked out the hand ax. He half clambered, half rolled down the bank, then set to work hacking a sizable hole in the ice. When he'd finished, he cut loose the leather traces from the sled, grabbed the harness at the shoulder of the lead dog, and dragged it down the embankment.

One by one, with little resistance, he pushed the dogs under the ice and held them down there with a length of broken tree limb. Soon they stopped their feeble pawing attempts at survival. As the last dog kicked away its last seconds of life, the man sank to his knees, howling in surprise at his madness, wondering what he had done, not just to the dogs but to his wife and children, and to the men from whom he had stolen. And the farm his father had left to him—he had squandered it away, transforming the rich river-bottom land into a dung pile of debt too big to ever get on top of.

And now this. . . . He sat down by the side of the trail and wondered if he was any use to anyone anymore.

THE DEAD HORSE TRAIL.

During the brutal winter of 1897–98, three thousand ill-used beasts of burden were dumped, dead and dying, along White Pass Trail during the rush to get to the gold fields of the Klondike. The corpse-choked river and ravines along this stretch came to be known as Dead Horse Trail and Dead Horse Gulch. *Courtesy Alaska State Library*

Oliver D. Silks, budding young journalist, regarded the corduroyed path he trod, then looked at the huffing fat man walking beside him. "I have to say, this trail is not nearly as bad as I was led to believe."

"That's 'cause the ground is still a bit seized up in spots." The fat man's cheeks ballooned with each step. "Wait 'til she gets soft, you'll see sights that'll make your eyes pop."

"What sort of sights?" said Silks, regretting that he'd opted to buy the least-expensive backpack of the several models available when he was outfitting himself back in New York. He hadn't counted on hiking so far with this one.

"Sights—well, let's see. How about the fact that the trail you're now tramping is mostly the hides and bones of dead horses."

Silks sneered at the thought. "That's not even funny."

"Wasn't meant to be. If you scratch at the snow a bit, you'll find a dead horse staring up at you. Sometimes the dead on this trail are so close together you can step from one to another."

"But they're living creatures."

"Not any more, they ain't. And the kicker is, most of these men dragging all this junk along these treacherous trails would be thrilled to find five hundred dollars' worth of gold. And you know what?"

"No," said Silks, choosing his path with more care.

"Most of these men paid five hundred dollars, seven hundred dollars, or more for a single pack horse, so scarce are they. Blew their stake on a horse, thinking all their prayers were answered, now that they had something to carry all their gear. But most of them conveniently forget that the feed to keep the horse alive is as dear as the horse is. Last time I heard, it was running a hundred-and-a-half per ton. And it gets worse."

"What do you mean?" Silks began to slow down, suspecting something awful.

The fat man said nothing in response. The path had become more uneven, the ground a half-frozen, squelching mess, calf-deep brown muck interspersed with soft hummocks.

Another minute passed in silence, then the fat man spoke. "Look where you're stepping, boy."

Silks looked down, and a horse stared straight up at him—a leather bridle clamping its mouth shut tight, the lips partially torn away, a muddied eye staring upward, the lid fluttering, breath wheezing through its one visible distended nostril. Silks saw that he was standing on the beast's neck. Even as he paused, gazing toward his muddied boots in horror at what he saw, he was aware of the crush of thousands behind him, forever moving to swarm over him, push him aside, and stamp into muck the rib cage of the still-living horse.

The snow had largely melted off, and it was nearing June. The shuffling line of men, women, horses, mules, donkeys, oxen, seemed to never end. At the base of a defile, the trail widened enough to accommodate two or three people abreast. As soon as the path widened, individuals struck off the trail a few feet to either side trying to gain ground and leap ahead in line.

Jeers met such attempts by a man and his wife. They were but three or four feet to the side of the squelching, knee-deep mud path when their horse began to mire. Within two paces, it had sunk deeper.

The man shouted, shrieked at his wife. "Pull, dammit! Get the horse's head up out of the muck! Keep it out, else all is lost, woman! All is lost!"

Their anger boiled, but it was apparent to everyone on the trail just a few feet away that they had already lost everything. Like all the others, the horse was overloaded. Blood seeped out from under its load, rivulets of it ran over a bone-tight hide already crusted with blood, fresh scabs pushed off every time the load shifted. And the load shifted with each step.

The man took to lashing the beast with the studded leather quirt. The horse made a final lunge, then everyone within earshot heard a popping noise as something tight succumbed to puncture. Seconds later, crimson bubbled and swirled, pluming up into the brown swamp water. The beast's eyes rolled and its rotted teeth ground in its foaming mouth. It thrashed side to side, slapping its head into the mud until it could only lay still in the muck and slowly sink. All that remained was a bubble of its still-panting midsection, an ear, and one white staring eye, the lid flickering even as the dank brown muck water pooled across it.

The man screamed and lashed at the horse in a renewed frenzy, his own eyes wide, spittle flecking his matted beard. Another man just ahead of Oliver Silks shouted, "The horse is gutted! She's snagged on a jagged stump, you fool! Get yourself and your wife out of there before you sink out of sight, too."

Certain strenuous stretches of the trail were lined with all manner of men and beast too exhausted to move on. They lay back against the mud- and snow-banks, panting and wheezing. Silks noticed that some merely sat and stared ahead, as if at nothing. Then he noticed there was no clouding breath coming from one man's sagged mouth. "My God!" he said. "I think that man is dead."

"You would be dead too if you had a hole in your chest," said his portly companion.

"What do you mean?" Silks struggled to look back, but the crush of people around him made it impossible. Someone behind him grunted an angry oath. Silks assumed it was directed at him, so he faced forward and picked up his pace.

"I mean," said the fat man, "that he shot himself."

"What? But we nearly stepped on him . . . we stepped over his legs."

"Mighty big of you, but I'd guess it won't be long before his legs are trampled into the damn ground, along with the rest of him."

"All for gold," said the young journalist, shaking his head.

"Bet your life on it." The fat man rubbed his hands together and laughed.

◈

It has been said that regardless of one's chosen route, White Pass (aka the Skagway Trail, and alternately called "Dead Horse Trail" and "Dead Horse Gulch") or Chilkoot Pass (a twenty-five-mile-long trail that rose two thousand feet, half of that in the last half mile), the bone-weary traveler invariably wished he had chosen the other trail. Alas, their beasts of burden did not have the luxury of choice.

Greedy men, desperate to be the first to exploit the riches of a wilderness, reduced themselves to base creatures, thrashing and flogging the life out of their pack animals. That included horses, burros, mules, oxen, dogs, and even goats. Eventually the overloaded beasts, their hides whip-stripped, trembling, frothing, and bleeding, collapsed under the weight and strain of round-the-clock torment.

And if it wasn't their "masters" brutalizing them, it was the elements, unpredictable and raw, that claimed the lives of too many of these unwitting creatures. The journey was a death warrant for thousands of pack animals. When they were no longer useful, though in many cases still alive, they were pushed off the trail or left where they dropped for the following stampeders to trample into the mud. The bleached bones of the dead beasts are still in evidence along these routes.

Interestingly enough, several other states lay claim to a "Dead Horse Gulch," among them Colorado, Wyoming, and Maine.

42

AVALANCHE!
(1898)

Though they had been warned of dicey conditions on the Chilkoot Trail due to a lengthy blizzard, on April 3, 1898, seventy men are buried under thirty feet of snow. Few are dug out alive.

◆

The blizzard had been at it for ages, pelting down hour after hour, day after day, building up along the tops of the surrounding peaks, the dollops growing fatter, lazier, more sluggish, until they began to sag during a lull early in the storm's third day. Despite warnings and then the outright refusal of experienced guides and Indians to travel the increasingly snowed trails, dozens of antsy stampeders, eager to get up the pass, weighed common sense with safety and found safety wanting. In the end, all it took was a handful of pack-laden men to take to the trail once again. The rest, in a fidgeting, milling herd, hated seeing those few get the jump on them, hated it so much they abandoned any good sense they might have had and took to the trail—even after the old-timers begged them to stay put.

As the morning brightened, a snowslide up the trail buried a dozen people. One old man saw a raft of snow slump; then with impressive speed, it covered a dozen surprised trekkers. It being early on a Sunday, the trail hadn't yet filled. The gathered crowd of rescuers needed many long minutes to dig through the ten feet of snow that had rafted down and covered the men. Despite their best efforts, they could only find nine of the twelve. Then, far-off rumblings, high in the surrounding peaks crowning the pass, drove everyone to look skyward in unison. In unspoken agreement, the straggling crowd bolted for Sheep Camp two miles below.

The word passed through the group that great masses of snow had been seen slumping off the peaks before hitting the glass-smooth ice sheets, acres and acres in size, and gaining speed as they rocketed downward. These were the sounds they had heard.

A preliminary slide had seeped down around their legs, and for the briefest of moments, it seemed as if the hip-deep deluge was all they were going to get. "Dish it out, we can take it" was the tough-minded sentiment that crossed more than one mind, even as they struggled to lift themselves up, out of the loose wash of snow. And then, a rush of cold air and a world of sound and darkness covered everyone on the slope.

That sound, mightier than anything any person within earshot had ever heard, boomed and echoed at them, through them. Soon it felt to the trekkers as if the entire mountain were being dragged out from under them. A wall of snow thirty feet high and compressed by the shape of the pass itself pummeled down on them as if it were a fist driven from the heavens.

It had begun from the cliff face twenty-five hundred feet above the trail, and within seconds a great raft of snow thirty feet thick covered a ten-acre area. Unheard screams of those running full-out downslope were pinched off with eye-blink speed.

The swarm of nearly one thousand men from Sheep Camp scrabbled its way toward the snowslide, which lay ahead of them upslope—a monstrous, wide mass of nearly pristine whiteness, so vast and complete an area did it seem to cover. Where moments before stood the jagged forms of boulders and clefts and ropes and animals and people, all straining downslope to avoid the rolling, roiling mass of snow, now there was little more than a sea of unbroken snow.

It took the men, on snowshoes and skis and punching holes in the increasingly deeper snow, nearly half an hour to reach the snowslide where they had last seen most of the victims. Below them they could see breathing holes opening, saw the legs and arms of the luckiest, those who somehow had managed to stay near the surface of the slide. But most were not so lucky, and they lay buried far beneath the surface. Some at thirty feet down.

The men began digging trenches several feet apart in hopes of adding logic to the dizzying field of snow. They worked with caution, lest in sinking

The long, steep route known as the "Golden Trail" threaded its way up Chilkoot Pass in Alaska. Once exhausted prospectors reached the top, Canadian Mounties checked that each man possessed the requisite two thousand pounds of goods and gear, enough to sustain a body in the interior for a year. This required numerous trips up and down the trail. *Courtesy Library of Congress*

their shovel blades they lop off a victim's head, arm, or fingers, and they also worked in as much silence as they could, because early on they realized they could hear the cries of trapped people.

"Dig for it!" one man shouted into a hole in the snow. He was an older gent, and he and his son had come north in hopes of striking it rich. His wife had died the year before, and the boy had not yet married. But Kentucky now seemed a faraway place. He looked up, his face a mask of confusion and rage.

"Help me! My boy is down there!" The old man scrabbled into the snow like a dog digging up a bone. Every few seconds he would stop and shout, "You hear me, boy? I'm coming—hold on, hold on now, boy." And he would resume his gruesome task. "I hear you, boy. In the name of God, I will get to you."

Soon, though, he heard his boy's voice no more. Men with shovels had helped him, but the snow proved too dense, and as the rescuers dug all over the snowslide, they realized that the survivors might not be that way for long. There was no way the trapped could help themselves, their limbs were pinned, their bodies packed in as if for shipment. The snow had lodged so tight around everything. One digging man said to another a few feet away, "It's like mud, rammed and baked hard."

From what the rescuers could tell, very few people had been killed in the initial snowslide. But within minutes, the depth and the crushing effects of it would claim the lives of many more. Breathing became difficult; then as the oxygen slowly became a recycled, poisoned cloud of carbon dioxide, they succumbed to drowsiness, and drowsiness gave way to death.

Rescues were limited, but some made it through, including an ox that was found in a snow-formed grotto, standing upright and chewing its cud as if nothing much had happened.

"Leave her be, by God. If she wants to labor over him, that's her business. He was her man, after all."

"But Joppe's dead. It's been pretty near three hours since we dug him out, and he ain't moved a lick."

"What's the harm in it?" The man said to another who had hefted an end of a travois. He'd been hauling bodies downslope, piling two and three on at a time, to the makeshift coroner's tent. The men there were laying out the bodies, arranging snapped and mangled limbs into some order. But he knew who had appointed himself coroner, and he had little regard for the scoundrel, Soapy Smith. And this buffoon dragging the travois was getting on his nerves, for he too was one of Soapy's men. He knew he'd seen him before, at Smith's saloon, in Skagway.

The man with the travois headed toward Vernie Woodward, the weeping girl, and tried to pull her from the body of her man, Joppe. But he didn't reckon whom he was dealing with. Vernie was well known among the men who had made a business of hauling freight up and down the pass for the travelers. She was as rugged as a man and kinder than she had a right to be.

She'd been crying and working diligently on Joppe's lifeless form for hours, breathing into his mouth, rubbing his blue-tinged limbs, flopping him forward and pounding on his back, massaging his head and feet, and whispering frantic prayers and oaths of love to the dead man. The man who had defended her earlier had to admit that three hours was a bit much, but who was he to interfere? And he'd be damned if he was going to let one of Soapy Smith's vulture boys bother her any longer. He lunged at the man, shouting, "See here, you—" when the queerest thing happened. . . .

Joppe's eyes flickered open, and he croaked out, "Vernie!" All the men surrounding them on the slope stood widemouthed and staring at this miracle. Vernie's defender felt his head shaking, as if his body were telling him, "No, this is not possible, don't believe what you're seeing, man." And yet, he could see that Joppe was alive. How was another story. But it seemed to hit the crowd all at once. Cheers arose, and the men raised their wool hats and voices in happiness.

All was not lost, they seemed to be saying. And while there is breath left in our bodies, we will endeavor to find each and every person, to account for every life, and if Joppe can live after three hours of seeming dead, then surely we can find others, too.

For a week following the avalanche, frozen bodies were pulled from the snowpack, many of them wide-eyed and with legs and arms akimbo, as if running from the terrible rushing snow. When the last of the dead had been interred as composed as possible in a declivity in the mountainside, close by the Chilkoot Trail, the tenants of Sheep Camp turned out for the services. There was little else that could be done for the dead. As for the living, the seemingly neverending column of expectant gold-rushers snaked its way upward, glancing at the grotto and thanking their good fortune that they weren't caught in the famed avalanche. Then they turned their attentions back to the trail before them and, step by hard, trudging step, they groped their way upward.

Later, as summer bloomed, the tragedy of months before once again made itself known. The grotto in which the avalanche victims' bodies had been laid to rest filled with water. In selecting the site, no one had known that in the warm months, the hollow became a lake. As the summer's stragglers trudged up the muddy slopes of the pass, they saw dozens of corpses, bloated and drifting, on the surface of the little lake.

43

CHEECHAKO DEATH TREK
(1898)

Eighteen New Yorkers set out in April 1898 to gain the Yukon gold fields by their own route, traversing the fifty-mile bulk of Alaska's largest glacier. By April 1899 accidents, disease, starvation, and stupidity whittle the group to four. They are found starving, addled, and blind.

◆

The man Arthur Dietz, a robust, thick-shouldered fellow with short hair and piercing eyes, radiated vigor, and it was his undeniable enthusiasm for the grand adventure awaiting them all that had helped him recruit the seventeen New York City men. Their long, arduous journey to get to the West Coast and then their travels on a boat north were buoyed by his infectious spirit, which rubbed off on every member.

And now here they were, clustered in a tight group, the bold, cold-looking shoreline of Alaska in the distance. With each passing minute, their steamer brought them closer to her. Dietz called them all together in a huddle and rubbed his hands, more out of excitement than to ward off the chill of being on the water. He pointed at the map, a document each had seen so often they knew every detail by rote. "One more time before we disembark, gentlemen, if you please."

His remark brought nods from most, a few wry smiles from some, and barely concealed contempt from a few others. He took in all the reactions, filing them away, each man knew, for possible use later. Dietz was nothing if not predictable, methodical, and, they all hoped, effective.

They each remembered his recruitment speech. His was to be the most singularly prepared-for expedition to Alaska's gold fields ever launched. He had planned every moment of the trip, and he knew the maps intimately, well before he even approached potential members. Furthermore, and more importantly, he was convinced, according to various firsthand reports that few others had access to, that he knew exactly where vast quantities of gold resided, and he said he knew how to retrieve it. They could all go there, spend a year, longer if the find turned out to be extraordinary, as he fully expected it would, and then they could all return to New York as millionaires. How did that suit them? he had asked. Right down to the ground, most of them responded.

And so they had signed up, these men, fully aware of the risks but fully aware that their leader, Arthur Dietz, a YMCA director of physical education, was a robust specimen of a man both physically and intellectually. He exuded such confidence that they in turn were convinced that any unfortunate eventualities, while not negated, would be minimized by the preparedness they all underwent before the trip west. And now here they were, on the ship, within sight of Alaska. Soon their adventure would begin in earnest.

The cold months were the most propitious time to travel to the interior, as trails that would normally be impassable due to mud and clouded with unbearable biting insects in summer would be bug-free and hard-packed, ideal for travel in winter. He had assured them that one thousand pounds of food per man, regardless of what the Canadian government demanded of travelers going through normal routes to the interior, would prove more than sufficient.

"It's a squall, nothing more!" but Arthur Dietz's words were whipped from his mouth as soon as he uttered them. Just as well, he thought, for he didn't believe what he was saying anyway. Truth is, we're lost, exhausted, and caught in weather I never imagined I'd see, he thought. I assumed it would be more pleasant than this. It is April, after all. But he was beginning to realize that April in Alaska is not April in New York City.

They had traveled for days now, across Malaspina, Alaska's largest glacier. And there had been no respite from the wind slicing down the flanks of the glacier above them. Even the dogs on their sleds quivered and had trouble advancing in the teeth of this constant onslaught. And the sun, which he had hoped would provide them with warmth, had skipped the warming part and went straight to burning them. It reflected and blazed off the brilliant white surface of the snow across which they trekked. What flesh they had exposed, on their faces, soon burned red and brown, peeling and painful.

To add another layer of insult, just the night before, a blizzard had struck. Should have realized something was amiss, thought Dietz, as the wind finally ceased its howling. He had chosen to take advantage of the lull to gain ground before they had to camp for the night. And then it had begun—a thick, dense snowfall. In the morning they discovered more than two feet of snow had fallen, burying their gear and delaying their start.

Mere days later, Dietz had been following along behind the doctor's sled, and then the man had simply disappeared. A scream that rapidly winked out was the last anyone in the party heard of the man, his dogs, and their entire store of medical supplies. (Dietz realized too late that he should have made them separate such loads so that, should something happen to one, all would not be at a loss.)

Within seconds the crew members had gathered and looked straight down for what seemed miles into a crevasse. The death of a member of the team was not something any of them had counted on. That he was their sole medical expert hammered an icicle of fear into every man's heart. If he could die, so could they all. Indeed, so might they all.

Over the following weeks, and despite their overt caution, another crevasse seemed to open before their very eyes and suck down two more men, their sleds, gear, and dogs, all tumbling, screaming, and yowling into the bottomless maw that by then they were all convinced led straight to a frozen hell.

And yet many of them had begun to feel that's where they were—in a living hell. How could it get any worse? But for a time they were given a reprieve, for summer came, and with it, a melt. But so too did the warmer temperatures bring with them vicious biting insects that attacked them in swarms so thick they could part the bugs with their hands. They tried various promising spots and panned them with little success, all the while working to procure meat, to learn the skills that they had painfully begun to realize could not be acquired in books.

Near the end of the summer, snow appeared in the elevations above them as if by magic, dusting the mountaintops. It was a pretty time, with long, cool nights and fewer biting insects. And then another man died, gripped by a fever. He had thrashed in his bedding for days before succumbing. The foremost

Because the gold-rich Klondike region of northwest Canada's Yukon Territory was so difficult to get to—it was five hundred miles from Skagway to the Klondike—prospectors faced arduous climbs up steep mountain passes. Their own backs were the most reliable means of transporting their gear. *Courtesy Library of Congress*

thought on each man's mind was when the fever would take them, for surely it would spread through the group and lay them each low, one at a time.

The short autumn gave way to winter, and the group finished building a cabin and prepared to settle in for the coming cold. Despite their losses, most of them felt sure that it was but a matter of time before they found the gold that would make it all worthwhile. But not all of them felt this way. Three men, in defiance of their oath to each other at the beginning of the venture, packed up one day before severe snow prevented their plans and announced they were off to find an Indian settlement.

"At least with the Indians," said one of them, "we stand a chance of surviving the coming winter." There was nothing the others could do to dissuade them. It would be the last time they ever saw those men.

Soon the fullness of winter settled on them with a series of blinding storms the likes of which they hadn't yet experienced. The long, dismal days in their cramped, dark, low-ceilinged cabin were nearly unbearable. For long, frustrating months on end, no matter how much wood they burned in their crude fireplace, they never felt anything approaching warmth.

Except for essential reasons, the men spent most of their winter in their bedding, wrapped tight against the all-pervasive cold. And before spring finally peered around the corner at them, another of their number died, this time of scurvy. Many of them felt the effects of it—bleeding gums, weakness—but he had been the first to succumb. Soon, while the snows were at their drooping heaviest, as the beginnings of the spring melt compressed the snow all about them, three more men were crushed under an avalanche while out hunting.

April arrived and found the remaining seven men reduced to eating the last of their sled dogs. They realized their grand expedition had been doomed from the start. They had realized this for the better part of a year, in fact, but only now did they feel utterly defeated. The remaining seven swore they would head toward the coast in the most expeditious manner possible. Three of them soon died of starvation and severe exhaustion.

Of the remaining four, two men became blind, the permanent effects of exposure to the sun reflecting off the snow. The other two men had suffered severe sight loss as well, Dietz among them. They traveled for weeks, were given some assistance by native tribesmen of the region, and subsisted on dead fish washed up on the beach. Eventually none of the four were fit to move any longer, so they built a fire and prayed that someone might see the smoke. And a passing US revenue cutter, the *Wolcott*, did.

A deadly mix of ignorance, excitement, and hubris convinced the members of the ill-fated New York City expedition that they could go it alone. They

set a course that would take them across the vicious face of Alaska's largest glacier, a fifty-mile trip on which crevasses, snowblindness, and killing winds were a daily occurrence. But their disregard for the nature of the place caused the deaths of most of them. Expedition leader Arthur A. Dietz kept a journal throughout the expedition, and in 1914 he published Mad Rush for Gold in Frozen North, *his highly readable account of the harrowing journey.*

Stories of unqualified, inexperienced people trekking into the interior abound in the history of the great white north. Cheechako, or greenhorn in the Chinook jargon, was not only a name of derision, but it was also a warning to others that this newcomer probably had more enthusiasm than good sense. The only ones who made it through the long, vicious northern winters were the ones who early on assumed a role of quiet humility and who were willing to learn the many and varied ways of the natives and of the old sourdoughs who had been there for years. Intrepid but naïve souls from the States all too often looked down their noses at the natives, who were among the few who knew how to survive in the interior. Most old sourdoughs built up their caches of backwoods skills by keeping their mouths shut and their ears open when around the natives.

44

WHITE HORSE RAPIDS
(1898)

After the difficult winter, and soon after ice-out, thirty thousand eager Klon-dikers travel five hundred miles down inland waterways in seven thousand homemade boats, shooting through the treacherous waters of the Yukon's White Horse Rapids. Some make it.

◆

The Argonauts waited weeks for ice-out, their camps lining the banks of Lake Bennett. Finally, on May 29, 1898, after days of round-the-clock cracks and rumbles as if a thunderstorm were taking place beneath their very feet, great rafts of slush-covered ice began to float, spinning almost impercepti-bly, toward the lower end of the lake. Ice-out had come. And within forty-eight hours, the choked waters would flush clean of the bobbing hunks of slushed, softening ice. And even before then, 7,124 boats would also be on the move.

Sam Steele, of the North-West Mounted Police, surveyed the scene, shak-ing his head and wondering not for the last time how all these people could have ended up here, at this lake that, a year before, had been as untouched a lake as one could hope to find in the wilderness.

"Took long enough," groused one man who watched the loosening ice. Everyone called him "Sour Ed." But no one heard him, for great rousing cheers filled the air as people rushed to jam the last of their shoreside gear into their motley assortment of boats. The sudden din was that of men making ready to embark on yet another fantastic leg of their voyage to the interior of Canada's Yukon Territory.

The assembled frenzying masses had spent the preceding weeks and months not in leisure but in anticipation and construction and argument. Few of the boats they built resembled traditional watercraft, though some were legitimate boats, such as the massive scows, weighing in at twenty tons, ferrying livestock of all ilk, and they bumped and competed and jockeyed for position with lashed-log rafts.

Darting between them were canoes that had doubled as sleds, their bottoms nearly worn through—but not quite. A good many of the boats, ruminated Sam Steele, barely looked able to float. He'd seen men of all shapes and sizes whipsawing green logs into planks that seemed as if they would be ill-suited to the task.

From his vantage point, the Canadian lawman was occasionally distracted from his reverie by prospectors seeking mediation. He watched all manner of sails rise over the water, from the bloomers two women sewed together that caught the wind nicely to the flags, blankets, even winter mackinaws, which all filled and tugged in the steady, daylong breezes. The desperation of the travelers to reach the Klondike's promising riches, still five hundred miles and more distant, was tempered somewhat by the gold seekers' complete humility before the wind.

It wasn't the boaters' travel on the lakes that bothered Sam Steele. It was the fact that Miles Canyon, and the two sets of hellish rapids beyond—Squaw Rapids and White Horse Rapids—were not far ahead, once the travelers left behind the relative safe travels of the chain of mountain lakes. He knew that some of these thirty thousand people would die there.

By the time the North-West Mounted Police arrived at Miles Canyon, hundreds of boats had already ventured into the narrow, foreboding, steep-walled fissure, few of them knowing of the whirlpool swirling in its midst. Just three years before, two Swedes had unwittingly been swept into the hellish gyre and spun there for six hours before they were able to launch themselves out of it.

As Sam Steele arrived at the scene two days after the first boats floated into view, more than 150 craft had swamped, smashed, and lay ruined, bobbing in the shallows along with the sodden wreckage of gear, snapped and shredded planking, and animal carcasses bloating and eddying in the side currents. In that time, ten men lost their lives, their heads and torsos slamming into jagged rocks like the teeth of great beasts just below the surface. Or else the stamped-ers were unable to swim out of it and eventually became worn out, tumbling round and round in the current before their lifeless rag-doll bodies spurted out of the narrowed, lower end of the canyon into the air above Squaw Rapids.

Among the wrecked boats were the three that made up Major Walsh's party. As people watched from shore, eager to see at least one boat slip through the rapids, they saw each of the three boats rise up, surrounded by the great ten-foot-high sprays of whitewater fluming skyward—and for which White Horse Rapids was named. Then each boat dropped back down, lost from sight for long moments as the mist and froth churned in the air about the boat. Then came the sounds of collective disappointment as the boats were revealed for a moment, belly-up like turtle shells, their gear boiling in the current and their human occupants sputtering and gasping.

The river above Miles Canyon was choked for miles with thousands of watercraft. Many stampeders, not knowing what else to do, pitched camp along the riverbank. Like children, they avoided making the inevitable deci-sion of portaging their gear over seemingly insurmountable, unforgiving ter-rain. Instead they sat and stared at the frothing, pounding rapids.

What they couldn't see was the clutter of human wreckage five miles downstream. These were the people who had ventured down the rapids, and now most had little to show for it. Their bashed boats and what gear they could salvage lay drawn up on the shore, their money gone, their journeys at an end.

Steele knew he had to do something. And so, as the top representative of the law of Canada in that place at that time, he instituted laws that ensured as safe a passage as was possible. He made sure that each boat allowed to venture through the rapids was piloted by experienced men, was built to the satisfac-tion of the officers under his command, and bore a number that corresponded with the passenger list one of his officers made for each boat. He hoped it would be enough. He knew it would not prevent every death, but perhaps it might help reduce the number of needless deaths at the rapids—and beyond.

Among all the ramshackle watercraft that bobbed their way through the rapids in death-defying displays that challenged the very notion of flotation,

there were vessels that carried much more than the obligatory one-ton-per-man rule enforced by the Canadian government. Two of the boats ferried full printing presses for the not-quite-inaugurated Klondyke Nugget and the Midnight Sun.

A good many other boats carried loads that were more often than not luxury items the owners intended to mark up and charge exorbitant prices for, including eggs (it is estimated that eggs formed the primary cargoes of three dozen boats). Another carried fifteen hundred pairs of boots; still another was loaded with live chickens that had been packed up the Chilkoot. Other enterprising folks carried such bizarre loads as cats and kittens— bizarre until a plague of rats and mice in the mine camps became a concern. That man sold his feline friends for hefty profits. Another fellow, Signor R. J. Gandolfo, floated in sixteen thousand pounds of candy, fruit, and vegetables. And still another person hauled a milk cow on his scow.

All along the watery route to Dawson, what had been pristine wilderness prior to the arrival of so many gold-seeking whites within months became a stripped, savaged place. The trees for hundreds of feet lining the rivers had been chopped and used for building or burning for cookfires. When they left their makeshift camps behind, the stampeders frequently neglected their campfires. At the height of summer, the region raged with wildfires that covered everything with thick, choking smoke and an unrelenting yellow haze.

Many people died along the harsh, unforgiving water trail. But a good many more made it through, if not without incident, then at least with stories to tell. On Lake Bennett, a storm piled an overloaded scow onto shoreside rocks. The boat's occupants were Mabel Long and her husband, of California, and a young man named Rossburg, who had agreed to help them in exchange for passage.

When the boat crashed, poor Mabel was tossed into the water while her husband dithered in the stricken craft, yelling for assistance. Young Rossburg dove in and saved Mabel from drowning. It should be noted that Mabel was eighteen and her husband, a choice foisted on her by her parents, was two decades her senior. Rossburg, however, was somewhat closer to Mabel's age. Mabel, being a woman who had seen and experienced much in recent weeks, left her ineffectual older husband then and there and fled with young Rossburg. Though her husband gave valiant chase, his efforts proved useless.

Mabel divorced him, stuck with her savior, and later found him to be heir of a well-heeled Boston family.

The tens of thousands of men and women who ventured to Dawson spent thirty million to sixty million dollars just to get there. At its peak, in 1898, the Klondike's gold yield was approximately ten million dollars, and only one in ten people that year found gold.

45

DO IT FAST, DO IT NOW
(1898)

In twenty-six months, Michael J. Heney and his crew blast through moun-
tains, build trestles, and lay track—110 miles of it—to form the White
Pass & Yukon Route railway. Miners move from the port at Skagway to
the gold fields of the Klondike in record time. And the Yukon will never be
the same.

Well, it's obvious that something needs to be done, Sir Thomas." Big
Mike Heney shook his head. The topic was well known but still one
that aggravated him, especially when he knew of a solution. He turned back
to Sir Thomas Tancrede, the man representing Close Brothers and Company,
the London-based financiers of the proposed railway. "Thousands of animals, mostly pack horses, are dying along the White Pass Trail because these
damned stampeders were lied to back in the States, in Seattle, when they were
getting outfitted."

"So . . ." said Sir Thomas.

"So, we can change all that by building the railway. And it will be White
Pass and not the Chilkoot, as the pass gets us up and over the range at the
lowest altitude. That doesn't mean it's going to be easy. Far from it. We'll have
fifteen hundred workers at any one time, and with the twenty-two hours a day
of daylight, we'll run double, triple shifts."

"Where will you get that many men?" The Londoner paused with his
unlit cigar halfway to his mouth, his eyebrows arched high.

"Why, for the specialized tasks, I already know the best men for the jobs.
But for the common laborers, the majority of them, we'll get them from the
very men who are looking to get to the interior."

Sir Thomas poked his cigar into his mouth. "No, I think not. Those men
will abandon us as soon as they are able, mark my words."

"Not if we treat them right," said Heney. "I am the labor foreman of the job, after all. I give my word on it."

"Understood, but by 'treat them right,' I presume you mean to pay them well?"

"And why not? You get what you pay for in this life. Why, you give me enough dynamite and snoose and I'll build a railway to hell itself!"

Sir Thomas laughed, patted his vest pockets for matches. "Big Mike, you keep this up and one of these days I just might begin to believe you."

Heney felt good about this. He also felt a bit nervous, not that he'd ever admit to such a thing around the men, his laborers, or the backers. Though he was the labor foreman on the job, he'd been known as the "boy contractor," because of his age, still a youthful thirty-four. Though everyone, including himself, knew that he could be the contractor of the entire job itself.

He went on to tell the London financier that the 110-mile route, while not a walk in the park, was certainly well within his capabilities. If he planned it all accordingly, with two crews working toward each other from opposite ends of the project, they should meet at Carcross, roughly in the center. One crew would be headed north, another from the north working southward.

He'd read the press, and they were calling it the "railway built of gold."

They'd already made understandable but annoying concessions—the railroad itself was to be a narrow-gauge, with three-foot rails and a ten-foot-wide track bed. This would save substantial amounts of money over the course of the project. And it was truly a joint effort. The British were financing, the Americans had engineered it, and the Canadians were seeing that it would get built. And that's where Heney came in.

He knew that if he could pull this off—when he pulled it off, he told himself with a smirk—he would have managed a mighty feat, having been a key figure in constructing the northernmost railroad in the Western Hemisphere. Now that would be something to tell his father. He knew the old man was still miffed that he didn't finish his engineering degree, but he'd gambled that nothing anyone could show him as theory in a classroom back east could take the place of honest-to-god, hands-on experience building railways. So far, he'd been proved right, in more ways than one.

But this would prove his biggest challenge yet: The WP&YR would rise from sea level at Skagway to three thousand feet at the summit of White Pass in less than twenty miles. That was some grade to conquer—just shy of 4 percent, if his math was correct, and he knew it was. Then there were the sixteen-degree curves on sheer cliff faces, plus bridges, trestles, and two hard-rock tunnels to blast. He'd have to gut two mountains. And by golly, he said with a grim smile as he pulled on his coat, he and his men were going to do it.

But that wasn't the part that had him worked up—he was going to ask the men to do something next to impossible. They would have to work round-the-clock and round-the-calendar, in the most unforgiving temperatures known to man.

"Mike? Bad news . . ."

Heney's foreman stood in the doorway of the railcar Heney used as an office. He turned his hat in his hands and pulled a wide grimace.

"What's the worry?" Mike set down his pen and reached for his coat. Though it was only September, the weather had become increasingly raw for weeks, and the snow was pilling up. He did not look forward to the coming winter.

"You know that gold strike at Atlin?"

Heney's face sagged, and he shook his head. "Tell me you're pulling my leg."

"Not kidding, Mike. They up and left sometime in the night."

As they descended the steps to the track bed, Heney asked, "How many?"

"Don't know yet, but . . . I'd say most of them."

"What?"

"That's not all—"

Heney stopped and grabbed the other man by the sleeve. "Out with it, man. Tell me the whole story."

The other man sighed. "They took most of our shovels and picks, too."

The 110-mile White Pass and Yukon Route railway, carved out of raw wilderness in twenty-six months, succeeded in getting men and gear into the mountains and raw ore out of the mountains at a much faster—and safer—rate than did dogsleds and pack mules. *Courtesy US Geological Survey*

Big Mike clenched his fists, his jaw muscles bunching.

"Mike?"

"How about the law?" Heney said through gritted teeth. "Any help there?"

"I've sent two men to fetch 'em. And another man to track down the men who left, try to talk sense into them. But I don't hold out hope."

"No, neither do I. All for gold, gold, gold. . . . Do we have enough shovels and picks to get us by until I can get more up here?"

"Not really, but we'll limp through."

"Good," said Heney as the two men walked toward the job site. "And I want trusted people to guard the tools and men until this silly boom in Atlin is over with."

The foreman nodded. "Already on it. But we'll need more men and tools soon, Mike."

Heney nodded. "You know, I promised our backers that these men would be reliable. I guess the allure of the unknown is more tempting than the decent wage we're paying. But I gave my word, and that's what bothers me most."

Both men stood staring at the skeletal crew, then Heney said, "Well, let's get them to work."

"We're at mile sixteen, men, and in the midst of tunneling into a frozen rock face. We haven't stopped much yet for the damned weather, and I don't really want to stop now." Heney knew the temperature because he'd checked before he crawled out of the tent's relative warmth. It was a balmy sixty degrees below zero out here. Machinery and men were seizing up left and right, and there was more snow than he could have imagined he'd ever see in one place. Not only that, but the old-timer on the crew predicted there was more on the way. Snuffy had rarely proven himself wrong, even if he did rely a bit too much on his "rheumatism" as his diviner of weather.

They'd had one minor mishap the day before, when one of the men had loaded the charge hot. The blast had oversprayed, peppering the entire area with more scattershot than they'd expected, but thankfully there hadn't been any serious injuries.

"Well Mike, you did it. We never doubted your ability to pull it off. I knew you began the project as labor foreman, but truth be told, we were all very pleased when you were able to become contractor of record one-third of the way along and steered the ship, as it were, through to the end."

"Well, thank you, gentlemen. It was indeed a mighty undertaking." Big Mike Heney raised his glass. "I'd like to take a moment to remember the thirty-five thousand men who worked on this grand project."

"Hear, hear," said someone. They all sipped.

Then he cleared his throat and said, "And I think it's worth mentioning that we ended up spending a bit of money, about ten million dollars, if my figures are correct."

The men laughed, and some of them drew tight faces, as if the money had come from their own wallets. Then Mike continued. "But it's also worth noting that we did save an awful lot of money by making certain decisions on the fly, by deciding to go with narrow gauge, for instance. That saved not only money but also substantial time and effort expended. And all that said, we still managed to use 450 tons of explosives to get the job done!"

Again, a mighty cheer rippled through the crowd. Mike smiled. "Where is Sir Thomas? There he is. Do you recall, Sir Thomas, that night when we met more than two years ago, you had your doubts about a railway along the coastal mountains?"

The florid man at a front table nodded, a big smile on his face.

Heney continued, "Do you recall what I told you?'

Sir Thomas stood and addressed the room. "Indeed I do, ladies and gentlemen. This man you see before you said something to the effect that if given enough dynamite and, ah, snoose, he could well build a railroad to hell."

A rousing cheer echoed through the place, and Heney, red-faced, grinned and nodded.

Sir Thomas continued, "And gentlemen, I am here to tell you that I didn't much doubt him then, and I certainly have no reason to doubt him now!"

Cheers again rocked the building, and then he said, "Three cheers for Big Mike Heney!"

<hr/>

By 1898 the White Pass & Yukon Route connected Skagway, Alaska, with Whitehorse, the capital town of the Yukon. This saved untold numbers of pack animals' lives, since Canadian authorities demanded that prospectors each have one ton of supplies with them before they would be allowed into Canada. This sound law helped prevent the cheechakos—Chinook for greenhorn—from starving to death in the interior.

By late 1897 and early 1898, more than one hundred thousand gold seekers had ridden steamers up the Inside Passage and disembarked in Dyea and Skagway, frenzied for their chance at the waiting riches of the Klondike gold fields. Despite this, only one-third of them ended up making the overland trip to the Klondike, and even fewer found color in significant quantities.

But it was these numbers of stampeders that convinced investors to build the WP&YR railway. And though it was built in an astonishing record time—twenty-six months from first to last, using thirty-five thousand men and 450 tons of explosives—the ten-million-dollar undertaking came at the tail end of the great rush. It still managed to fulfill its primary mission of ferrying passengers inland in a most expeditious manner.

In 1994 the White Pass & Yukon Route railway was designated an International Historic Civil Engineering Landmark, making it one of only thirty-six such honored man-made marvels in the world, among them the Eiffel Tower, the Panama Canal, and the Statue of Liberty. The WP&YR railway still runs today as Alaska's most popular shore-based excursion, ferrying nearly a half-million tourists along 67.5 miles of the original 110-mile route, from May to September, from Skagway, Alaska, to Carcross, Yukon.

46

THE SCOURGE
OF SKAGWAY
(1898)

Infamous con man Jefferson "Soapy" Smith becomes the unofficial mayor of Skagway, Alaska's most boisterous gold-mining boomtown. The bunko king rules the burg from his saloon, ruthlessly conning locals out of their hard-earned profits. Eventually townsfolk tire of his heavy-handed ways, and vigilantes instigate a showdown on Juneau Wharf.

Jeff Smith's Parlor," Young Scott Maher said aloud as he read the sign on the freshly built little saloon. Looks clean and tidy. OK, here I go. One drink and then I'll get outfitted, top up the provisions, and off I go to find my fortune.

Within seconds of stepping into the bar, Maher felt as if he had made a mistake. There was nothing specific he could point to, but he felt a sense of unease. He reached back to put his hand on the doorknob, ready to leave, when a tall, thin man with dark, kind eyes and a dark beard with a cigar poking out of the middle of it smiled at him from the bar. "What'll it be . . . newcomer, are you?"

Maher nodded. "I'm Maher, Scott Maher."

The man's smile broadened. "Well, then, Mr. Maher. Let me buy you a drink."

The young man must have looked confused, because the man at the bar said, "You have every right to be suspicious. This town is teeming with flimflammers, but I can assure you, you've stepped into a nest of mostly decent folks." He winked at a table full of men engrossed in a card game. "Ain't that right, boys?" The men offered up vehement testament to the bearded man's statement.

"Come on over, one drink. Maybe I can point you in the right direction. Skagway can be confusing at the best of times."

The man put an arm around the youth's shoulders and ushered him over to the bar. "Well now, as to why I'm buying you a drink—simple. I own this place. And you're new in town. And it's good business to treat new citizens with a bit of respect. And besides," the man plucked the brown cigar from his mouth and licked his lips. He leaned close to the young man. "I was new in town once myself, and I know how difficult it can be. So I vowed I'd do my best to make all newcomers to Skagway feel a bit welcome. Though we are not without our conveniences, here in Skagway, Mr. Maher."

"How do you mean?"

"I mean telegraph, good sir."

"But I didn't think there was telegraph service anywhere in Alaska yet."

"You must be reading old news, then. For I own a telegraph office, and I can assure you, my fine fellow, that Jefferson Davis Smith's telegrams always make it through! It's not a luxury you'd want to indulge in frequently, but the occasional telegram from here back to families in the States has put many a mother's heart at ease and saved more than a few marriages, I can assure you."

Scott Maher considered this for a moment. He had to admit, it made sense. "How much to send a telegram?"

"That's where it gets a little embarrassing," said Smith. "At five dollars, it's not cheap. But for that, I will reduce the rate of a response, should one be required."

The young man found himself in a smaller room off the back of the saloon, sending a telegram to his brother. As he lifted free his wallet from an inner coat pocket, Smith casually glanced over.

"Boy, don't take this the wrong way, but," he gestured with a nod toward the bulging wallet, "you ought not to keep your entire stake in your wallet like that. There is a nefarious element in this town, much as it pains me to say so, being the unofficial mayor and all. But these devils will roll you for your stake as sure as I'm standing here giving you free advice."

"Well, I, uh, it's not all here in my wallet. I also have a money belt."

"Good, good. Keep it tight about your person and safe, promise me that?"

The youth nodded, handed Smith the five dollars, and thanked him profusely.

"I assume you'll be around town for a day or so, outfitting yourself," he said to the boy as they walked back into the saloon.

"Yes, I thought I'd find a room, then see about getting ready for the interior."

"Good plan."

"Well, I thank you, Mr. Smith. Much obliged to you."

"Say no more about it, son." Smith stuck out his hand. They shook, firm grips, and both smiled. "Welcome to Skagway."

He waved his cigar as the young man departed, then slid a chair over to the card game. "Palmer and Hopkins, I want you both to roll him tonight. Kid's got a wad on him that could choke a brace of mules. Wallet in his coat pocket and a money belt around his midsection. Got it?"

Both men smiled and nodded, looking back to their cards.

"Oh, and those contributions we sort of collected from the good people of Skagway on behalf of the new parson?" He waited until his men all looked at him.

One of them said, "Yeah, boss?"

"Well, I gave it to him this afternoon."

"You did what?" Reverend Bowers stood up, his ruddy jowls inflamed.

Smith laughed. "Settle down, Reverend. I was merely buying his goodwill."

The men appeared confused. Soapy sighed and said, "Tonight the poor new preacher will be robbed in his sleep. Shame that, really. Skagway's such a nice little town. But these things will happen."

The men joined their boss in laughter.

<hr />

"I tell you, men, we need to do something and do something damn quick about Soapy Smith and his gang. They've got a stranglehold on this town, and every time they lead another man down the garden path like they did to good Mr. John D. Stewart here, why, that's one step closer we all are to ruin and decay."

The speaker, Frank Reid, paused, his arms folded across his chest. A surveyor by trade, he was also an outspoken firebrand who, as most folks could attest, had long ago reached his snapping point with regard to the Soapy Smith conundrum. But he needed the help of other concerned citizens.

Reid held up his hands, "Now look, if we let this band of thieves lop off our horns and corral us, we'll have nothing left. I say we take action while we still can!" Reid pounded a fist on the table in front of him and gestured at the

Top: America's most famous con man, king of the bunko artists Jefferson Davis "Soapy" Smith, held court in his Skagway bar, "Jeff Smith's Parlor." He also controlled the boomtown's purse strings with heavy-handed, illegal tactics and a gang of thugs.

Bottom: A grisly peek at con man Soapy Smith's autopsy after he lost his life in the infamous shoot-out on Juneau Wharf on July 8, 1898. *Courtesy Alaska State Library*

angry miner who stood beside him. "Mr. Stewart here worked his back to the breaking point for that poke of twenty-seven hundred dollars, and he gets to Skagway and who does he encounter? That rascal 'Reverend' Bowers, Soapy Smith's right-hand man."

Angry oaths filled the air in the little meeting room. One of the men spoke, "What do you propose we do, Reid? Smith already ignored the judge from Dyea."

"Then we take him by force, brace him. We're all fair enough with a gun. If we can get the drop on them, we can get the judge to serve warrants."

"Meeting at the pier, are they?" Soapy Smith buckled on his twin six-guns and snatched up his rifle. "Come on along now, boys. I've need of each and every one of you. I will show you how it's done. Why, I'll chase the sons-of-guns into the bay!"

Within minutes his long legs carried him across the little town to the waterfront. He stormed onto the pier, and his footsteps hammered hard against the timbers lining his path.

"Halt there!"

"That you, Frank Reid?" said Soapy.

"It is, and I know your vile voice, Smith. Get on back. This meeting isn't for the likes of you."

"Why you insolent—I run this town, you hear me? You think you and your vigilantes will change that?" Smith quickened his pace and brought his rifle to bear on Reid's chest, even as he stepped in close. Reid tried to knock it aside with a chopping forearm as he raised his own rifle. It was the wrong move to make.

Simultaneous shots cracked the night air, and the two men collapsed in a pile on top of each other, bleeding and twitching.

Soapy Smith, shot in the chest, was nearly dead when he hit the pier. Reid, gutshot, writhed in his own private agony, delivered to him by the man who had caused him such great personal and civic torment for the previous year.

Jefferson Davis "Soapy" Smith died almost immediately during the brief gundown on Juneau Wharf on the evening of July 8, 1898. Frank Reid lingered for five days, then succumbed to his wound. Today Soapy Smith and Frank Reid are buried in the local cemetery, not all that far apart. It is also not surprising to note that Soapy Smith's grave sees far more visitors than does Frank Reid's.

During the hellish night that followed, Skagway teemed with citizens suddenly filled with the feeling of freedom from the oppression they endured under Smith's reign. They ran rampant throughout the town, tracking down anyone who had been in Soapy's employ. Stewart's gold was returned to him, as most of it was found among Smith's possessions, locked in a trunk. Smith's cohorts were rounded up, and eleven of them were transported to Sitka. They were put on trial and all received light sentences, as proof of the numerous murders of miners for their pokes they committed could not be substantiated.

Within a year of the gunfight on Juneau Wharf, Skagway had established a town council, and a low crime rate and was well on its way toward civic stability. Schools were built, and cultural events became top-shelf affairs. By 1899 Skagway was home to debating clubs, literary societies, and a band of the Arctic Brotherhood, a fraternal order that helped settle claim disputes among members.

❖

In 1887 Captain Billy Moore settled on the spot that would become Skagway a decade later. The former riverboat captain staked a claim on 160 acres of waterfront, moved his family there, and waited, hoping that should the Yukon open up with the sort of massive gold strike he wanted to see, his claim would be well positioned as the most ideal landing place for ingress to the interior. So confident was Captain Billy of his assessment of the Yukon's impending gold bonanza that he built a wharf and slashed trails through White Pass. News of a gold rush came, all right, but the newcomers overwhelmed the good captain and ousted him from his hard-won land. He did eventually sell his wharf for $175,000 and later sued the town—and won—for reimbursement for his lost land.

Three months after the first gold hounds arrived in Skagway in 1897, Soapy Smith and five of his most faithful cohorts wandered into town, having *already grown fat bilking greenhorns in Denver and Seattle. Skagway, in its first official year in existence, was called "a nightmare of lawlessness." And no one contributed to and nurtured that lawlessness more than Soapy Smith.*

Oddly enough, Soapy Smith's shooter, the upstanding vigilante Frank Reid, was the same man who, barely a year before, had led a group of influxers in seizing Captain Billy Moore's land. That he had become, one year later, one of Skagway's leading citizens is indicative of the town's rapidly transforming identity from roughest-of-the-rough mine camp to a respectable town people weren't afraid to live in.

47

CLAIM JUMPER EXTRAORDINAIRE
(1900)

In the largest-ever case of claim jumping, Alexander McKenzie of North Dakota heads a big-money conglomerate that swindles, bilks, and thieves hundreds of Alaskan miners working backbreaking hours, seven days a week. The outcome is anything but predictable.

◆

The big, brooding brute that was Alexander McKenzie stood on a rock above the mud by one of the three wagons that moments before had disgorged the gangs of thugs he had hired just for this purpose. This was going as well as he could expect, considering he was in an uncivilized place, surrounded by raw wilderness and people who would very soon want to kill him.

But now that he had his friend, Minneapolis lawyer Arthur H. Noyes, on the bench, and another friend, Joseph K. Wood, of Montana, appointed as federal district attorney in Nome, per orders from Washington, he knew there was truly very little that could slow him down in his appropriation of promising claims. And the best part of it all, he thought, nearly giggling at the notion, is that it was all legal. Well, close enough for government work, as he'd heard said. That did bring a laugh from him, though he quashed it in time to see the foreman of the thugs heading back toward him. "How did it go?"

"About as you would expect, Mr. McKenzie. The Wild Goose is about the richest mine up back of Nome. But they weren't expecting us, so after letting fly with a few choice words you wouldn't use in front of your sister, these men saw the value in backing off. My boys are escorting them down off the property just now."

They watched a silent procession of a few men being directed by the armed thugs down the trail and off the claim. "We had a bit of a tussle with them over the fact that they no longer own anything setting on the claim."

"That's right. As the judge said, I am entitled to any and all personal property residing on the claim, including dust and nuggets. I assume you have them."

"Yes, sir. Here's what I gathered, and there's more, too."

"Then you're a fool. In business you should always keep a little for yourself."

The thug foreman didn't quite know what to make of his new employer. But he kept the man's words in mind and determined to get his share in the future, come hell or high water.

"Let's get on up there. I sent you all ahead because I don't relish the idea of men trying to kill me."

"What makes you think they would do that, Mr. McKenzie?"

"My God, are you really a protector and security guard?"

"Of course, sir. Why do you ask?"

"Well, no man in his right mind would give up his hard-won claim without a fight. I, for one, would kill for it."

"Kill, sir?"

As they talked, they walked and soon found themselves at the cabin of the Wild Goose Mine's foreman, Gabe Price. The men entered, and McKenzie paused in the doorway, taking in the interior of the cabin, well lit by a lantern. "What is that heavenly smell?"

"He was just about to set down to his afternoon meal, sir, when we caught up with him. You want me to have his belongings burned?"

"What? No, no, nothing so drastic as that. Never let it be said I'm a cruel man. I only want his gold. He may keep the rest—once I've finished searching through it all, of course." But first things first, he thought. I will personally see to it that his meal doesn't go to waste. McKenzie pulled out the chair at the table, sat down, picked up the man's utensils, and tucked into Gabe Price's meal. Hmm, he thought as he chewed. Still tolerably hot.

Once he'd finished with the meal, McKenzie left a few thugs at the Wild Goose, then went on to the Pioneer and seized control of that mine as well. The owners of the mines set their lawyers on the cases, but by then Judge Noyes had moved on to the Yukon Delta to visit other portions of his new domain.

Later, at his hotel in Nome, McKenzie shared a drink with Judge Noyes. "Do you know, Noyes, that we now control most of the best mines in Nome? And as for most of the rest, well, we could probably have them if we wanted. I don't like to be spread too thin, though. Give me a barnyard of Swedes, and I'll drive them like sheep." He lifted his glass. "To these damnable Swedes," he said, raising his glass high. "They've worked so very hard, and now we're reaping the rewards. Lucky us."

"Why, he's nothing but a claim jumper!" The thin miner named Rupe leaned on his shovel and looked at his mining partner, who stood before him reading an official document.

"It appears," continued the other man, as his bushy eyebrows arched high above the tops of his wire-rim spectacles, "that this high-binding claim jumper McKenzie also knows the president of the United States and has the two new Alaska lawyer-types in his trouser pockets—for safekeeping, of course."

"Don't they all." The thin man nodded. "But what does this mean for us? I got too much invested in this claim to go and give it all away. Besides, she's just about paying off now. We're clearing pretty near a thousand dollars every three days. Now, you tell me where I'm going to be able to do that again."

"The wife, she ain't a-gonna like this, not one bit."

"I told you not to marry, didn't I?"

"This ain't funny, Rupe. I'm sunk."

As they spoke, a wagonload of ham-fisted men, most of whom they had never seen before, rolled to a stop just up the rutted, mud lane from their claim, to the claim of their neighbor and friend, Big John the Basque.

"What do you suppose they're going to do?"

"I don't know, Rupe, but whatever it is, they'll be fixing to do it to us next. Let's get our pokes and get ourselves clubs. You still got that revolver?"

"Yes, well . . . it won't do us no good."

"Why's that?"

The Merchant's Bank in Nome, Alaska, shows off its gold holdings in June 1906: $1,250,000, a sizable sum even by today's standards. A few years earlier, Nome was in the grip of acute gold fever—and the largest case of claim jumping in US history, courtesy of the crooked politico Alexander McKenzie and his heinous henchmen. *Courtesy Library of Congress*

Rupe looked at his wet boots. "I forgot to buy them bullets you said I should. Just plumb neglected it last time I was in Nome."

"Well," sighed his partner. "I guess we'll find out soon enough." He secreted several buckskin pouches into his waistband and waited for the wagonload of thugs to arrive.

In San Francisco, forty-five hundred miles south, an honest judge received word from the lawyers representing the Wild Goose, the Pioneer, and other mines "appropriated" by McKenzie and associates. He recognized the blatant thievery taking place, cloaked in thinly veiled lawfulness, so he sent two federal marshals northward, passage booked on the very last ship of the season to arrive from the south in Norton Sound before ice up. They were armed with a warrant for McKenzie's arrest.

McKenzie watched the two smartly dressed men enter the front doors of the dining room of the Golden Gate Hotel. He was halfway through his meal, and as he watched them shift their glances around the crowded room, their eyes settled on him and locked for a moment. They walked toward him, slight smiles playing on their faces. McKenzie finished chewing the steak in his jowled mouth and washed it down with half a glass of red wine.

"Alexander McKenzie?" said one of the men standing before his table.

People at surrounding tables watched. This was fast becoming annoying. McKenzie reached for the wine bottle. "What might I help you with, gentlemen?"

The man who spoke slipped a hand into his inner breast pocket and pulled out a leather wallet. He flipped it open and flashed a badge. "Federal marshal, McKenzie. Let's go."

"What? What's the meaning of this?" McKenzie felt his shirt collar tighten, knew he may have overplayed one of the many hands he'd kept on the table for the past few lucrative months in Alaska. But keep playing it, Alexander, my boy, he told himself. Keep playing it, to the very end. . . .

The men stared at him. He was about to offer them a glass of wine, and began to motion them to sit down and join him, when the second man spoke. He sounded remarkably like the first. Did they stamp them out in a tool and die? wondered McKenzie. The thought almost brought a smile to his lips, then he heard what the man said.

"You can come with us now, or we can make a bigger scene and you can still come with us. Your decision, McKenzie."

The big man leaned back in his chair, pretending not to notice the stares from nearly every damn face at the other tables in the place. He ran his tongue over his lips, sucking bits of food from between his teeth. Then he snatched his white linen napkin from his lap, tossed it on the table, and said, "Splendid idea, gentlemen. Let's take a stroll, shall we? Perhaps I can interest you in a fine cigar. I always find it's the prefect way to top off a meal."

He strode between them toward the door. They clung to either side of him as if they were attached. Once on the street he turned on them and gritted his teeth. "Do you have any idea who I am?"

The two men didn't change their expressions.

Press on, Alexander, he told himself. Play out the hand. "I hope you both enjoy your jobs, because after tonight, you will have them only as pathetic little memories."

One of the men sighed. "Mr. McKenzie, let's go to your bank, shall we?"

Within the hour, representatives from the Wild Goose and Pioneer mine companies had possession of the six hundred thousand dollars recovered from the vault. And Alexander McKenzie was bundled onto the last southbound vessel out of Nome, along with his two federal marshal escorts.

At its core, the bill McKenzie helped push through Congress removed language that protected aliens' rights to own land in the United States. This enabled the crooked McKenzie and his cronies to gobble up Nome's numerous—and profitable—legitimately held claims, many of which were established primarily by Swedes and other foreigners. McKenzie became puppet master behind the appointment of the two new judges, positions conjured to help Alaska become a more regulated, less roguish territory. The two judges happened to be two of McKenzie's old friends, because he was acquainted with people in President McKinley's administration.

Alexander McKenzie was sentenced to prison for one year on conspiracy charges in his role as mastermind of the plot to assume control of Nome's richest gold claims. He served three months of his sentence before being pardoned in May, 1901, by President McKinley. McKenzie eventually became one of North Dakota's wealthiest men. He even had a county and two towns named after him.

48

KLONDIKE HELL RIDE
(1900)

Within months of each other, two men attempt the same ludicrous pursuit—
and live to tell the tale of how they rode twelve hundred miles, from Dawson
to the new Nome diggings, in the middle of an Alaskan winter . . . on bicycles.

◆

You can't be serious! You'll be killed before you get ten miles!"

· Ed Jesson laughed as he wheeled the bicycle out of the front door of the Alaska Commercial Company general mercantile in Dawson. "Why, sir, you don't sound much like someone who wants to make a sale. What did you think I was spending $150 on this bicycle for? To wheel it around Dawson?"

The clerk shook his head. "But . . . Nome, man! Don't you know how far that is from here?"

"As a matter of fact, I do. It's about one thousand miles, give or take a few hundred."

"It's only February, you could get yourself a sled, a team, and mush out."

Hmm," said Jesson, rubbing his chin, his eyebrows arched together. "That's not a bad idea." Then he turned to the clerk. "Except that decent dogs are going for $350 and more, and you still have to feed them."

The clerk said nothing.

Jesson continued. "So I'll take my chances with this here contraption."

"Well, do you know how to ride it, then?"

Jesson stopped on the porch out front and looked down at the bicycle. "No, can't say that I do." He looked up, hopefully. "Do you?"

The clerk shook his head and disappeared back inside the store.

It was February 23, 1900, and Ed Jesson had been gone a day from Dawson, riding down the frozen Yukon River toward Nome, site of the latest gold rush. Early word was that at Cape Nome, clear on the other end of Alaska, on the Seward Peninsula, there had been a slew of promising strikes. Jesson had known that if he didn't act soon, he would regret not trying. Although he'd been in Alaska for four years, he'd not yet struck it. And he darn sure wasn't making much hunting caribou.

All this he thought about and not for the last time did he doubt his decision to make the trek . . . and on a bicycle. It had taken him the better part of a week of practice until he felt confident enough to try the bike on the frozen Yukon River, which was to be his primary roadway. He'd figured that if he could travel fifty miles a day, he would be able to stop at every other roadhouse, since they were located approximately twenty-five miles apart.

But now as he rolled but a few miles away from the first night's roadhouse, he began to have serious misgivings. It wasn't that the bicycle wasn't working. On the contrary, it was working just fine. Yesterday had been twenty degrees below zero, and she still rolled ahead. But this morning, it had been forty-eight degrees below zero, and as he pumped ever harder on his stiffened wheels, he could see that the bicycle's rubber tires were frozen straight through and that the oil in the bearings had seized. The last straw came when he found he could not both steer and raise his arms to warm his frostbitten nose.

He was saved, a short time later, by a native and his dogsled team. Soon the thermometer began to reflect a warming tendency, at least for a little while, so Jesson once again took to his river route on the Yukon. And the day was a good one for him—he traveled fifty miles before stopping for lunch.

One day in the middle of his journey, a particularly severe blast of arctic wind pummeled into Jesson and lifted him off the ground, spun him in the air, and slammed him down hard on a stretch of toothy ice. After extricating himself from the wreckage, Jesson found that his hands had been skinned and his knees had rapped hard against the unyielding surface. He swayed on all fours for a few moments, watching the blood drip from his battered, stinging nose and waiting for his vision to spiral back into something close to normal.

There has to be an easier way to live, he thought. Then he saw his bicycle—one of the handlebars had snapped off. He groaned and stood, steadying himself against the wind and the bike, at the same time. "Curse my foul luck," he said and then he laughed. "Could have been worse—I could be dead!"

He looked the bicycle over and determined that he would need to effect substantial repairs. But first he'd try to make it to a camp or the next roadhouse,

Dog teams were a vital mode of transporting food, people, gear, and gold in the Yukon, where much of the landscape was plugged tight with snow six months or more a year. Alternate means of transport—ice skates, sails on sleds, and even bicycles—were also employed to travel the long, frozen miles. *Courtesy Library of Congress*

though he doubted he might find such shelter. They were never around when you needed them. But he kept his fingers crossed in his fur mittens for a passing sled team with which he might hitch a ride. His knees ached him something fierce, and he had to limp the entire way, though he did manage to limber up after a bit.

He estimated he'd gone nearly four miles before he saw the wavering light of a campfire. "Halloo the camp!"

A handful of cautious shouts greeted him. As he approached, he found it to be a ramshackle lean-to with a welcoming fire blazing before it. The men, haggard prospectors by the looks of them, welcomed him to the fire, and within seconds of seeing his conveyance, barraged him with questions. He soon supplemented their meager tea, beans, hot cakes, and mush with butter, two cans of milk, bacon, crackers, and a fry pan. A great repast was had, and Jesson's flagging spirits rose, buoyed by the companionship and curiosity of the prospectors. In the morning they helped him find suitable cedar and he repaired his handlebars.

Days later, Jesson departed from the river route at the little settlement of Kaltag and headed due west, the subsequent frozen tundra not quite as rewarding to travel on as the smoother river. And worse, there were no roadhouses, though he did manage to bunk frequently with native Indians. And so it went until, a month after he departed Dawson, he rolled, plagued by a recent bout of near-snowblindness, into Nome. The newspapers from the States that he had packed along for the ride made him as much a celebrity as did his incredible feat. So popular did he become in Nome that he rarely had to buy a drink for himself all winter long.

Max Hirschberg knew he was about to get a dunking in the Yukon River. He'd been warned that this might well happen, and he knew it was a distinct possibility, having left so late in the year. But there was no turning back, he told himself, as he pedaled harder and fought to stay upright, as he had for hundreds of miles over seemingly endless days.

And through it all, even when the weather slowed him, or when he had broken a series of pedals, he managed to keep the gold in mind. He had to get to the diggings at Nome, for that's where fortunes were found, no matter what the old sourdough back in Dawson had said to him. Max secretly doubted if the old man understood the way things operated anymore. Max was in the grip of the gold fever, and he knew he had to get there as soon as possible. The old-timer had told him, "You'll get there in plenty of time. And when you do, there'll still be plenty of the dust for you, mark my words."

Easy for him to say, thought Max. He wasn't the one on the bike, risking life and limb for a chance at the gold. As he pedaled, despite the hardships he'd been through on this trip, Max knew he didn't want to be anywhere else. Especially now that he was almost there.

As if to emphasize that thought, Max felt the patched and battered bike slip sideways and his conditioned reflexes automatically jerked to correct for the slide, as he had so many times on this trip. But within that split-second, he knew something else was wrong. As he laid the bicycle down on the wet surface of the frozen bay, Max saw the reason for the slipup: His chain had snapped. Of all the lousy luck. He dragged the bicycle upright, untied his parcels and scant gear, then upended the contraption and set to work, confident that he could effect a repair.

Long minutes later, and with cold, aching fingertips, Max had to admit that he was licked. He stood up and stretched his back as he looked around at the landscape. As always, it stunned him with its beauty, a mixed vista of mountains, and flat as could be stretching toward the coast. Here I am, he thought, still east of Nome, and the cursed chain couldn't have held out just a while longer. He sighed, flipped the bicycle upright, and lashed his gear onto the frame in its usual positions. As he secured the various wrapped parcels, he fastened the top button of his mackinaw against the buffeting winds that pressed it close to his body.

Then an idea hit him. He retrieved a solid pole, shucked his coat and rigged it, and, with this new mast and sail at his back, he climbed aboard. After a few false starts, Max found himself rocketing toward Nome, despite the broken chain. In fact, the injured piece meant no speed control. He traveled so fast at times that he was forced to steer into the softer, slushed snow at the edges of the track to help control his speed. He howled into the wind as he rocketed along. Of all the long moments on this journey that had been equally harrowing and thrilling, this was easily the most exhilarating.

◆

On May 19, 1900, Max Hirschberg rolled into Nome, having traveled twelve hundred miles since his departure from Dawson, on March 2, 1900. During the trip he celebrated his twentieth birthday. In his later years, at his wife's urging, Hirschberg wrote an account of the journey so that his children and grandchildren might know of his amazing adventure. He passed away in 1964, and his firsthand tale was later published in Alaska magazine.

If it can be said that one of these two adventuresome men had an easier time than the other, perhaps it is true of Ed Jesson, for he was able to travel on the Yukon River when it was fully frozen, unlike Max Hirschberg, whose trip took place later in the season and so, unfortunately, subjected him to stretches of thawing ice and rougher going.

In addition to Jesson and Hirschberg, it is reported that at least two other men made the same amazing bicycle trek that winter.

49

NOME'S WORST STORM
(1900)

In September 1900 a three-day tempest ravages the overpopulated beach at Nome, ripping away tents, equipment, and supplies. An unknown number of miners are swept out to sea, and four ships are brutally peeled apart in the roiling surf.

◆

L awrence Filbertson pulled his eyes from the fascinating scene emerging before him and returned to his task of writing to his mother. The letter was the latest in a long string of weekly dispatches he had promised to send to her from Alaska's gold fields. Or "the promised land," as he'd referred to it before he left that small town in Kentucky two years before. He'd heard that the gold seekers went as far as Dawson City, clear up in the Klondike, in Canada. He'd never made it that far, his money having given out in Skagway, but he had managed to keep body and soul alive working odd jobs and eventually getting hired on as an amalgamator with a mining firm. It was his job to combine the found dust with quicksilver, wrench it until it formed into lumps, then weigh it.

> *It is tedious work, mother, but rest assured I am making a little something now and should have money to send to you before long.*

Even as he painstakingly penciled those words, he knew that it might be longer than he suspected. Nome was fit to burst, and all because of the dust at the beach. He'd never seen so many tents in one place, nor beasts of burden, nor stacked crates from all the barges that seemed to get dragged to shore without letup. Where do they all come from?

> *And the contraptions these newcomers brought with them to Nome, the City of the Golden Sands, mother, well I heard one man*

refer to it all as "jackass machinery," and I cannot quibble with his assessment. All of these machines make a lot of noise and require fuels of some sort, come in varying girths and colors. Some have windmills for their power needs.

Most of them have long pipes which the operators stick into the watery sands and then this sand gets sucked up to the machine, which is supposed to sift it out. All well and good, you say, but this is the sort of thing that a man and a shovel can do all day without much letup. These machines, from what I can see, take constant fussing and fidgeting. And I guess I wouldn't make such a hue and cry over someone else's machinery except that I heard that one company, the Mongollon Exploration Company, spent seventy-four thousand dollars on their machine. Yes, you read that right, mother. I just hope they know how much sand that thing has to sift in order to begin paying for itself.

I have taken to wearing my money on my person, for it is a hard thing to work all day and come home and find not only that your savings are gone, but that your tent and belongings are gone, too. But that is the way of things here on the beach at Nome. I daren't venture into town, either, for I have heard that it is much the same and worse, with all manner of unspeakable activity and lowbrow characters slow-walking the muddy lanes the townies are calling "streets." But really, the theft is the worst. Am nearly exhausted lugging all my own gear with me to work each day for fear someone will walk off with it while I work. But the thieves must have their day, I suppose. I have heard that law will arrive at some point. I am not holding my breath.

The hardest is to see grown old sourdoughs break down and cry—one even shot himself—because in the night someone had made off with their dogs. I was told just this morning that the crime isn't relegated to the beach, though here it is most rampant. But the miners inland have taken to lowering their food down their shafts in an effort to save a morsel for themselves.

One store in town suffered a mighty loss, and with it the savings of a good many hardworking folks here on the beach. It seems that when thieves couldn't figure out how to open the storekeep's safe, they hooked onto it and dragged it straight out the wall, taking the wall with it. They were not caught.

In another instance, someone had built up a fire in their stove, in their wall tent, then went to retrieve a bit of something to cook for supper. When he returned, he found that his stove, with the fire still smoking and puffing, was gone. I tell you, mother, life here is a dire thing.

My biggest fear is that when the stormy season comes, the beach will be a place of desolation and ruin. An old-timer who has lived in these parts for decades told me that southern storms ravage the land hereabouts on a twice-yearly basis, in the fall and again in the spring. He has been up and down this beach, telling folks, warning them to beware and clear off, but they laugh at him and tell him he just wants their claims and anyway he's not getting their claims, nor gold, nosiree. He looks as though he's about to weep, but he ends up walking away, shaking his head, near tears. I shared a meal with him, and he told me all about the storms.

It is August now and fall is coming. And after that, winter's wrath. I have been through enough of these. I'm not so sure I want to put up with Alaska's cold shoulder any longer. But I'll have to make up my mind soon, else I will be iced-in with the rest of the criminals and people with more hope than sense. On second thought, perhaps this is just where I belong.

Your loving son, Lawrence

P.S.: Tell my young cousins that a genuine sourdough wishes them well and tells them to work hard and do not travel to the Land of the Midnight Sun!

The discovery of gold in Nome by the three "Lucky Swedes" in 1898 caused Alaska's biggest gold rush. By the summer of 1900, twenty thousand gold seekers set up a crude tent city along the shore. On a whim, someone panned the beach. Soon, one million dollars had been panned from the reddish-black sands of Nome Beach. Placer mining in the Nome region continues today. *Courtesy Library of Congress*

Dear Mother,

As you may have surmised, I am still here in Nome. And I am still alive. I almost wasn't, however. Do you recall that letter I sent to you in late August? Well, in that letter I mentioned that an old sourdough who is familiar with such things mentioned to all and sundry here on the beach that fall and spring storms came at the beach from the south. Well, it turns out he was correct. But there is so much gold fever clouding peoples' minds hereabouts that they ignored him.

Late in September, I will never forget it, for it was hell, there were thousands of people on the beach, in tents, and many of them had their own mules and oxen and donkeys and dogs and lord, I don't know what else.

If you cannot tell by my tone, then I will let you know that the storm came in with the vengeance of an angry bull grizzly, wide as all Alaska, and as long as a three-day train. And not only did it hammer hard at the coast, but every time the waves pulled back, there was less and less to see.

It hit so suddenly at the beginning that people were caught unawares. Some of them, I fear, never woke up until they felt the cold clinging fingers of death caress them—death in this case in the vicious, killing waves. Shipping crates as big as two ox wagons and filled with machinery and goods of all sorts were there one moment and gone the next.

People who could have made it to the safety of the high ground foolishly waited too long, scrabbling for one last thing to load into their arms, hoping to get their goods to safety, and then they were just gone, ripped from the earth as if they'd never been here among us.

When the storm passed, after three days, we went out, though there was very little we could do. Still, we tried, going out there, forming human chains and looking for survivors. And all we found were a few dead people wedged underneath stubborn timbers sticking up out of the sand like the rib bones of some poor, picked-over beast long since dead. And that's about what Nome looks like now.

The entire length of Front Street, our fair city's main road, was washed away, and when I say that, I mean it was taken away and no longer exists. The buildings, the people in them, all gone. The biggest shock for me was seeing the ravaged hulks of the four great ships that were anchored in the harbor.

I had been told by more than one old sourdough that they would be safe, as that's what ships are meant for and built for, to ride out such storms, for they bob and wobble, but they don't topple. Well, Mother, that is not what happened. For those ships were mostly gone, and what was left were the gaping, ravaged hulls dashed in the surf and washed ashore. There were bodies in them too, whether they were from the beach or the bodies of sailors, I do not know. But it was a bad storm. That old sourdough was right, after all. Cold comfort to him, I am sure. I hope he is well, wherever he is.

Mother, I am forever a changed man and as soon as I can, I am coming home to ol' Kentuck. There is nothing for me here but death, bad memories, and a long, cold winter of starvation and sadness ahead. I do not know if I will make it out before we are iced-in. But I will try.

Your loving son, Lawrence

Lawrence Filbertson set down his pencil and regarded the letter for a moment. Then he folded it and tucked it into the envelope. He propped it against his little oil lamp and pulled on his coat. He felt like taking a walk, and one quick visit to McMann's claim couldn't hurt. He had offered to let Lawrence buy in, after all. What harm could one peek do?

◆

By the summer of 1898, word leaked out that gold had been found in and around Nome, and a handful of men ventured to the region. They struck enough gold to convince them that filing a claim would be worth their while. A small band of men were more convinced than others and filed ninety claims. In September 1898 three Scandinavians called the "Lucky Swedes" hit pay dirt at Anvil Creek. Within a few months, word truly leaked out and the rush lived up to its name. Within a year a tent city, home to thousands of gold seekers, bloomed on the previously barren beach.

By the end of 1899, Nome had become the epitome of a thrumming, thriving gold town, with one hundred saloons (twenty-two of which bothered to apply for licenses in that largely lawless place), a half-dozen bakeries, as many laundries, a dozen general mercantile stores, numerous smaller specialty stores including bootmakers, butcher shops, a bookstore, a bank, plus four hotels, six restaurants, barbershops, a hospital, and more. If that weren't enough, all manner of specialists plied their skills, including but not limited to two paperhangers, two photographers, tinsmiths, sign painters, three watchmakers, two dentists, a dozen doctors, twenty lawyers, and one massage therapist.

50

BLUE PARKA MAN
(1905)

In 1905 a man wearing a blue parka and toting a Winchester rifle gets the drop on a number of miners along well-traveled trails near Fairbanks. Though he takes their pokes and other valuables, this highwayman of the Alaska Gold Rush is regarded by many—even some of his victims—as a throwback to another era, a Robin Hood of the icy trail, for his tendency toward leniency.

◈

Hey!"

The three other shotgun-toting gold-dust guards all spun their attentions from scanning the low-rolling, arid hills surrounding Fairbanks. They looked at the youngest of their quartet, Billy Timmins.

"What are you on about now?" The senior guard, Old Rolf, scowled at the youth.

"I know what you're thinking, but I swear this time I seen a snatch of blue, just there, back in the trees." The young man pointed, excitement writ large on his light features.

They all spun in the direction he pointed.

"Well, fine, but who cares? I ain't stoppin'," said the driver. "We was hired by the miners and the banks to get the dust from these mines all over Fairbanks, and if you think I'm going to set still and jaw about it, well, that ain't getting the job done, is it?" The driver spoke the truth. Hearty strikes had been made in Fairbanks Creek, Easter Creek, Dome, Gulch, and Fox since 1902, three years prior, and showed no signs of slowing up.

On this day they all shared the same thought: Until 1905 it had been business as usual, with people such as themselves hired to haul the mines' gold into Fairbanks for safekeeping, and on all manner of conveyance too, from mules towing sleds, and often in packs on the miners' backs. But then came the new year and the damnable Blue Parka Man and his damnable Winchester rifle. Old Rolf spit out his chaw, angry at the very thought of the bandit.

Rolf could well understand the boy's nervousness. The Blue Parka Man had so far made a mockery of Fairbanks's marshal, George Perry, to the point where the people were beginning to rumble and squawk about starting a vigilante group. The populace was sick to death of getting robbed by the rascal every time they wanted to stretch their legs.

Even groups of people weren't safe. All they knew was that it seemed that if you were a traveler and you were carrying your poke of dust on your person, he'd have it one way or another. That and anything of value you might have with you—he'd been known to steal rings off women, pocket watches from men, and whatever else of value he took a liking to.

◆

"You been held up by him, Mr. Barber?"

The bartender pursed his lips for a moment, then nodded. "Yes, yes, Billy, I have. I won't ask you how you knew, but I will tell you. It's a damn shame when a hardworking man has to give over his hard-won gold to someone just because that person has a gun held to you. It ain't right and it ain't fair. Rest of us have to work fair and square. Why, just because everybody's pockets got some amount of gold in 'em, does that give this common thief the right to take it? And what about rings and watches passed down to men from their fathers and grandfathers?"

"Aw, Mr. Barber, you remember that old man a few weeks back? Come into town from Pedro Dome, walking down through the woods trail." He paused to wait for a response. The bartender reluctantly obliged him.

"Well, he come into town saying that when the Blue Parka Man—he was wearing a mask, remember the old man said that? That he was wearing a mask? Anyway, found out his poke only had ten dollars in it, why, he tossed it to back to the old man . . . and he tossed him coin enough out of his own pocket, told him to buy himself a drink. Then he slipped off, quiet as you please, back into the woods."

"We all heard that story, Billy. Hell, it was my saloon the old man came to. What's your point?"

"Well, my point is that, far as I knew, he's never shot no one. Hell, I heard he never even cocked that Winchester of his." Billy turned his back to the bar and looked at the small crowd, all eyes on him, everybody listening. "Hell!" The blond boy was smiling now, warming like a lit log to his subject, "For all we know, that Winchester of his might not even be loaded."

"Loaded gun or not Billy, I stared into them eyes of his," said the bartender. "Blue they were, like his damn coat, but they weren't the eyes of a man who would put up with any shenanigans."

"Aw, Mr. Barber, you're just afraid that he's stealing so that he can give it to those folks less what's the word . . . ? Privileged?"

The bartender shook his head and walked down the bar. He either had to get away from the boy or hit him, he told himself. But he couldn't let it go. He stormed back down the bar and poked a finger in the surprised youth's face. "The Blue Parka Man ain't a hero, Billy. He's a thief, and one of these days, he'll be caught and sent to prison—or hung. And I for one will be there cheering."

"Stand your ground and deliver your goods, ladies and gentlemen. This is indeed a holdup. Be sure to toss all your valuables in this sack, and we'll get along just fine."

The sack was passed around the little group. The last man to drop in his meager offering said, "Have you no shame, bandit? I am a man of the cloth."

The Blue Parka Bandit stiffened, and his rifle, which had been leveled at the man's chest, shifted a foot to the side. "Why, so you are. You are Bishop Rowe of the Episcopal Church in town! I am a member of your congregation, sir."

"Well, what are you going to do about it?"

"Why, I can tell you one thing, sir. I'll not rob you. Take your poke and the rest of it, too." He addressed the rest of the party, saying, "You have all made a donation to the church. Good day to you. Now, gather up your winnings there, bishop, and get off down the road with you all, and don't look back, or I may be tempted to shoot you."

The bandit watched the group of agitated citizens bustle away from him, then he stepped off the trail and into the woods.

The Blue Parka Bandit had escaped from this paltry little log jail before Judge Wickersham could bring him to trial, thought Marshal George Perry. And if these townsfolk or Judge Wickersham still think I am to blame, why they ought to let me hire more deputies, for I cannot be everywhere at once. Perry gritted his teeth and swore that if he ever had the chance to deal with Charles Hendrickson again, he would by gum let him have it right on the sniffer. Just for the satisfaction of it.

And you would think that such a close call would be enough for a man to turn his back on his former ways as a road agent. But not so with Hendrickson. That rogue seemed to relish the game of it all; meanwhile Perry had half of Fairbanks shouting down his neck for justice and the other half shouting in his face.

But this morning, he thought with a smile as he strode toward the courthouse, this morning, it would seem that we have him. The evidence had been enough to convince the judge that Hendrickson was the Blue Parka Bandit and that he should be remanded to prison—somewhere other than Fairbanks.

Less than an hour later, Marshal Perry got his wish, for the judge had found Hendrickson guilty and sentenced him to federal prison on McNeil Island near Tacoma, Washington. A more fitting place, Perry couldn't think of. He personally saw Hendrickson aboard and watched from shore as the boat steamed away down the Yukon River.

It wasn't until hours later that young Billy Timmins, breathless and not a little excited, and wearing a smile that Perry would later recall with contempt, burst through the jailhouse door to tell him the impossible—that Charles Hendrickson had escaped.

"What?" Perry leaped to his feet, knocking to the floor his favorite straight-back chair. "How is that? I saw him onto the steamer myself!"

"Yes, yes, you may well have—"

"I did, I tell you."

"Oh, I don't doubt you, marshal, but the bandit—"

"Stop calling him that! He's Charles Hendrickson, a common thief!"

"Yes, well, be that as it may. The band—ah, Hendrickson jumped into the river. The boat was too big and moving too fast to give chase."

"No!"

Billy nodded and smiled. "Yes, I swear it."

Marshal George Perry sat down hard in his chair and rubbed his face with his hands. He didn't doubt for a moment that Charles Hendrickson, the Blue Parka Bandit, would return to the mine trails around Fairbanks and continue to menace the populace. He just knew it.

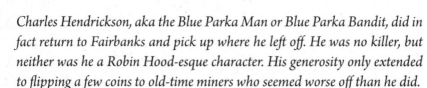

Charles Hendrickson, aka the Blue Parka Man or Blue Parka Bandit, did in fact return to Fairbanks and pick up where he left off. He was no killer, but neither was he a Robin Hood-esque character. His generosity only extended to flipping a few coins to old-time miners who seemed worse off than he did.

By the time he was finally captured, Hendrickson's notoriety had achieved widespread fame, and he was written about in newspapers throughout the States and Canada. On September 2, 1906, he was sentenced to fifteen years at the federal penitentiary at McNeil Island. Once there he tried again to escape but was unsuccessful. He was then moved to Fort Leavenworth, Kansas, where he served out his sentence.

The Fairbanks region proved especially lucrative and served, when its rush was announced, to draw gold seekers by the thousands from the playing-out diggings at Dawson City, in Canada's Yukon Territory, as well as the dwindling diggings at Nome, Alaska. By 1905 Fairbanks boasted a population of five thousand, and the hills and creeks surrounding Fairbanks were riddled with six thousand claims that generated six million dollars in dug gold in 1905 and nine million dollars in 1906. But to get at the real gold, located deep in the bedrock, big-money investors were brought in.

As a reaction to the well-earned reputation of lawlessness and debauchery that so many other Alaska mining towns had gained and cultivated, Fairbanks's citizenry worked hard to maintain a stiff, upright civic presence that did not tolerate lawlessness. And this proved largely to be the case, until the spring of 1905, when the road agent known as the Blue Parka Man began sticking up innocent travelers on the still-undeveloped trails leading in and out of town.

From January to mid-August 1905, there were at least fourteen holdups. Though not all of the robberies are attributed to the Blue Parka Bandit, it appears that he conducted most of them—and probably inspired the rest.

A BRIEF GLOSSARY OF PROSPECTING TERMS:

Argonaut: One who pursues gold; from Greek mythology, the heroes who accompanied Jason onboard the ship *Argo* in the quest for the Golden Fleece.

Assaying: The testing of ore to determine its content and quality.

Cheechako: Chinook jargon for newcomer or greenhorn.

Claim: A plot of land in a gold-producing region legally held by a person who has staked it out and officially recorded the title.

Claim Jumper: One who steals another miner's claim, often after it has been staked but before it has been officially recorded.

Color: The gold remaining in a pan after mud, sand, and gravel have been washed away.

Coyoting: A practice in which miners sink a vertical shaft, then dig tunnels that radiate outward, as if spokes on a wheel.

Drift: A mine tunnel cutting across an ore vein, often used for ventilation and communication.

Dry Gulcher: One who devalues another's property, then pays pennies on the dollar for it; also one who kills from a distance to avoid a fair fight.

Greenhorn: An inexperienced newcomer, usually ignorant of local ways and customs.

Grubstaking: The act of supplying a miner with gear or financial backing in exchange for a share of his findings.

Hard-Rock Mining: Working to extract ore that can only be removed by drilling, chipping, and blasting, often taking place underground.

High Grading: The theft of ore by miners who often take only the highest-grade ore.

Hydraulic Mining: Removing precious material from sand, mud, or gravel using pressurized water.

Lode: An obvious vein of rich ore; often the "mother lode" from which nearby veins originate.

Mother Lode: A high-yielding, primary vein of ore.

Ore: A solid material, such as quartz, from which valuable metals can be extracted.

Placer Mining: Pronounced "plasser"; the removal of minerals from the surface by washing, panning, or dredging.

Poke: A small bag or pouch used to hold a miner's gold dust or nuggets; can also refer to the contents of the pouch.

Prospecting: The search for mineral deposits, as in gold, through panning, digging, washing, and drilling.

Rocker: A cradlelike piece of equipment used to sift sand through screening; used in placer mining.

Salting: Planting rich ore samples in an unproductive mine to attract unwary buyers.

Sluice Box: A grooved wooden trough through which water is directed, separating gold from sand.

Snoose: Swedish "snus" or moist snuff tobacco, held in the lip; popular with miners.

Sourdough: A seasoned prospector wise in the ways of the trail; also fermented dough, a bit of which is used to leaven the next day's bread.

Stampeder: One who, in the grip of gold fever, races for the gold fields, largely oblivious to the harm he causes to himself or others.

Tinhorn: A contemptible person, often a card sharp, cheat, or gunfighter who goads lesser gunhands into drawing.

Yee-haa!: The favored proclamation used when a miner strikes a mother lode.

ART AND PHOTO CREDITS

Page 3: Coronado's March. Reproduction of drawing by Frederic Remington, 1897. Library of Congress, LC-USZ62-37993.

Page 16: "We have it rich." John C. H. Grabill, 1889. Library of Congress, LC-DIG-ppmsc-02669.

Page 31: The way they go to California. Illustration by N. Currier, 1849. Library of Congress, LC-USZ62-104557.

Page 40: Funeral Mountains. View is southwest from the forks of Furnace Creek. Death Valley is in the distance on the right. Photographer's shadow in the lower right. M. R. Campbell, 1901. US Geological Survey.

Page 56: Gold Fever. John C. H. Grabill, 1889. Library of Congress, LC-DIG-ppmsc-02668.

Page 63: Mining life in California. *Harper's Weekly,* October 3, 1857. Library of Congress, LC-USZ62-130289.

Page 73: A Pikes Peak prospector. William Henry Jackson, 1900. Library of Congress, LC-D4-13794.

Page 90: Loads of gold coming down trail from Tomboy Mine to Telluride, Colorado. Underwood & Underwood, 1910. Library of Congress, LC-USZ62-110843.

Page 101: Hydraulicking bench deposit on Woodin claim. Skagway district, Southeastern Alaska region, Alaska. C. W. Wright, 1903. US Geological Survey.

Page 119: In the "Bobtail" Mine, Black Hawk Canyon, Colorado. B. L. Singley, 1898. Library of Congress, LC-USZ62-55738.

Page 131: Wells-Fargo Express Co. Deadwood Treasure Wagon and Guards with $250,000 gold bullion from the Great Homestake Mine, Deadwood, South Dakota. John C. H. Grabill, 1890. Library of Congress, LC-DIG-ppmsc-02598.

Page 141: Nellie Cashman. Alaska State Library, Alaska State Library Portrait File, ASL-P01-4024.

Page 154: Tired Prospector. National Park Service.

Page 164: Man working at entrance of gold mine, Goldfield, Nevada. Waldon Fawcett, 1907. Library of Congress, LC-USZ62-65270.

Page 179: A burro train bringing gold from the mines near Ouray, Colorado. W. S. Smith, Standard Scenic Company, 1906. Library of Congress, LC-USZ62-110841.

Page 186: Prospectors returning to camp, 62 [degrees] below zero, Alaska. B. L. Singley—Keystone View Co., 1899. Library of Congress, LC-USZ62-57296.

Page 197: Miners prospecting. Frederic Remington, 188–. Library of Congress, LC-USZC4-2483.

Page 212: Mrs. Clara Dunwoody on the "Clara" variscite claim; 10 miles SW of Sodaville. Mrs. Dunwoody is a prospector and socialist leader. Mineral County, Nevada. D. B. Sterrett, 1910. US Geological Survey.

Page 224: Dead Horse Trail. John M. Blankenberg, 1898. Alaska State Library, J. M. Blankenberg Photograph Collection, ASL-P125-018.

Page 230: Miners and packers climbing the "Golden Stair" trail, Chilcoot Pass, Alaska. B. L. Singley—Keystone View Co., 1898. Library of Congress, LC-USZ62-60565.

Page 237: Miners bound for the Klondike gold fields: close-up of men with heavy packs near summit of Chilcoot Pass. Keystone View Co., 1898. Library of Congress, LC-USZ62-41761.

Page 248: White Pass and Yukon train with freight and passenger cars on a trestle, with mining operation below the bridge. L. M. Prindle, 1906. US Geological Survey.

Page 255: Top: Soapy Smith's Saloon. Peiser. Skagway, Alaska. Flashlight. 11 p.m. 2/26/1898. Larss & Duclos, 1898. Alaska State Library, Wickersham

State Historic Site, ASL-P277-001-009. Bottom: Autopsy on body of Soapy Smith, showing bullet wounds. Case & Draper, 1898. Alaska State Library, William R. Norton Photographs, ASL-P226-786.

Page 262: $1,250,000 in gold bullion at Miners and Merchants Bank. Lomen Bros., 1906. Library of Congress, LC-DIG-ppmsc-01961.

Page 267: Prospector with dog team. Public Photo Service, between ca. 1900 and 1923. Library of Congress, LC-DIG-ppmsc-01558.

Page 274: Mining on beach at Nome, Alaska. Between ca. 1900 and 1930. Library of Congress, LC-DIG-ppmsc-01651.

BIBLIOGRAPHY

Adams, Brewster. *The Prospector: Values in the Rough*. Reno, NV: Reno Printing Co., 1940.

Allen, Robert Joseph. *The Story of Superstition Mountain and the Lost Dutchman Gold Mine*. New York: Simon & Schuster, 1971.

Anderson, Elliott and Robert Onopa. *TriQuarterly 48,* Spring 1980. Evanston, IL: Northwestern University, 1980.

Balcom, Mary G. *Creek Street*. Ketchikan, AK: Lind Printing, 1975.

Basque, Garnet. *Gold Panner's Manual: A Complete Guide for the Novice*. New York: The Lyons Press, 1991.

Batman, Richard. *The Outer Coast*. New York: Harcourt, Brace, Jovanovich, 1985.

Belden, L. Burr, and Mary DeDecker. *Death Valley to Yosemite: Frontier Mining Camps & Ghost Towns: The Men, the Women, Their Mines & Stories*. Bishop, CA: Spotted Dog Press, 2000.

Bennett, Estelline. *Old Deadwood Days: The Real Wild West of My Childhood*. Santa Barbara, CA: Narrative Press, 2001.

Berton, Pierre. *The Klondike Fever: The Life and Death of the Last Great Gold Rush*. New York: Carroll & Graf, 1989.

————. *Stampede for Gold: The Story of the Klondike Rush*. New York: Sterling Point Books, 2007.

Birmingham, Stephen. *California Rich*. New York: Simon & Schuster, 1980.

Black, Martha Louise. *My Ninety Years*. Anchorage, AK: Alaska Northwest Publishing, 1976.

Bristow, Gwen. *Golden Dreams*. New York: Lippincott & Crowell, 1980.

Brown, Dee. *The Gentle Tamers: Women of the Old Wild West.* Lincoln: University of Nebraska Press, 1968.

———. *Hear That Lonesome Whistle Blow: Railroads in the West.* New York: Holt, Rinehart, and Winston, 1977.

———. *Wondrous Times on the Frontier.* Little Rock, AR: August House Publishers, 1991.

Brown, Robert L. *An Empire of Silver.* Denver, CO: Sundance Publications, 1984.

Clappe, Louise Amelia Knapp Smith. *The Shirley Letters from California Mines in 1851–52.* New York: Ballantine Books, 1971.

Corbett, Christopher. *The Poker Bride: The First Chinese in the West.* New York: Atlantic Monthly Press, 2010.

Crampton, Frank A. *Deep Enough: A Working Stiff in the Western Mine Camps.* Norman: University of Oklahoma Press, 1993.

Davis, William C. *The American Frontier: Pioneers, Settlers & Cowboys (1800–1899).* Norman: University of Oklahoma Press, 1999.

Death Valley Tales. Death Valley, CA: Death Valley '49ers Inc., 1970.

Demlinger, Sandor. *Mining in the Old West.* Atglen, PA: Schiffer Publishing, 2006.

Dixon, Kelly J. *Boomtown Saloons.* Reno: University of Nevada Press, 2006.

Dobie, J. Frank. *Apache Gold and Yaqui Silver.* Austin: University of Texas Press, 1996.

———. *Coronado's Children: Tales of Lost Mines and Buried Treasures of the Southwest.* Austin: University of Texas Press, 1984.

Drabelle, Dennis. *Mile-High Fever: Silver Mines, Boom Towns, and High Living on the Comstock Lode.* New York: St. Martin's Press, 2009.

Eberhart, Perry. *1536–1968: Treasure Tales of the Rockies: Lost Mines and Buried Bonanza.* New York: Ballantine Books, 1969.

Fisher, Vardis, and Opal Laurel Holmes. *Gold Rushes and Mining Camps of the Early American West*. Caldwell, ID: Caxton Printers Ltd., 1968.

Gibbens, Byrd, Elizabeth Hampstein, and Lillian Schlissel. *Far From Home: Families of the Westward Journey*. New York: Schocken Books, 1989.

Grant, Marilyn. *Montana Mainstreets, Volume 1: A Guide to Historic Virginia City*. Helena: Montana Historical Society Press, 1998.

Griffith, T. D. *Deadwood: The Best Writings on the Most Notorious Town in the West*. Helena, MT: TwoDot, 2010.

Hand, Dana. *Deep Creek*. New York: Houghton Mifflin, 2010.

Hardesty, Donald L. *Mining Archaeology in the American West*. Lincoln: University of Nebraska Press, 2010.

Holliday, J. S. *The World Rushed In: The California Gold Rush Experience: An Eyewitness Account of a Nation Heading West*. New York: Simon & Schuster, 1981.

Hollihan, Tony. *Gold Rushes*. Edmonton, AB: Lone Pine Publishing, 2002.

Horwitz, Tony, ed. *The Devil May Care: Fifty Intrepid Americans and Their Quest for the Unknown*. New York: Oxford University Press, 2003.

Hughes, John L. *Wyatt's Gold: The Story Tombstone Missed, and Bisbee Never Told*. Mustang, OK: Tate Publishing, 2006.

Hunt, William R. *North of 53: The Wild Days of the Alaska-Yukon Mining Frontier 1870–1914*. New York: MacMillan Publishing, 1974.

Jackson, Donald Dale. *Gold Dust*. Edison, NJ: Castle Books, 1980.

Jackson, Joseph Henry. *Anybody's Gold: The Story of California's Mining Towns*. San Francisco, CA: Chronicle Books, 1982.

Johnson, Dorothy M. *The Bloody Bozeman: The Perilous Trail to Montana's Gold*. Missoula, MT: Mountain Press, 1983.

Kelly, C. Brian. *Best Little Stories from the Wild West*. Nashville, TN: Cumberland House Publishing, 2002.

Knowles, Thomas W., and Joe R. Lansdale, eds. *The West That Was*. Avenel, NJ: Wings Books, 1993.

Levy, Joann. *They Saw the Elephant: Women in the California Gold Rush*. Hamden, CT: Shoe String Press, 1990.

Mabee, Sourdough Jack. *Sourdough Jack's Cookery and Other Things*. Nevada City, CA: Argonaut House Inc., 1971.

MacKell, Jan. *Red Light Women of the Rocky Mountains*. Albuquerque: University of New Mexico Press, 2009.

Marks, Paula Mitchell. *Precious Dust: The Saga of the Western Gold Rushes*. Lincoln: University of Nebraska Press, 1994.

Mayer, Melanie J. *Klondike Women: True Tales of the 1897–1898 Gold Rush*. Athens, OH: Swallow Press, 1989.

Mayo, Matthew P. *Cowboys, Mountain Men & Grizzly Bears: Fifty of the Grittiest Moments in the History of the Wild West*. Helena, MT: TwoDot, 2009.

McMurtry, Larry. *Oh What a Slaughter: Massacres in the American West: 1846–1890*. New York: Simon & Schuster, 2005.

Meeker, Ezra. *Ox-Team Days on the Oregon Trail*. Yonkers-on-Hudson, NY: World Book Company, 1932.

Morgan, Lael. *Good Time Girls of the Alaska-Yukon Gold Rush*. Vancouver, BC: Whitecap Books, 1998.

Murphy, Clair Rudolph, and Jane G. Haigh. *Gold Rush Women*. Portland, OR: Alaska Northwest Books, 2003.

———. *Gold Rush Dogs*. Portland, OR: Alaska Northwest Books, 2001.

Nokes, R. Gregory. *Massacred for Gold: The Chinese in Hells Canyon*. Corvallis: Oregon State University Press, 2009.

North, Dick. *The Lost Patrol: The Mounties' Yukon Tragedy*. Vancouver, BC: Raincoast Books, 1995.

O'Brien, Mary Barmeyer. *Across Death Valley: The Pioneer Journey of Juliet Wells Brier.* Helena, MT: TwoDot, 2009.

Oppel, Frank, ed. *Tales of Alaska and the Yukon.* Edison, NJ: Castle Books, 1986.

————. *Tales of the Canadian North.* Edison, NJ: Castle Books, 1984.

Pace, Dick. *Golden Gulch: The Story of Montana's Fabulous Alder Gulch.* Virginia City, MT: Dick Pace, 1962.

Place, Marian T. *The Yukon.* New York: Ives Washburn Inc., 1967.

Raymond, C. Elizabeth, and Ronald M. James. *Comstock Women: The Making of a Mining Community.* Reno: University of Nevada Press, 1997.

Roop, Connie and Peter, eds. *The Diary of David R. Leeper: Rushing for Gold.* Tarrytown, NY: Benchmark Books, 2001.

Sagstetter, Beth and Bill. *The Mining Camps Speak.* Tarrytown, NY: Benchmark Books, 1998.

Secrest, William B. *Dangerous Trails: Five Desperadoes of the Old West Coast.* Stillwater, OK: Barbed Wire Press, 1995.

Seelye, John D., ed. *Stories of the Old West: Tales of the Mining Camp, Cavalry Troop & Cattle Ranch.* Norman: University of Oklahoma Press, 2000.

Service, Robert W. *Best Tales of the Yukon.* Philadelphia, PA: Running Press, 2003.

Shepherd, Jill. *The Last Frontier: Incredible True Tales of Survival, Exploration, and Adventure from Alaska Magazine.* Guilford, CT: Lyons Press/Globe Pequot Press, 2002.

Shermeister, Phil, and Noel Grove. *National Geographic Destination: The Sierra Nevada.* Washington, DC.: National Geographic Society, 1999.

Siringo, Charles A. *A Cowboy Detective: A True Story of Twenty-Two Years with a World-Famous Detective Agency.* Lincoln: University of Nebraska Press, 1988.

Steele, Volney, M.D. *Bleed, Blister & Purge: A History of Medicine on the American Frontier.* Missoula, MT: Mountain Press, 2005.

Time-Life, eds. *The Old West Series.* 26 vols. Alexandria, VA: Time-Life Books, 1973–80.

Titler, Dale M. *Unnatural Resources: True Stories of American Treasure.* Englewood Cliffs, NJ: Prentice-Hall, 1973.

Townshend, R. B. *A Tenderfoot in Colorado.* Boulder: University Press of Colorado, 2008.

Vestal, Stanley. *The Old Santa Fe Trail.* Lincoln: University of Nebraska Press, 1996.

"Vigilante Justice, 1851." Eyewitness to History, www.eyewitnesstohistory .com, 2006.

West, Elliott. *The Saloon on the Rocky Mountain Mining Frontier.* Lincoln: University of Nebraska Press, 1996.

Willard, John. *Adventure Trails in Montana.* Billings, MT: John Willard, Publisher, 1986.

INDEX

A

Adams Museum, 18
Alaska Commercial Company, 265
Alder Gulch, 104, 115
American River, 19
Anaconda Vein, 121
Antler Creek, 87
Anvil Creek, 276
Apache Indians, 105–9, 151, 206–7
Arapaho Indians, 75
Arcane and Bennett Party, 39, 40
Arctic Brotherhood, 257
Atlanta Mine Camp, 214
avalanches, 228–33

B

backshooters, 94–98
Baja, CA, 28–29
Baptiste Louie, 175, 176
Battle of the Little Bighorn, 18
Bell, H. A., 102
Bigelow, Alfred, 116–17, 120
Bigelow, Marta, 120
Black Hills, 13–18, 128–32, 133–38
The Black Hills, or, The Last Hunting Ground
    of the Dakotahs, a Complete History of
    the Black Hills of Dakota, from Their
    First Invasion in 1874 to the Present
    Time (Tallent), 137–38
Black Stephen, 2
Blue, Alexander, 71–76
Blue, Charlie, 71–76
Blue, Daniel, 71–76
Blue Parka Man (Charles Hendrickson),
    278–83
Bodey, W. S., 77–80, 81
Bodie, CA, 77, 80–81
Boise Basin, 94, 98
Boyett, Johnnie, 218–19, 220
Bremner, John, 194–99

Bremner River, 199
Brewer, John, 108
Brown, Sam, 82, 83–86
Brown, Tom, 14, 17
Brown, William "Swede," 54–58
Bruff, Joseph Goldsborough, 44–48
Buck, Norman, 182
Bucke, Robert, 68–70
Bullock, Seth, 149, 150
Bullock Hotel, 150
Bunker Hill Mine, 80, 182
Burns, Jimmy, 200–204
Burton, Elijah, 89–91
Butler, Jim, 182
Butte City, MT, 121

C

Calamity Jane, 115
Camp Huachuca, 151
Camp Robinson, 136
Canadian Army, 139–40
Canadian government, 222, 235, 243
Canadian Mounties, 230
Canary, Martha Jane, 115
Canary children, 115
cannibalism, 10–11, 74–75, 91, 92–93
Cantons, 60
Cape Horn, 33
Carcross, Yukon, 245–58
Carson City Rangers, 85
Cashman, Nellie, 139–44
Cassiar Mountains, 139
Cheechako, 239, 250
Cheechako Death Trek, 234–39
Cherry Creek, 159
Chief Nana (Apache Indian), 105, 106, 109
Chilean War, 34–38
Chilkat Indians, 186–87
Chilkoot Pass and Trail, 183, 184, 187, 188,
    227, 228–33

Chinese Exclusion Act, 193
Chinese miners and gangs, 49–53, 60–65,
    189–93
claim jumping, 259–64
claim salting, 50, 53
claim tampering, 53
Clark, William A., 121
Close Brothers and Company, 245
Comstock, Henry, 66, 70
Comstock Lode, 70, 85, 120
Copper Indians, 198–99
Copper Kings, 121
Coronado, Francisco Vásquez de, 1–6
Cottonwood Crossing, 76
Crampton, Frank, 159–61
Cricket Saloon, 148
Cripple Creek, 162–66, 200–204
Crow Indians, 99–104
Crown Point Mine, 119
Custer, George Armstrong, 18, 128–32

D
Dawson City, AK, 265, 282
Day's Creek, OR, 155, 156
Dead Horse Gulch, 222–27
Deadwood, Dakota Territory, 145–50
Dease Lake, 140, 142, 143
Death Valley, 39–43
Deep Enough (Crampton), 161
Dietz, Arthur, 234–36, 238, 239
dog teams, 267
Dolphin (schooner), 28–29, 32
Donner Party, 23
Doyle, James, 200–204
dry gulchers, 85, 87, 88, 90, 189–93
Dunwoody, Clara, 212
Dutch Em, 210–13, 214

E
Earp, Allie, 219–20
Earp, Josephine Marcus, 216, 217–18, 221
Earp, Morgan, 220
Earp, Virgil, 219–20

Earp, Warren, 218–19, 220
Earp, Wyatt, 216–21
El Paso Mine, 162, 163–66
El Rosario, Mexico, 32
Emigrant Gulch, 115

F
Fairbanks, AK, 278–83
Filbertson, Lawrence, 271–76
Filkins, Dicky, 57
floats, 163
flour gold, 189–90
Fort Leavenworth, 10
Fort Sutter, 23
Fortymile River, 183, 187, 188
French Creek, 129, 130, 133
French expedition, 7–12

G
Gandolfo, Signor R. J., 243
Gang of Innocents, 92
Gem Variety Theater, 145, 146, 147, 148,
    149, 150
Gird, Richard, 152
Golden Trail, 230
*Gold Rush: The Journals, Drawings, and
    Other Papers of J. Goldsborough Bruff*
    (Bruff), 48
Gordon Party of prospectors, 133–37
Granite Mountain, 121
Grant, Ulysses S., 143
Griffith, John W., 28–32
Griffith, William, 152
Grimes, George, 94–98
Grosh, Ethan Allen, 66–71
Grosh, Hosea Ballou, 66–71

H
hard-rock mining, 119, 121, 164
Harnan, John, 200–204
Harper, Arthur, 183
Hauser, Samuel Thomas, 100–104
Healy's Post, 186, 187, 188

Hearst, George, 132
Heinze, F. Augustus, 121
Hells Canyon Massacre, 189–93
Helm, Boone, 87–93
Heney, Michael J., 245–49
Henry, Guy V., 136–37
Hirschberg, Max, 268–70
Homestake Mine, 132
Hong Kongs, 61
Hook, George, 167–68
Hope Diamond, 204
Hungry Winter (1864-1865), 111
hydraulic mining, 101

I

Idaho City, ID, 98, 115
I Married Wyatt Earp (Earp), 221
Indian Bar Mining Camp, 54, 55
Inside passage, 250
International Historic Civil Engineering
    Landmark, 251
Isthmus of Panama route, 33
Ives, George, 99–100, 104

J

Jayhawkers, 39, 40–41, 42, 43
Jesson, Ed, 265–66, 270
Johnson, Peder, 196–99
Juneau Wharf, 252, 255, 257

K

Kansas Territory, 75
Kellogg, Noah, 177–82
Kent, Robert, 14, 17
Kentuck Mine, 117, 119
Kerbyville, OR, 182
Kind, Ezra, 13–18
Klondike, 59, 188, 222, 224, 240–44, 250
Kong Mun Kow, 189–92

L

Lake Bennett, 222, 240, 243
Lake Manly, 43

Lakota Sioux, 13–17
Lakota (Teton) Sioux Indians, 128–32
Leadville, CO, 167
Little Pittsburg Mine, 168
Long, Mabel, 243–44
Lost Adams Diggings, 110
Lost Dutchman's Mine, 205–9
Lost Mine at Treasure Mountain (now the
    Summitville ghost town), 11–12
Lost Pegleg Mine, 209
Lost Spanish Silver Mine of St. Marie's River,
    172, 176

M

Mad Rush for Gold in Frozen North
    (Dietz), 239
Maher, Scott, 252–54
Malaspina Glacier, 235–36, 239
Manly Beacon, 43
Manly Peak, 43
Manuel, Moses and Manuel, 132
Marshall, James, 19, 20, 21–22, 53
Matchless Mine, 170, 171
Mazatlán, 29
McClintock, James, 155–56
McCracken Mine, 152
McKenzie, Alexander, 259–64
McLaughlin, Patrick, 70
Meehan, Paddy, 199
Mendoza, Viceroy Antonio de, 1
Mikelson, Judge, 54–58
Miles Canyon, 241, 242
Miner's Boarding House, 143
Miners' courts, 59
Mojave Desert, 39, 42, 43, 216, 218
Mongollon Exploration Company, 272
Monterey region, CA, 24, 25, 27
Moore, Billy, 257, 258
Morrow, Annie "Pegleg Annie," 210–15
Murietta, Joaquin, 38

N

Nebraska Territory, 75

New France (now southern California), 7
Newhall, Henry Mayo, 33
New Spain, 2, 5
New York City Expedition, 234–39
Nome, AK, 216, 259–64, 265, 268,
    271–77, 282
North Butte Mining Disaster, 121
North Ophir Mine, 53
North-West Mounted Police, 241–42
Noyes, Arthur H., 259, 260, 261

O
Ophir Mine, 122–27
O'Riley, Peter, 70
Ormsby, William, 85
O'Rourke, Phil, 177–80

P
pack animals, 179, 182, 227
Packer, Alfred, 92–93
Paiute Indians, 85
Penrod, Immanuel "Manny," 70
Peralta, Don Miguel, II, 206
Perry, George, 279, 281–82
Pikes Peak, 71–76
Pikes Peak Rush, 75
Pioneer Mine, 260, 263–64
placer mining, 274
Plains Indians, 76
Plummer, Henry, 92
Price, Gabe, 260

Q
Quesnel Forks, 88
Quivira (now central Kansas), 3, 4–5, 6

R
Reid, Frank, 254–57, 258
Reminiscences of Alexander Toponce
    (Toponce), 115
Rische, August, 167–68
Rock Springs, WY, 193
Rocky Bar Mine Camp, 213, 214

Roosevelt, Teddy, 150

S
Sam Yup Company, 189
San Diego, CA, 32, 33
San Francisco, CA, 27, 33, 221, 263
San Francisco Vigilance Committee, 89
San Gabriel Mountains, 42, 43
Santa Rosa Mountains, 209
Schieffelin, Ed, 151–56
Schieffelin, Mary Brown, 156
Seven Cities of Gold (Seven Cities of
    Cibola), 1–6
Seward Peninsula, 265–66
Sexton, Inez, 146–48, 149
Sheer Camp, 228–29, 232
Sheridan, Phil, 128–29, 130
Sherman, William Tecumseh, 24–27
Shoshone Indians, 94–95, 98
Sierra Nevada, 39, 44, 45, 48, 68
Silks, Oliver D., 224–27
Silver Bow Creek, 121
Sioux Indians, 135
Skagway, AK, 245–51
Skagway Trail, 222, 227
Smith, George, 102
Smith, Jefferson Davis "Soapy," 231–32, 252,
    253–58
Smith, Lynn, 199
Smith, Thomas "Pegleg," 209
Smoky Hill Trail "Starvation Trail," 71,
    72–73, 76
Snake River, 112, 114, 189
sourdoughs, 151–56, 194–99, 239
Splawn, Moses, 94–96
Squaw Rapids, 241, 242
Standard Company, 80
Steele, Sam, 240–41, 242
Stewart, John D., 254, 256, 257
Stuart, Granville "Mister Montana," 104
Stuart, James, 99–104
Sullivan, Con, 177–80
Sullivan Mine, 182

Superstition Mountains, 205–9
Sutter, John Augustus, 19–21, 22–23, 53
Swearengen, Ellis Albert "Al," 145–50

T
Tabor, Augusta, 167–71
Tabor, Elizabeth Bonduel Lillie, 170
Tabor, Elizabeth McCourt "Baby Doe," 167, 169, 170–71
Tabor, Horace, 167–69, 171
Tabor, Rose Mary Echo Silver Dollar, 171
Taiya Inlet, 186, 187
Tallent, Annie D., 133–34, 135, 137–38
Tallent, David, 133–35
Tancrede, Sir Thomas, 245–46, 250
Taylor, "Black," 77–80
Temple of the Forest Beneath the Clouds, 65
tent city, 274, 276
Theakston, Ned, 60–65
Thoen, Louis, 18
Thoen Stone, 17–18
Thomas, Julia, 205–9
Timmins, Billy, 278–80, 281–82
Tiwa, 2, 5
Tombstone, AZ, 151–56, 220
Tonopah, NV, 182, 217
Toponce, Alex, 111–15
Treaty of Fort Laramie, 130
trespassers, 133–38
The Turk (Indian), 3–4
Twain, Mark, 85

U
US Army, 24–25, 27, 105, 131–32, 133
US government and Indian treaties, 128–32, 134, 135
US Navy, 27

V
Vanderbilt Line (shipping company), 33
Van Sickle, Henry, 86

vigilantes, 172–76
Virginia City, MT, 92, 111, 113, 114
Virginia City, NV, 75, 82, 85
Virginia City Rush, 75

W
Wallace, John, 174, 175
Walsh, Thomas Francis, 204
Waltz, Jacob, 205–9
Ward, Joshua and family, 157–61
Washington City and California Mining Association, 44, 47
Wayne, John, 221
Weaver's Needle, 206
Weaverville, CA, 60–65
Weaverville Tong War, 60–65
White Horse Rapids, 240–44
White Pass Trail, 222, 224, 227, 245
White Pass & Yukon Route railway (WP&YR), 245–51
Wild Goose Mine, 259–60, 263–64
Willcox, AZ, 218, 220
Williams, James, 172–76
Williams, Tom, 183–88
Wilson, William S., 95, 96–97, 98
Wimmer, Jenny, 53
Wolcott (US revenue cutter), 238
Womack, Crazy Bob, 162–65
Wood, GW, 14, 17
Wood, Joseph K., 259
Woodward, Vernie, 231–32

Y
Yellow Jacket Mine, 116–21
Yellowstone Expedition, 99–104
Yellowstone River drainage, 99
Yukon River, 266–68

Z
Zorro legend, 38

ABOUT THE AUTHOR

Matthew P. Mayo is the author of numerous novels and nonfiction books, including the Westerns *Winters' War; Wrong Town; Hot Lead, Cold Heart;* and *Dead Man's Ranch,* and the critically lauded nonfiction books *Cowboys, Mountain Men & Grizzly Bears; Bootleggers, Lobstermen & Lumberjacks;* and *Haunted Old West.* His short stories have appeared in a variety of anthologies and magazines.

Matthew is a Western Writers of America Spur Award Nominee and a Western Fictioneers Peacemaker Award Nominee. He recently collaborated with his wife, photographer Jennifer Smith-Mayo, on the coffee-table books *Maine Icons, New Hampshire Icons,* and *Vermont Icons.* Mayo lives with his family (and Ned, the imaginary burro) on the coast of Maine. Visit him on the Web at www.matthewmayo.com for a chin-wag and a cup of mud.